CRITICAL ESSAYS ON

MACBETH

William Shakespeare

D1322403

Editors:
Linda Cookson
Bryan Loughrey

LONGMAN
LITERATURE
GUIDES

Longman Literature Guides

Editors: Linda Cookson and Bryan Loughrey

Titles in the series:

CONTENTS

PREFACE

Like all professional groups, literary critics have developed their own specialised language. This is not necessarily a bad thing. Sometimes complex concepts can only be described in a terminology far removed from everyday speech. Academic jargon, however, creates an unnecessary barrier between the critic and the intelligent but less practised reader.

This danger is particularly acute where scholarly books and articles are re-packaged for a student audience. Critical anthologies, for example, often contain extracts from longer studies originally written for specialists. Deprived of their original context, these passages can puzzle and at times mislead. The essays in this volume, however, are all specially commissioned, self-contained works, written with the needs of students firmly in mind.

This is not to say that the contributors — all experienced critics and teachers — have in any way attempted to simplify the complexity of the issues with which they deal. On the contrary, they explore the central problems of the text from a variety of critical perspectives, reaching conclusions which are challenging and at times mutually contradictory.

They try, however, to present their arguments in a direct, accessible language and to work within the limitations of scope and length which students inevitably face. For this reason, essays are generally rather briefer than is the practice; they address quite specific topics; and, in line with examination requirements, they incorporate precise textual detail into the body of the discussion.

They offer, therefore, working examples of the kind of essay-writing skills which students themselves are expected to develop. Their diversity, however, should act as a reminder that in the field of literary studies there is no such thing as a 'model' answer. Good essays are the outcome of a creative engagement with literature, of sensitive, attentive reading and careful thought. We hope that those contained in this volume will encourage students to return to the most important starting point of all, the text itself, with renewed excitement and the determination to explore more fully their own critical responses.

How to use this volume

Obviously enough, you should start by reading the text in question. The one assumption that all the contributors make is that you are already familiar with this. It would be helpful, of course, to have read further — perhaps other works by the same author or by influential contemporaries. But we don't assume that you have yet had the opportunity to do this and any references to historical background or to other works of literature are explained.

You should, perhaps, have a few things to hand. It is always a good idea to keep a copy of the text nearby when reading critical studies. You will almost certainly want to consult it when checking the context of quotations or pausing to consider the validity of the critic's interpretation. You should also try to have access to a good dictionary, and ideally a copy of a dictionary of literary terms as well. The contributors have tried to avoid jargon and to express themselves clearly and directly. But inevitably there will be occasional words or phrases with which you are unfamiliar. Finally, we would encourage you to make notes, summarising not just the argument of each essay but also your own responses to what you have read. So keep a pencil and notebook at the ready.

Suitably equipped, the best thing to do is simply begin with whichever topic most interests you. We have deliberately organised each volume so that the essays may be read in any order. One consequence of this is that, for the sake of clarity and self-containment, there is occasionally a degree of overlap between essays. But at least you are not forced to follow one — fairly arbitrary — reading sequence.

Each essay is followed by brief 'Afterthoughts', designed to highlight points of critical interest. But remember, these are only there to remind you that it is *your* responsibility to question what you read. The essays printed here are not a series of 'model' answers to be slavishly imitated and in no way should they be regarded as anything other than a guide or stimulus for your own thinking. We hope for a critically involved response: 'That was interesting. But if *I* were tackling the topic . . .!'

Read the essays in this spirit and you'll pick up many of the skills of critical composition in the process. We have, however, tried to provide more explicit advice in 'A practical guide to essay writing'. You may find this helpful, but do not imagine it offers any magic formulas. The quality of your essays ultimately depends on the quality of your engagement with literary texts. We hope this volume spurs you on to read these with greater understanding and to explore your responses in greater depth.

A note on the text
All references are to the New Penguin Shakespeare edition of *Macbeth*, ed. G K Hunter.

Michael Gearin-Tosh

Michael Gearin-Tosh is Fellow and Tutor in English Literature at St Catherine's College, Oxford. He is also Associate Director of the Oxford School of Drama.

ESSAY

The treatment of evil in *Macbeth*

Macbeth is evil, yet pity is essential to tragedy. Two ways in which Shakespeare reconciles these opposites so that we pity a 'hellhound' (V.6.42) are the use of soliloquy and the strategies of the last two acts.

Macbeth contains more soliloquy as a proportion of the play than any other drama by Shakespeare. Soliloquy can create intimacy with those we do not like, as it does in Shakespeare's other tragedy whose hero is evil, *Richard III*, which was written some fifteen years before *Macbeth*. Richard is also called a 'hellhound' (IV.4.48) but he is a 'hellhound' from the start. He declares his villainy in the soliloquy which opens the play and we soon learn that he has already moved against his first victim in the play, his brother Clarence. Macbeth *becomes* evil, and his soliloquies chart the stages of this degeneration.

The opening lines of Macbeth's first soliloquy show his excitement at the prospect of gaining power:

> If it were done when 'tis done, then 'twere well
> It were done quickly. If th'assassination
> Could trammel up the consequence, and catch
> With his surcease success . . .

(I.7.1–4)

The strenuous activity of 'trammel up' — trapping game birds or fish in a net — is followed by the thrilling energy of sound in 'catch' which draws together and concentrates the earlier sounds in the line as well as their meaning. 'Success' almost wrestles for a moment with 'surcease', words well matched in weight, and when 'success' succeeds (in both senses), there is a note of triumph. Macbeth at once corrects this with:

> But in these cases,
> We still have judgement here — that we but teach
> Bloody instructions, which, being taught, return
> To plague the inventor.

(I.7.7–10)

It is an old political truth that assassins show others how to get rid of them. Macbeth's tone is sober, until he considers how good a king Duncan has been:

> Besides, this Duncan
> Hath borne his faculties so meek, hath been
> So clear in his great office, that his virtues
> Will plead like angels, trumpet-tongued, against
> The deep damnation of his taking-off;
> And Pity, like a naked new-born babe
> Striding the blast, or heaven's cherubin, horsed
> Upon the sightless curriers of the air,
> Shall blow the horrid deed in every eye,
> That tears shall drown the wind.

(I.7.16–25)

This is a mental earthquake — Macbeth is torn apart by conscience and his harrowing is enacted in the surreal metamorphoses: a new-born baby who suddenly gains the muscular power to ride astride the wind; tears which begin as a reaction to dirt blown in the eye, but are then so forceful that, like torrential rain, they drown a gale.

In the terror of these lines, Macbeth intuitively discovers enough about himself to abandon the idea of murdering Duncan:

> I have no spur
> To prick the sides of my intent but only

Vaulting ambition which o'erleaps itself
And falls on the other.

(I.7.25–28)

Yet when Lady Macbeth enters, he cannot tell her why:

We will proceed no further in this business:
He hath honoured me of late, and I have bought
Golden opinions from all sorts of people,
Which would be worn now in their newest gloss,
Not cast aside so soon.

(I.7.31–35)

This idea played no part in his soliloquy and it is scarcely persuasive: if you are going to carry out a secret murder, the best time may be when you have 'bought golden opinions' since people may suspect you less. Macbeth is now in great danger. As Shakespeare wrote of another man tempted to commit evil, Tarquin, who is mentioned in Macbeth's second soliloquy:

Then where is truth, if there be no self-trust?

(*The Rape of Lucrece*, line 158)

Those who lack the self-trust to speak out are often made to listen, and what Macbeth hears from his wife is:

I have given suck, and know
How tender 'tis to love the babe that milks me;
I would while it was smiling in my face
Have plucked my nipple from his boneless gums
And dashed the brains out, had I so sworn as you
Have done to this.

(I.7.54–59)

Lady Macbeth makes against him the move he should have made first: she has invoked the depths of her being. Even now his chance of saving himself is to speak the truth which he discovered in the soliloquy, that his inner being felt terror at the prospect of murdering Duncan. But his response dwindles to 'If we should fail?' (line 59) and he is lost. He has smothered the voice of his deepest intuitions. His tragedy is that he will hear it no more.

Perhaps the most striking word in his next soliloquy is 'withered':

> Now o'er the one half-world
> Nature seems dead, and wicked dreams abuse
> The curtained sleep. Witchcraft celebrates
> Pale Hecat's offerings; and withered murder
> Alarumed by his sentinel the wolf,
> Whose howl's his watch, thus with his stealthy pace,
> With Tarquin's ravishing strides, towards his design
> Moves like a ghost.

(II.1.49–56)

Vision has lessened to dream — and dreams which abuse. Where previously Pity and heaven's 'cherubin' crowded before his imagination, now Macbeth scans the landscape in order to detect the stirrings of evil in a world which 'seems dead'. This is Macbeth's world now he is a murderer, and it is a world which blights. Macbeth has cauterised his ability to grow. The word 'wither' primarily refers to a plant which shrivels through lack of light and moisture. Murder's world has no sun. It is grey like his wolf, pale like Hecate — and separation from the earth is death to a plant. Macbeth ends the soliloquy with:

> Thou sure and firm-set earth,
> Hear not my steps, which way they walk, for fear
> Thy very stones prate of my whereabout

(II.1.56–58)

With heaven's 'cherubin', it was rain which drowned the wind: they brought terror which was creative, and they had the energy of the cosmos itself. Macbeth's new world is one not of terror but horror. Tarquin committed rape and murder's world has a rapist's energy: less appetite than craving; no giving, scarcely even taking, but alien infliction to force a moment's rest from what Macbeth will soon call the 'scorpions' of the mind (III.2.36); a festering which poisons the heart and swells to action on the incantation which we first hear in these lines, and later becomes a habit. In III.2.50–55 the excitedness of the language tells us that Macbeth now needs this world in order to feel alive:

> Light thickens
> And the crow makes wing to the rooky wood;
> Good things of day begin to droop and drowse,
> Whiles night's black agents to their preys do rouse.

Macbeth's third soliloquy is a masterpiece of dramatic strategy. A man who withers must be given appropriate poetry. It is revealing to compare the climaxes of Macbeth's three soliloquies. The climax of the first soliloquy is the vision of heaven's 'cherubin', and the climax of the second is the invocation of murder's world. Both are visual. But the climax of the third soliloquy is oratorical. There is a change of tone in the middle of the speech. The earlier part is reflective:

> To be thus is nothing;
> But to be safely thus! — Our fears in Banquo
> Stick deep; and in his royalty of nature
> Reigns that which would be feared. 'Tis much he dares,
> And to that dauntless temper of his mind
> He hath a wisdom that doth guide his valour
> To act in safety.
>
> (III.1.47–53)

The movement is fitful, the half-line at 47 catching the rhythm of probing thought, uneasy but leisured. The conclusion is different:

> If it be so,
> For Banquo's issue have I filed my mind,
> For them the gracious Duncan have I murdered,
> Put rancours in the vessel of my peace,
> Only for them; and mine eternal jewel
> Given to the common enemy of man,
> To make them kings, the seed of Banquo kings!
>
> (III.1.63–69)

The phrases flow and fill the lines which are broken not through the early conclusion of a thought as at 'feared' in line 50, but for rhetorical climax as in line 67. The repetitions, 'For Banquo's issue', 'For them', 'Only for them', 'To make them kings' are the marks of an orator's manipulative emphasis. Yet Macbeth is alone. His oratory is aimed not at a jury, but himself. Nor is the first part of the soliloquy as detached as it seems.

'There is none but he/ Whose being I do fear': this is one of those statements which are never made unless they are false. If it were true, who would Banquo lead against Macbeth? How could he be a threat? The truth is revealed later that day when Macbeth tells his wife he has spies everywhere:

> There's not a one of them, but in his house
> I keep a servant fee'd.

(III.4.130–131)

The soliloquy continues with the rebuking of Macbeth's genius 'as, it is said,/ Mark Antony's was by Caesar'. Since the issue at stake is no less than whether Banquo should be murdered, it matters where the comparison falls short: Caesar and Antony were both emperors but Banquo is Macbeth's subject; Caesar had vast armies, Banquo has none; neither Caesar nor Antony gained power by murder; so far it is Macbeth and not Banquo who seems to have gained the greater glory. The comparison is false. The truth lies in a combination of factors. There is the Witches' prophecy. Macbeth also envies Banquo because he cannot corrupt him — a perennial irritant to evil minds.

Macbeth now needs to kill, just as he needs the world of night, in order to confirm his identity. His language becomes agitated in lines 60–63:

> Upon my head they placed a fruitless crown
> And put a barren sceptre in my grip,
> Thence to be wrenched with an unlineal hand,
> No son of mine succeeding.

'Grip' sounds harsh and the near rhyme of 'thence' and 'wrenched' is vehement. No doubt Macbeth preferred to be succeeded by a son, but he does not have one. The argument is a justification, not a motive, and Macbeth moves to a peroration in lines 63–69 of which the substance is breathtakingly frivolous. He articulates the fact that he has defiled his mind (line 64) at the moment when he plans to defile it further. He refers to Satan (line 68) without even considering the Christian defence which was at least tried by Claudius, another king who murdered a king: 'Try what repentance can. What can it not?' (*Hamlet* III.3.65). Macbeth's style is crucial: Satan is 'the common enemy of man', a phrase which links the orator as closely as possible to his audience.

In his first soliloquy, Macbeth was able to think through a problem in a way which related it and himself to the whole universe, earth, heaven and hell. Now he is reduced to constructing for his own excitement an oration whose vehement sequences are necessary to conceal the absurdity of its premises. His mind is feeding on its own cravings. Its workings have become what Macbeth later calls a 'strange and self-abuse' (III.4.141).

Indulge such cravings and they become insatiable. Macbeth's last speech in Act IV shows him in a more repellent light than any other tragic hero in Shakespeare. The First Apparition at IV.1.71–72 tells Macbeth to 'beware Macduff' but the Second Apparition tells him 'to scorn/ The power of man' (lines 78–79). Macbeth decides to spare Macduff, but then changes his mind, to 'make assurance double sure' (line 83). When he is told that 'Macduff is fled to England' (line 142), he declares:

> The castle of Macduff I will surprise,
> Seize upon Fife, give to the edge o'the sword
> His wife, his babes, and all unfortunate souls
> That trace him in his line.

> (IV.1.149–152)

It was never suggested that Macduff's family were a threat; indeed, the confirmation that Banquo's children will reign might have directed Macbeth's attention elsewhere. Even Richard III who kills all who oppose him, and his wife when she becomes an obstacle, does not sink to extraneous butchery. Macbeth's language is also repellent. 'Unfortunate' is a sadist's caress. It is like Satan saying that he 'could pity' Adam and Eve, although he is determined to destroy them (*Paradise Lost*, Book IV, line 374). Not only do we hear Macbeth's lines, we are made to witness the murders in the next scene. How can we pity him?

Shakespeare's first strategy is his use of the scene in England — IV.3. The scene has often been attacked for its length, but it is astutely planned. In the main, it tells against

Macbeth. We hear that Scotland 'cannot/ Be called our mother, but our grave' (IV.3.165–166); we share Macduff's grief; we breathe the air of a sane world and for this purpose leisure is vital. Yet there are at least two effects which prepare the way for Act V. By the end of the scene we do not doubt that Macbeth will be defeated by the English army. We are told twice that Seyward has ten thousand men (IV.3.134, 190); he is a most able leader (lines 191–192); and in the eloquent passage about King Edward's 'most miraculous work' (lines 146–159), we are reminded of the huge presence of the divine in the world of *Macbeth*. The likelihood of English victory makes a difference: we do not view Macbeth the oppressor in the same way as when he is 'ripe for shaking' (line 238). The length of the scene also puts a distance between the horrors of IV.2 and our return to Macbeth's world in V.1. We do not forget the horrors, but there is space for other effects to grow.

Shakespeare's next strategy is his use of Lady Macbeth. Holinshed, the source of the play's history, does not mention when she died: she disappears from the narrative once Duncan is killed. Shakespeare brings us back to Macbeth's world in Act V with the sleep-walking scene. This is a coup of genius. Perhaps only pathos of this intensity could demand to be heard after the pathos of Lady Macduff and her children. Further, because Macbeth and Lady Macbeth have been through so much together, we transfer to him part of what we feel for her, not least when he asks the Doctor in V.3, as much on behalf of himself as his wife:

> Canst thou not minister to a mind diseased,
> Pluck from the memory a rooted sorrow,
> Raze out the written troubles of the brain,
> And with some sweet oblivious antidote
> Cleanse the stuffed bosom of that perilous stuff
> Which weighs upon the heart?

(V.3.40–45)

V.1 also reminds us of the scene when Macbeth seemed mad: after hearing the terrible voice which cried 'Sleep no more' (II.2.34), he made the futile but most vulnerable wish:

Wake Duncan with thy knocking! I would thou couldst!

(II.2.73)

To have Lady Macbeth talk in her sleep is an effect which is finely calculated. She is not deranged as Ophelia is in *Hamlet* IV.5. What we hear occupies a no-man's land between sanity and breakdown, yet the effect is intimate in the sense that nobody knows what takes place during sleep and we are all subject to those strange processes of psychic reworking, guilt and regeneration which make sleep 'great nature's second course' (II.2.38). With Lady Macbeth there is both an eerie intensity at being witness to what is secret, and a shared vulnerability: would we wish to be exposed in the same way?

Lady Macbeth's lines are exceptionally rich. They tell us more about her character and in a way which condemns it yet generates pathos:

> Out, damned spot! Out, I say! — One: two: why, then, 'tis time to do't. — Hell is murky! — Fie, my Lord, fie! A soldier, and afeard? — What need we fear who knows it, when none can call our power to accompt? — Yet who would have thought the old man to have had so much blood in him?

(IV.1.34–39)

The near rhyme of *two* and *do't* is like a nursery jingle. The puerility of its associations is most apt for the immature nature of her taunts to Macbeth in I.7 of which we are reminded in 'Fie, my Lord, fie! a soldier, and afeard?' This puerility modulates into naïveté with 'Yet who would have thought . . .?' The question is child-like, yet its self-condemnation is total. Shakespeare characteristically exploits the vulnerability to give us pathos which, if it does not lessen the condemnation, yet makes it pitiful:

> Here's the smell of the blood still. All the perfumes of Arabia will not sweeten this little hand. Oh! Oh! Oh!

(V.1.48–49)

We see Lady Macbeth's delicacy and sensuousness only now that it is lost, and we see the loss from the cruellest perspective, through her own eyes.

The delineation of Macbeth's mental condition is concentrated in V.5. There is a 'cry of women' and learning that his wife is dead, Macbeth tells us:

> She should have died hereafter.
> There would have been time for such a word —
> Tomorrow, and tomorrow, and tomorrow,
> Creeps in this petty pace from day to day
> To the last syllable of recorded time;
> And all our yesterdays have lighted fools
> The way to dusty death.

(V.5.17–23)

The living mind conducts a dialogue of past, present and future. But the present is not where Macbeth lives because he can react to his wife's death only by banishing it from the present. Will the future serve him better? If 'tomorrow' creeps in at this torpid, unvarying pace, how can the future rise to the occasion? As for the past, his victims were not 'fools' then:

> Here lay Duncan,
> His silver skin laced with his golden blood,
> And his gashed stabs looked like a breach in nature
> For ruin's wasteful entrance . . .

(II.3.108–111)

If he distorts the past, he can scarcely be helped by memory, whose 'use', as T S Eliot wrote, is 'For liberation' ('Little Gidding', lines 156–157). There is no dimension in which there is mental ground for him to grow. In 'The Wreck of the Deutschland' Hopkins expressed the terror of a similar lack of ground for his mind. Faced with God's fury, Hopkins is saved by his heart:

> The frown of his face
> Before me, the hurtle of hell
> Behind, where, where was a, where was a place?
> I whirled out wings that spell
> And fled with a fling of the heart to the heart of the Host.

(lines 17–21)

But Macbeth's heart has long since shrivelled. There is no 'place' left. The 'withering' of the second soliloquy is in effect complete.

Shakespeare ends Macbeth's speech with an effect which is characteristically generous to his hero:

> Out, out, brief candle!
> Life's but a walking shadow, a poor player
> That struts and frets his hour upon the stage
> And then is heard no more. It is a tale
> Told by an idiot, full of sound and fury,
> Signifying nothing.
>
> (V.5.23–28)

The contemporary audience was alert to biblical echoes. Some of these echoes refer to the wicked but others refer to everyman. Thus in Job 18:6 it is written of the wicked man that 'his candle shall be put out with him', but in Job 8:9 it is written of all men that 'our days upon earth are a shadow'. Again it is of all men that Psalm 39 declares:

> . . . verily every man at his best is altogether vanity.
> Surely every man walketh in a vain shew . . .
>
> (5–6)

It is the height of Shakespeare's art to remind us of our human bond with Macbeth in the very speech which shows us the terrifying desert of Macbeth's mental condition. We hope we may avoid the latter but, faced with eternity, who does not feel an 'idiot'? In blessed moments, the prospect of eternity will give us joy; more often it will tease us 'out of thought' as it did Keats ('Ode on a Grecian Urn', line 44); but if the saints, as many holy men and women have written, feel themselves 'the greatest of sinners', it is a dangerously proud man who does not feel, in this context, Macbeth's suffering as his own.

Soliloquy is a two-edged weapon. It reveals mental processes but it creates such intimacy that we are on the side of the soliloquiser. Shakespeare needed its powers of revelation to make us understand the fierce sterility of Macbeth's evil, its ability to evolve a parody of mental life which acquires greedy energy. Then Shakespeare boldly destroys our sympathy by the scene with Lady Macduff's children in order to create a response which is like sympathy but different. Today, sympathy implies approval. But in ancient Greece, sympathy meant, on the whole, to suffer with someone, to share their pain because of a common human bond, and not for any other reason: the question of approval was left open. In a famous discussion of 'the poet described in *ideal* perfection', Coleridge observed that the poet's power 'reveals itself in the balance or reconciliation of opposite or discordant qualities' (*Biographia Literaria* XIV). In *Macbeth* Shakespeare creates sympathy in the ancient sense and the question of approval is not merely not left open: it is absolutely decided in the negative. He then creates pathos which is itself remarkable for being without approval yet also devastating. We feel the terror of tragedy in the condition of Lady Macbeth and Macbeth and we feel its pity in this new pathos which is rigorous yet most sorrowing.

AFTERTHOUGHTS

1

On page 12, Gearin-Tosh draws special attention to the word 'withered' (II.1.52). Why?

2

Do you agree with the distinctions drawn in this essay between 'pity' and 'sympathy'?

3

How does Gearin-Tosh relate detailed analysis of individual speeches to the play as a whole?

4

The closing pages of this essay refer quite widely to other works of literature. What effect does this have?

Charles Moseley

Charles Moseley teaches English at Cambridge University and at the Leys School, Cambridge. He is the author of numerous critical studies.

ESSAY

Macbeth's free fall

> All hail, Macbeth! Hail to thee, Thane of Glamis!
> All hail, Macbeth! Hail to thee, Thane of Cawdor!
> All hail, Macbeth! that shalt be king hereafter!

The Witches' prophecies in I.3 are fulfilled to the letter. Macbeth, almost immediately Thane of Cawdor, is soon king. Banquo would indeed beget kings: James I, early in whose reign the play was written, was one of them. So was everything that happened to Macbeth inescapable? Did he ever have a chance? Faced with a masterful wife who twits him about his own manliness, Witches lying in wait in odd corners of the country-side, the motive of huge ambition, an ideal opportunity and a dagger conveniently at his belt, could he have resisted, avoided his fate and not killed Duncan? The question of Macbeth's freedom of will and action is central to the play. I shall suggest that not to see Macbeth as a free agent is to destroy any coherence and dignity the character might have.

But to begin with we need some discussion of terms to clear the undergrowth. First, free will and predestination. Predestination has usually been understood as man not being free to alter the future course of events and his own conduct in them, both of which being controlled by some higher power. Free will, on the other hand, means the capability of choosing, within the constraints of circumstances — among which are the results of the free will of other beings — between alternative courses of action and response. The opposition seems complete: if there is free will, there can be no predestination, for the outcome cannot be known in advance; if the outcome is determined in advance, goodbye free will. But in fact the mutual exclusion is only apparent.

The problem with the concept of predestination lies in the idea of time implied in the syllable 'pre-'. Some analogies may help to sort this out. For example, when we watch a play for the first time and do not know its plot, we cannot know in advance what the characters are going to do. When we see it again — and nothing *in* the play has changed — we know, as by definition the characters cannot, just what they will do: we can see their future, but they can't. The sequence of time in the play is present in our minds as a single completed whole. This of course allows the possibility of irony; but it does not and cannot mean the characters are predestined by us to behave as we know they will, for in their imaginary and illusory world they are still ignorant of the future, which for them at any given moment does not, strictly, yet exist. They are capable of acting and deciding as free beings, which is why we find them interesting. To put it another way: if we see a man sitting on a chair, he must be sitting on it. But his sitting on it is not controlled by our seeing him. In a similar way, in the sixth century, Boethius, in the *Consolation of Philosophy*, suggested the idea of predestination was simply a literal nonsense; God, who exists by definition in an Eternal Present, where there is no time, has knowledge of events in time but not *fore*knowledge of them, for all times are equidistant from him as all points on the circumference of a circle are equidistant from the central point of no dimension round which it is described. Thus it is possible to reconcile God's knowledge of all time, including the future, with the freedom of choice and action in time of human beings.

Macbeth could be seen as the puppet of forces external to the world of the play — the Witches, or the evil they represent, or of a malevolent Fate or a hostile Creator. But to do so would reduce him to the level of a doll without autonomy of action and choice; it would rob him of his dignity as a tragic hero. Our reaction could only be pity, and the play would be a statement,

literally, of no meaning — no meaning in the suffering and
ndeur of man, and because it would imply that all men are
similarly so controlled, the statement would itself be predestined
and therefore without any meaning that could logically be seen
as true or false. But to see Macbeth as a free agent with real
choices allows us to ask the much more interesting question of
how Macbeth was trapped into becoming the willing agent of his
own damnation. Before we can look at that damnation, it is
necessary to glance at what type of play *Macbeth* is, and the
nature of the Witches and what they represent.

Macbeth is a fundamentally religious play: that is, its main
area of interest is in the struggle in a man's soul between good
and evil courses, where the choice of good leads to his developing
his full potential, and the choice of evil to his utter and complete
loss of being and identity. It draws, indeed, for a good deal of
its material on the religious drama, the Moralities and
Mysteries, that were still being played in the towns of England
well into Shakespeare's manhood. The Porter scene, for
example, is built on and has verbal echoes of the comic scene
in the play of *The Harrowing of Hell*, where the devil-porter
hears a knocking on the gate and opens it — after much verbal
slapstick — to let in Christ the redeemer who will destroy the
power of hell for ever. (This gives us an interesting clue about
Macduff.) Like other art of the time, the play presupposes a
model of the order and degree of the universe that is the fruit
of centuries of speculation by Christian philosophers, where
every being has its allotted place and job to do, and sin consists,
basically, in refusing to do it. But most importantly, like
Marlowe's *Dr Faustus*, it is a play about a man being tempted
by appeals and suggestions to his overriding passion — in the
cases of both Faustus and Macbeth, power — to his damnation.
Shakespeare has clearly built Macbeth's motivation on an
understanding of the nature of sin as defined, for example, in
the work of the great theologian St Thomas Aquinas: the root
cause of sin is the commitment of the self to a good which is
changeable and imperfect, and every sinful act stems from an
uncontrolled desire for some such good. Desire like this results
from the fact that the sinner loves himself before all other
things (the name for that is the Deadly Sin of Pride) Macbeth's
inordinate ambition — of which he is fully conscious, (I.7.25ff)

— makes murder a lesser evil than not enjoying the kingship. Furthermore, Macbeth's career closes with an insight into the terrible despair and aloneness that is how the theologians define hell — for, as Marlowe's Mephistophilis reminded Faustus, it is only imagery to talk of the fires of hell, for hell is a state and not a place: 'Why, this is Hell, nor am I out of it'. *Macbeth* is thus the spiritual tragedy of a man who rejects his honoured and virtuous place in the hierarchy of Scotland and of the universe through the coveting of the throne, and reduces himself to nothingness. He is a man, moreover, who assumes that the knowledge of the future the Witches seem to have leaves him no escape from his destiny.

Shakespeare's understanding of evil in this play is also built on sound theological footings. It is philosophically and logically a grave mistake, as St Augustine demonstrated in the early fifth century, to see evil as independent, self-existing, a rival army, as it were, to the hosts of heaven, that might eventually win. Unfortunately the imagery we have to use in order to be able to think at all about those things beyond human reason does tend to make us visualise evil as a power capable of action, just as the metaphor of the fires of hell has misled thousands into a phobia about toasting forks. Evil, rather, is a privation of good, an emptying, rather than a filling with something else. Its character is fundamentally negative. But on stage this philosophical nicety is very hard to represent — though we do see a gradual emptying from Macbeth of all those qualities that made him so admired by other characters at the play's opening, and Lady Macbeth prays for a quite literal emptying of her womanly qualities. Shakespeare's device of the Witches was a way of getting round this difficulty as well as appealing to popular taste and preconceptions.

Among the educated, there was an underlying scepticism about the powers supposedly deployed by witchcraft. Even James I was beginning to modify the credulous position he had expressed in his youthful work *Demonologie*. In some circles, indeed, the whole concept of an invisible angelic/demonic world was under some attack. But there was a good deal of popular belief in the power of witches to do nasty things to people, and the annual consumption of harmless old women being burnt as witches was quite high for a good part of the seventeenth century. On the stage there was a fashion for plays with witches and devils in them, and though often the devils were comic (for Satan can't stand being laughed at) they were not taken without seriousness. The stage presence of Shakespeare's Witches combines something revolting and threatening with absurdity. The doggerel in which they speak emphasises the mindlessness of their malice — as for example towards the master of the *Tiger*; they represent in an externalised form the power *in* nature to turn to nothingness, away from true Good. The supernatural soliciting has no power of itself; they do not tell Macbeth to do anything, they do not control him in any way, they merely say what shall be and leave the chain of circumstance leading to it unsaid. Their prophecies could all come true — as does the first — without Macbeth doing anything at all except continue as 'noble Macbeth', 'Bellona's bridegroom'. He could even become king without doing anything — as he sees: 'If chance will have me king, why, chance may crown me' (I.3.143). (He is a member of the royal family, and even the designation of Malcolm as heir, which he sees as a major blow to his hopes (I.4.49ff) does not preclude the possibility. Malcolm, heir to the throne or not, through entirely natural causes might well fail to live to enjoy the crown.) All the portents and prophecies of Macbeth's second interview (IV.1.47ff) — which is initiated not by the Witches but by Macbeth — have, ironically, a logical and natural explanation. The ambiguity of these second prophecies extends to the first; they 'palter in a double sense', and Macbeth ultimately recognises that it is his hopes that have made him take that sense in a way that has led to his destruction (V.6.56ff). Their power derives from their initial articulation of Macbeth's overmastering passion, the ambition he has already at least hinted at to Lady Macbeth (I.5.16ff), and from his *wish*, his 'burn[ing in] desire' (I.5.3) to believe, understand, and know in a certain way. It is not the Witches but Macbeth himself who allows the prophetic utterance to enslave his mind.[1]

---

[1] The motif of prophecy being fulfilled by attempts to avoid it — as in *Oedipus Tyrannos* — is common enough. Shakespeare is using the motif the other way round.

Any power the Witches have is therefore parasitic upon Macbeth's own nature and ambition, and they externalise the deepest desires that he finds difficult to admit even to himself (I.3.136–137). Shakespeare is thus in a sense using them almost as a part of Macbeth's noble but flawed mind. A similar point is hinted at in V.3 and V.5: the Seyton (pronounced 'Satan') who arms Macbeth, and who tells him the news of the Queen's death that pushes him finally over the edge into despair, is an image of the real relationship between the Prince of Darkness and the moral being. The devil is powerless unless men give him power. The focus of the play thus centres in Macbeth's character, in the tragic mental and moral destruction and its effects. There was much theorising about tragedy in the sixteenth century which there is no space to go into here. What really concerns us is the consequent assumptions about the nature of the hero on which Shakespeare and his audience would be working. On a mature view a tragedy does not simply describe the fall of a man from high place to misery — which certainly happens to Macbeth, from 'noble Macbeth' to 'that dead butcher' — but also studies how he falls. His fall has to matter to us; we have to be convinced of his original grandeur, nobility and importance, see his fall as terrible and yet, because it proceeds from his own moral choice rather than merely from things done to him, ultimately just. And we have to feel a sense of terrible waste of human greatness and potential.

Both these premises, therefore, the religious and the dramatic, necessitate a Macbeth who is in a real sense free to choose. If he is not, he cannot be a viable hero of a tragedy; only if he is can the spiritual drama have any meaning.

As a tragic hero Macbeth has something in common with overreachers whose ambition brings about their downfall, like Marlowe's heroes Tamburlaine, Mortimer or Faustus — especially in their amoral pursuit of power. But he has more in common with a hero like Milton's Satan, where we see a being making an initial and entirely free wrong choice, and gradually being rendered less and less free by the consequences of that choice, to the point where he is unable to escape the prison of his own self. What is striking about Macbeth is the self-awareness he shows in his own self-destruction. He knows exactly what he is doing and is at all stages aware of his own progress.

Moreover, his progress is highlighted by the important use of two foils to him, Banquo and Lady Macbeth.

Banquo and Macbeth start the play off pretty much on the same level. Both are valiant soldiers, dutiful subjects, the saviours of their country, equal in their deservings (I.4.29ff). But when the Witches appear on the heath to both of them, their reactions begin to separate them, and it is worth illustrating how Banquo's cautious detachment preserves him from the fatal lust to know what devours Macbeth's mind.

Ironically, we know from I.2.66ff, before the Witches appear, that the thaneship of Cawdor has been granted (entirely understandably) to Macbeth. Their first prophecy is thus no prophecy, merely a statement of what is. But Banquo and Macbeth do not know this; and Macbeth's 'rapt' reaction, conveyed by bodily gesture (I.3.50ff) '... why do you start ...?') suggests that his interest has been passionately kindled and we are prepared for his desire to know more (lines 69ff). He has already, without examination, taken the statements at face value, and his desire to believe in the future greatness he covets means he is well and truly hooked: 'The greatest is behind' (line 116) is a clear hint of his passionate interest, and his eager turning to Banquo in the following lines elicits Banquo's prophetic warning (an important signal to us that the play is deeply concerned with the way Macbeth is motivated): 'That trusted home/ Might yet enkindle you unto the crown' (lines 119–120). His desire to talk of it more to Banquo (lines 153ff) confirms his acceptance of the reality and trustworthiness of the experience, and it is only after he has murdered Duncan that he dissembles his interest (II.1.21)

Banquo receives a similar but apparently contradictory prophecy in I.3.61ff; he too desires to hear more — he is understandably curious — but he is aware of the likelihood that the Witches are an illusion (lines 51–53), mere 'bubbles' (lines 78–79). He recognises something devilish in them (line 106), and remembers, as Macbeth forgets, that the 'instruments of darkness' can tell truth to make the soul trap itself — again, a useful guideline for the audience about what to watch out for in Macbeth (line 120). Nevertheless, he is intrigued by them (II.1.20) though he never loses his doubt about their status and reality — 'If there come truth from them ...' (III.1.6ff). Like Banquo, the audience may be being asked to remain uncommitted to the final reality of the Witches and the supernatural, but to recognise that the mind's consent to the illusion or whatever it is might enkindle all sorts of terrible things. It is, after all, Macbeth alone who sees the Ghost in III.4, and whatever else it is, it is one of the 'scorpions' of his mind.

The moral sense and caution shown by Banquo is constantly emphasised by Shakespeare to highlight the freedom of choice both men enjoy. Careful of his honour, Banquo is guarded at Macbeth's tentative suggestion that they should join forces:

> So I lose none [honour]
> In seeking to augment it, but still keep
> My bosom franchised and allegiance clear,
> I shall be counselled.
>
> (II.1.26–29)

He is clearly suspicious when Duncan is murdered, and declares his own position quite unambiguously (II.3.127ff): 'In the great hand of God I stand'. The point is that he is tempted, he is attracted to the idea of siring a race of kings, but he does not fall:

> Merciful powers!
> Restrain in me the cursed thoughts that nature
> Gives way to in repose!
>
> (ll.1.7–9)

Having one character who did not give way enormously heightens our perception of the one who did.

The Witches' prophecy is powerful only because Macbeth already has ambitions and desires that alarm him. I.3.129ff shows that he wants to believe that he will be king, but he sees a terrible way to achieve it: murder. He is aware that even thinking the thought — 'murder yet is but fantastical' (line 138) — is dreadful (though having the thought flash through the mind is not in itself sinful). It is consenting to it that revolts his whole physical frame, as the action itself will upset the very order of nature — a terrible 'yield[ing] to that suggestion':

> Whose horrid image doth unfix my hair,
> And make my seated heart knock at my ribs
> Against the use of nature
>
> (I.3.134–136)

Macbeth sees the appalling reversal of all values, of duty and nature implied in the action. And this time his conscience and his perception of the way the moral machine of the universe runs make him reject the notion of actively seeking the crown in this way; he rightly sees that he is not compelled to do anything (line 144).

Yet his desires, though 'black and deep', unfit for the eye of heaven to see, he does want accomplished. Clearly he has discussed them with Lady Macbeth at some point (I.7.48). She, indeed, has at this point no similar misgivings: there is no ambiguity about her when we first meet her. Indeed, Shakespeare had to develop her so rapidly as a foil to Macbeth's moral perplexity that in her first appearance she has to be clearly recognised as villainous. She is committed to the fulfilment of their joint ambition by any means. There is something utterly devilish in her rejection of all that is feminine in herself, something literally unnatural. Her terrible prayer (I.5.38ff) is fulfilled to the letter like all the prayers in this play are: she becomes a 'fiend-like queen'. But he is not willing to so commit himself — he reacts, 'We will speak further' (which is the polite formula for 'no') (I.5.69) to Lady Macbeth's clear assumption that he is eager to get on with the murder. She reacts with fury; but this is the last time we see her so confident. For as Macbeth grows in evil doing, she weakens. She needs Dutch courage before the murder of Duncan (II.2.1); she is agitated and nervous after it; by III.2.5–7 we are seeing the first crack in her, the first signs of the fear and insecurity that lead to her eventual madness. By V.1 she is in her own hell. The character whom Shakespeare presented to us at first as in many ways the simplest to understand is being shown to have a moral consciousness and awareness of her responsibility for her own actions.

By I.7.1ff the desire to be king is at the front of Macbeth's mind. He is even ready to murder to become so, but dreadfully afraid of consequences in this life and the next. He is aware that kingship won in such a way makes itself vulnerable to the very same breakdown in order and duty. He recites all the reasons why he should not murder Duncan (lines 12ff), and — in utter self-knowledge — he recognises that his ambition will, if not checked, ultimately destroy him (lines 25ff). (This concern for right conduct has been the means for him to be up till now 'noble Macbeth', and it is well known — and seen as a fault — by Lady Macbeth: I.5.16ff.) Sensibly, he determines to 'proceed no further in this business' (lines 31ff), in recognition that what he would be doing would destroy his humanity (lines 45–47). But as a result of Lady Macbeth's persuasion by the unfair argument attacking his self-esteem, his courage, and his love for her, by lines 80ff he consents. He knows exactly what he is doing. The horror of what he is about to do that he shows in his soliloquy II.1.33ff does not stop him; and by II.2.20ff the horror at what he has done is compounded by the awareness that his bodily and spiritual rest is destroyed for ever. He needs blessing, but has (without repentance) cut himself off from it. The consciousness of his own guilt for his own action is over-whelming, and remorse (line 73) is almost insupportable.

His action has made him in a real sense unfree, for as he himself perceived, no action is without consequences. His life is now a series of responses to those that flow from this initial crime. First he has to dissemble. Yet in his dissembling when Duncan's death is discovered he speaks, with a hypocrisy which must be self-aware, a truth he echoes sincerely on Lady Macbeth's death:

> Had I but died an hour before this chance
> I had lived a blessèd time . . .

> (II.3.88–89)

Fear makes him follow the first murder with two more, when he kills the guards to protect his own position; fear of Banquo, fear of the future — 'To be thus is nothing;/ But to be safely thus' (III.1.47ff) — becomes the controlling emotion in his mind. Fear makes him mistrust his peers so that he keeps spies in their houses (III.4.130–131). He is quite aware of what is happening to him: he recognises that his 'eternal jewel', his soul, is now:

> Given to the common enemy of man,
> To make them kings, the seeds of Banquo kings!

> (III.1.68–69)

And the reaction is not repentence, which can rescue the most hardened sinner, but defiance and despair: 'come fate into the list/ And champion me to the utterance' (lines 70–71). All the time he is conscious of the 'bonds' on him (III.2.16ff) which alone keep him human, and in his despair rejects them. In the agonies of remorse, in the hellish snake-pit of his conscience — 'full of scorpions is my mind, dear wife' (III.2.36) — he envies Duncan's peace. He knows what he is doing and what he is:

> I am in blood
> Stepped in so far, that, should I wade no more,
> Returning were as tedious as go o'er.
>
> (III.4.135–137)

The irony, which Shakespeare could count on his audience spotting, is that in his despair he forgets that true repentance can cleanse of the worst of sins. He has now truly lost his freedom, for he is trapped by his own mind in a hell of his own devising.

At this point he has overtaken Lady Macbeth in evil. He tells her to be innocent of the knowledge that he is planning to murder Banquo (III.2.45–46). When we see him meeting the murderers almost on their own level and persuading them, we are aware of the enormous lowering of status and dignity he has brought on himself (III.1.75ff). He has thrown all concern for anyone or anything except himself to the winds, and mere retention of power is all that matters. He decides to seek the Witches out 'to know/ By the worst means, the worst' (III.4.133–134) and in IV.1 he desires to know the future even if it entails the destruction of the world itself (lines 49ff; cf. lines 99ff).

By IV.1.149ff, when he vows to kill the Macduffs, his crimes have become merely vindictive, purposeless, vicious — and stupid. This cannot be to his advantage in any way. The violence is mindless, and even the nobility he had as a fighter at the opening of the play begins to dissipate in sheer bloodiness: the ugliness in V.3 of his nervous anger — supported by the significant oath 'death of my soul' (line 16) — does not argue a great commander men willingly follow any more, and he knows that he is alone and must always be so: all the things he had at the beginning of the play he has lost. His life is fruitless, in the 'sere, the yellow leaf' (lines 20ff). He has even lost 'the taste of fears' (V.5.9ff). His mind is now diseased as is Lady Macbeth's, and in V.3.40ff he is clearly talking about himself as well as her. Life has become meaningless, 'signifying nothing' (V.5.18ff). He has finally become both the traitorous Cawdor and 'merciless' Macdonwald, even to the composition of his army of kerns. The sense of waste and the terrible loss of something that was once grand and noble is profound.

Macbeth has been tricked by his own desires and ambition into projecting onto the ambiguity of the Witches' showings and speeches what he wanted to see and understand. He recognises at the end that the fiends are 'juggling':

> . . . palter[ing] with us in a double sense,
> That keep the word of promise to our ear
> And break it to our hope.

(V.6.59–61)

But by then it is too late; he is in hell, where the doors are firmly bolted — on the inside.

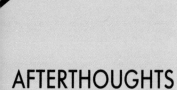

AFTERTHOUGHTS

1

What, according to Moseley, are the essential differences between free will and predestination?

2

What view of the Witches is given in this essay?

3

In what senses does Macbeth resemble the 'traitorous Cawdor and "merciless" Macdonwald' (page 33)?

4

Suppose a theatre director wished to present an interpretation of the play that saw Macbeth as victim rather than free agent. How might this be done?

Robert Wilson

Robert Wilson teaches English at Merchant Taylors' School. He is the author of numerous school text books and editions, his most recent publication being Novels *(Longman, 1987)*

ESSAY

The sense of society in *Macbeth*

> Each new morn
> New widows howl, new orphans cry, new sorrows
> Strike heaven on the face, that it resounds
> As if it felt with Scotland, and yelled out
> Like syllable of dolour.

(IV.3.4–8)

This is how Macduff describes the condition of Scotland when he visits Malcolm in England and hopes to rouse a military action against the evil dictatorial tyranny of Macbeth. At this stage in the play we know that its tragedy is not to be confined to the self-induced destruction of a man of great force, imaginative power and insight. The sense of waste and loss is not to be limited to that which follows the complete moral disintegration of the flawed hero, Macbeth. For the tragedy is not simply that of an individual of towering psychic force; it is the tragedy of a whole society.

Two images may be teased out from Macduff's words (above) and related to sentiments and actions in the rest of the play — that of the family and that of the victim and bully. And as we examine these two themes we shall become increasingly aware of the particular sense of society that permeates the play and contributes to its final tragic impact.

Firstly, then, Macduff chooses to present the agony of Scotland in terms of the decimated family: 'widows' and 'orphans' are all that are left of that primary and formative 'society', the family, which gives us the models for all other broader groupings of people living together. It is in families that our capacity for loving and relating to others and our appreciation of human values are first nurtured, as Malcolm implies in that same scene when he refers to 'wife and child,/ Those precious motives, those strong knots of love'.

Throughout *Macbeth* moments of horrific destruction are linked with an awareness of family and so reinforce our sense of a fundamental destruction of society at its very origins. Malcolm and Donalbain, the King's sons, are spiritually present at the murder of their father. They sleep in the next room to Duncan and, being woken at the moment of his death, they clearly respond to the presence of evil for Macbeth overhears them:

> One cried, 'God bless us' and 'Amen' the other

(II.2.26)

Fleance is present when his father is murdered but escapes to carry the generative power and values of Banquo forward into future generations, for his 'children will be kings'. At the very end of the play, the relief of Macbeth's death is not to be experienced without a further reminder of the fundamentally destructive effect of his career. Young Seyward is his last victim and another family relationship is severed, though here the sentiments expressed by his father and the manner of his death create a wholesomeness, that of stoical self-sacrifice in the service of the greater family, the good society.

But the most dramatically overwhelming destruction of family occurs in deeply moving and ironic juxtaposition to the quotation which is the starting point of this essay. When Macduff utters these words, he is unaware that his wife and children have been savagely butchered by Macbeth's men. Indeed, we have just witnessed this assault upon child-like innocence and feminine tenderness and care — so moving to Ross and even to one of Macbeth's minions. Consider the implications of that scene's (IV.2) final lines:

MURDERER	What, you egg.

Young fry of treachery!
He stabs him

SON	He has killed me, mother!

Run away, I pray you.

(IV.2.83–85)

The destruction of the hope of the family, its eldest son — we might assume — is made all the more poignant by his desire, even at the moment of his own death, that his mother should escape. The child is young, pre-adolescent in the tone of his conversation, yet he urges survival upon his mother rather than comfort for himself. This reverses the situation when Banquo is murdered and urges his son to escape. But both moments are intensely moving because they proclaim the values of the family and its selfless humanity at the point of its being threatened to absolute destruction. Notice too the connotations of the language used by the Murderer. He expresses his scorn for the diminutive size of the child who dares to oppose him by calling him an 'egg' and 'fry'. Yet these words also have positive associations, for it is the egg from which life comes and 'fry' — as well as meaning the eggs or recently hatched young of fish — may simply mean offspring, a man's children. The insult carries an implicit acknowledgement of the child's worth.

It is not only in the action of the play, in the enactments of family destruction, that we are aware of this theme. Notions of family permeate the sentiments and language of the characters. When Macduff, in the scene in England, wants to express his incredulous horror at the depraved character that Malcolm has assumed, he refers to family values:

Thy royal father
Was a most sainted king: the queen that bore thee,
Oftener upon her knees than on her feet . . .

(IV.3.108–110)

He cannot believe that such piety in the parents should not be inherited by the son. When Lady Macbeth conveys her ruthless self-assertion in the strongest possible terms and wants to overcome her husband's scruples, she frighteningly mutilates the most moving of family images:

> I have given suck, and know
> How tender 'tis to love the babe that milks me;
> I would while it was smiling in my face
> Have plucked my nipple from his boneless gums
> And dashed the brains out, had I so sworn
> As you have done to this.

(I.7.54–59)

Here is no casual reference to breast-feeding; the emotional reality of the physical act is fully present, even to the responsive and trusting smile of the defenceless babe. Contemplate the full horror of the sentence. Lady Macbeth does not say that she would have killed her child had she broken her word. She has apprehended a deeper truth, that the physical destruction of the family, its love, its hope for the future, is the *inevitable*, the *necessary* accompaniment of the act of self-aggrandisement to which Macbeth has sworn. But she is not thinking with her whole being: in her state of passionate ambition she denies the values that she shares — whether she likes it or not — with the rest of her society. For, a little later, it is reverence for the family that inhibits her murderous impulse:

> Had he not resembled
> My father as he slept, I had done't

(II.2.12–13)

And that very line concludes with a form of address which is a statement of a socially validated family relationship — 'My husband!'

These are but a few of the many instances in *Macbeth* where the image of the family suggests the values and the destruction of a whole society. We cannot leave it without noting the irony of Macbeth's not being apparently blessed with any living children and of his fear of the Witches' prophecy that the children of Banquo shall inherit the throne, 'a fruitless crown . . . No son of mine succeeding' (III.1.60/63). He longs for the very thing that he is everywhere destroying.

Our starting quotation offers another, equally fruitful, image which may likewise be traced as a persistent theme through the play. This is the idea of the victim and bully, an image of weakness. Macduff says that the cries of the widows and orphans 'strike heaven on the face'. The direct frontal attack, the blow that is a demeaning insult, asserts the dominance of the aggressor. And 'heaven' — in these lines responding like a child that is bullied and cannot give back blow for blow — 'yelled out/ Like syllable of dolour'. This is a fragmented inarticulated cry, a 'syllable' of pain and suffering. Such response from the bully's victim is likely to provoke only further aggression and Macduff's lines, extending Scotland's national agony into a cosmic state in which the victim's cry echoes or 'resounds' throughout the moral order of things, suggests a particularly hopeless, empty view of a passive state of goodness being persistently threatened by virulent evil. The only reality seems to be a hollow space echoing with the expression of impotent pain. The implication is that Scotland is essentially passive, weak and vulnerable.

Scotland's vulnerability is evident right from the opening scenes. A rebellion has broken out; a foreign predator has invaded in order to exploit this internal conflict and drawn the opportunistic support of a noble who had formerly been the close and loyal supporter of the King. The first lines of the second scene suggest this political uncertainty, a government on the brink of collapse. Such is the King's ineffective grip on events that he must stop a passing wounded soldier in order to find out what is happening in the battle. In the ensuing dialogue the King's responses are extraordinary in their brevity and nature. The fearsome carnage perpetrated by Macbeth and his slaughter of Macdonwald —

> ... he unseamed him from the nave to the chops,
> And fixed his head upon our battlements

(I.2.22–23)

— provokes from Duncan not wrath against the rebel nor any thought of political implications, military manoeuvres or horror of war, but a simple cry of almost naive admiration for the man who has become a killing machine in order to protect this weak but gracious society:

> O valiant cousin! Worthy gentleman!

(I.2.24)

His recalling of a familial relationship and of the whole set of values associated with 'gentleman' sounds oddly inappropriate in this context.

Duncan has neither been involved in directing the tactics of the battle nor in agreeing terms of surrender with the defeated invader and, as the scene unfolds, he displays no political awareness and makes none of those judgements that we might think appropriate to an effective and astute ruler. Instead he utters a few brief statements of praise and gratitude towards those that have defended him and he condemns the traitor:

> No more that Thane of Cawdor shall deceive
> Our bosom interest. Go pronounce his present death,
> And with his former title greet Macbeth.
> . . .
> What he hath lost, noble Macbeth hath won.
>
> (I.2.66–70)

Duncan's interest lies in valuing the person and the personal relationship. It is the breach of trust and loyalty that hurts and preoccupies him and the punishment for that disloyalty is withdrawal of close affection — 'Our bosom interest'. To counterbalance that loss of relationship, he must praise and reward the worthy subject.

The tragic passivity and naïve ineptitude of this society are evident everywhere in the play. When Duncan is murdered, his sons are, as I have pointed out, roused from sleep, spiritually alerted to the evil around them. Macbeth overhears their movements and describes them thus:

> There's one did laugh in's sleep, and one cried, 'Murder!'
> That they did wake each other. I stood and heard them.
> But they did say their prayers, and addressed them
> Again to sleep.
>
> (II.2.22–25)

Together they produce an ambivalent response — laughter and horror — that contradicts and so cancels out itself but, aroused from sleep, they take the way of prayer and contemplation to return as swiftly as possible to that state of unconsciousness. This passive retreat from evil reality is to be further acted out when, as potential victims of the bully, Malcolm and Donalbain flee the country rather than stay to fight for their rightful inheritance and to exact vengeance on the murderer.

Their action is but one version of a characteristic pattern of response amongst the Scottish nobles. When Duncan's murder has been discovered, Banquo takes the lead:

> ... when we have our naked frailties hid
> That suffer in exposure, let us meet
> And question this most bloody piece of work
> To know it further. Fears and scruples shake us.
> In the great hand of God I stand ...

(II.3.123–127)

His moral stand, his determination to find the truth, is counterbalanced by a feeling of weakness. He refers to 'frailties' and the effects of 'fears and scruples'. The use of 'scruples' is particularly interesting: it is a doubt or uncertainty in regard to right and wrong, especially one which causes a man to hesitate where others would be bolder to act. Hamlet refers to 'some craven scruple/ Of thinking too precisely on th'event' (*Hamlet* IV.4.40–41) and thereby offers a definition which is equally relevant to the outcome of the deliberations of the thanes and leaders of Scotland. For, in spite of private reservations and even shared suspicions of Macbeth, he is allowed to bully his way through to kingship. Banquo's sensitive apprehension of the moral ineffectiveness and weakness of his society is aptly symbolised in his description of their bodies, clad in the scanty clothing of the night. We see their physical vulnerability before us on the stage.

Later, Banquo allows himself to be hopelessly outmanoeuvred by Macbeth. He has not taken the moral stand he had promised and his own integrity is compromised as he utters the sentiments of the loyal subject:

> Let your highness
> Command upon me, to the which my duties
> Are with a most indissoluble tie
> Forever knit.

(III.1.15–18)

Even if we were to justify these words as issuing from Banquo's deep reverence for the office of the King rather than as a statement of personal loyalty to Macbeth — and that would run counter to the very *personal* basis of loyalty projected in Duncan's court — we have to see his reactions in the rest of this scene as very foolish. In spite of his deep suspicions of Macbeth — 'I fear/ Thou playedst most foully' (III.1.2–3) — he is sufficiently guileless for Macbeth to elicit information from him about his future movements. So he puts his own life and that of Fleance in jeopardy.

Macduff, similarly, muddles his way through to marshalling opposition to Macbeth, exposing and sacrificing his entire family on the way. A more worldy-wise and suspicious man would have carried out his duties to protect his wife and children as well as stimulated Malcolm to lead an army against the tyrant. Since he was himself able to leave Scotland, it should not have been beyond his resources to effect the safe exile of his family. It is as if this entire society colludes with Macbeth, supporting him in his domination and abandoning those arts of trickery and guile which are necessary for survival in the wicked world. Scotland identifies itself with the psychology of the victim, regressing to a childish cry of pain as its only response to aggression.

This is not all that is to be said about Duncan's court, for there are positive values that give it life. The tragedy issues from the destruction of what is of immense worth and potential: a sensitive, humane society and a tragic hero who shares those values in the early episodes of the play and never entirely abandons the memory of them. We shall consider the various instances where finer feelings, such as gratitude, are expressed.

Ross, greeting the triumphant Macbeth, refers to Duncan's reaction in these terms:

> . . . when he reads
> Thy personal venture in the rebels' fight
> His wonders and his praises do contend
> Which should be thine, or his.

(I.3.89–92)

The notion is complex, reflecting the particular tension involved in adequately expressing gratitude. The issue is whether Duncan will retain the sentiments of admiration within himself and so feed upon them, preserving them as perfect 'wonders' or impart his sentiments to Macbeth in the form of 'praises' which cannot do justice to the fineness of the original 'wonders'. It is, indeed, a refined moral conflict and what Ross says here of the King's feelings is borne out when Duncan does greet Macbeth:

> O worthiest cousin!
> The sin of my ingratitude even now
> Was heavy on me. Thou art so far before,
> That swiftest wing of recompense is slow
> To overtake thee.

(I.4.15–19)

He asserts that, like a runner leading a race who cannot now be caught, so Macbeth's merits are impossibly beyond Duncan's capacity to render him adequate thanks. It might be merely excessively polite, a fulsome and courtly way of dealing with a conventional moment — the king thanks his triumphant general in public — if it were not for the intensely personal and heartfelt language in which the sentiment is couched. Duncan greets Macbeth as 'cousin' and reminds him of family values and personal feeling. He need not even have spoken of his feeling of oppression at being unable to thank him before — he had not, after all, had an opportunity — and to describe a state of being pent up with thanks as 'sin' is to put the highest possible value on recognising the service and worth of others. A little later, the converse of his oppression is experienced: Duncan is able to say to Banquo that Macbeth:

> . . . is full so valiant,
> And in his commendations I am fed;
> It is a banquet to me.

(I.4.55–57)

The proper expression of praise is life-giving; indeed, an appreciation of the value of another person is as good as a satisfying communal celebration, a 'banquet'.

This truly civilised society is based on and animated by personal regard and trust, which means loyalty of subjects to their king and a recognition of the value of good feelings, particularly those of personal devotion. This scene (I.4.) is vital, establishing early in the play these qualities of human relationship. They are perhaps quintessentially captured in Duncan's words of mourning for the loss of relationship with the traitorous Thane of Cawdor:

> There's no art
> To find the mind's construction in the face.
> He was a gentleman on whom I built
> An absolute trust.
>
> (I.4.12–15)

The very foundation of government in Duncan's court is faith in the good will, the nobility and 'gentle' qualities of the other. That it is no secure foundation is acknowledged by Duncan in the very moment of his turning to greet the man who will utterly betray that trust.

Duncan wears his heart upon his sleeve. When, after welcoming Macbeth and Banquo, he attempts to stabilise his country by making clear the succession to the throne, he introduces the matter by describing his feelings:

> My plenteous joys,
> Wanton in fulness, seek to hide themselves
> In drops of sorrow.
>
> (I.4.34–36)

A state of overflowing joy is associated with one of delightful waywardness which must bring something fruitful to birth, as rain nourishes the soil or a child issues from loving. The King goes on to name Malcolm as heir after addressing his court as 'Sons, kinsmen, thanes,/ And you whose places are the nearest'. The appeal is to a close identification with the ruling family and a proper participation in this loyalty leads to a shared well-being, for Malcolm's naming as Prince of Cumberland, and therefore as heir, affects everyone:

> . . . which honour must
> Not unaccompanied invest him only,
> But signs of nobleness, like stars, shall shine
> On all deservers.
>
> (I.4.40–43)

Again the thought is complex and here, perhaps, ambivalent. The powerful words — 'honour', 'nobleness' — identify values which though experienced inwardly must be expressed publicly. Malcolm will be 'invested' with an honour much as one might wear ceremonial robes and Duncan asserts that this public title will be accompanied by a growth of inner virtues issuing in 'nobleness' beneficial to all. A parallel idea is that those of noble spirit will be likewise given publicly recognisable signs of their worth, as if hung with the star-like insignia of the chivalric orders.

Another cluster of images conveying the life of this gracious society concerns the natural world. Duncan tells Macbeth:

> I have begun to plant thee, and will labour
> To make thee full of growing.

(I.4.29–30)

In the nourishing and nurturing of good feelings and of a sort of growth which has more to do with the *spirit* of service and loyalty, Duncan sees himself as a gardener in touch with natural processes of growth and maturing. But it is Banquo, and not Macbeth, who is able to develop the image, for when Duncan embraces him — 'let me enfold thee/ And hold thee to my heart' — Banquo's intuitive sympathy with the King's feelings leads him to say, 'There if I grow,/ The harvest is your own' (I.4.33–34). The line most elegantly marries the twin notions of bountiful giving and of fruitfulness which permeate the dialogue of this scene.

Once again, before the blow falls on Duncan, we appreciate similar sentiments. As they approach Macbeth's castle, Duncan and Banquo remark on the beauty of its location, the freshness of the air and the presence of house martins nesting everywhere on the building. They delight in this harmonious interaction between the human and the natural world. For Banquo, the 'martlet', or house martin, is a 'guest of summer', the bird's seasonal presence described in the terms of a valued social relationship — echoed a little later by Duncan when he greets 'our honoured hostess'. Banquo delights in its nesting habits, its use of every ledge on the castle for the building of its nest.

> . . . no jutty, frieze,
> Buttress, nor coign of vantage, but this bird
> Hath made his pendent bed and procreant cradle.

(I.6.6–8)

Here again is a potent cluster of ideas which leads us back to the central paradox of this society and to its union of virtue and weakness. The martlet is resourceful in exploiting and trusting itself to a human artefact and its hanging nest is the place of rest and birth, an image of restoration and of growth; and it is also an image of extreme vulnerability, for what is weaker than an infant in its cradle or more defenceless than a sleeping man in his bed?

Macbeth destroys this society knowing, as he does so, all that he is losing. In his powerful soliloquy at the start of Act I, scene 7 he rehearses all the reasons against killing the King: the claims of kinship, of loyalty, of hospitality, the virtues of the man whose murder he contemplates. And, above all, he senses the moral strength and the physical weakness of his country, for he talks the same language as Banquo and Duncan:

> . . . Pity, like a naked new-born babe
> Striding the blast, or heaven's cherubin, horsed
> Upon the sightless curriers of the air,
> Shall blow the horrid deed in every eye,
> That tears shall drown the wind.

(I.7.21–25)

This resonant image pulls together so much of the rest of the play. The tender emotion of 'pity', most sensitive and delicate of feelings, epitome of finely tuned humane responses, is appropriately that most weak, touching and defenceless of creatures, 'a naked new-born babe', the babe whose brains Lady Macbeth would dash out. Yet it rides the winds, the blast that announces the final judgement, and, like the avenging angels, it forces all of mankind to face the vicious storm of evil. Its power is elemental and overwhelming and its moral force produces an obliterating flood, reminding us of the mythical purging of the world which Noah survived.

Remarkably, these perceptions, this intuition of the moral beauty and strength of his nation and of its vulnerability, are voiced by the man who will allow a deadly ambition to overwhelm him. That is his tragedy and it is the tragedy of a whole society.

AFTERTHOUGHTS

What parallels does Wilson draw in this essay between domestic relationships and society as a whole?

How important are children in *Macbeth*?

Wilson describes Duncan as 'ineffective' (page 39). What grounds does he give for this judgement? Do you agree with him?

Consider the final sentence of this essay, where the word 'tragedy' is used twice. Does it have the same meaning on each occasion?

Christopher Mills

Christopher Mills is Head of English at Larkmead School in Abingdon, and author of several critical studies.

ESSAY

The relationship between Macbeth and Lady Macbeth

Macbeth is a classical tragedy which plots the fall and death of a once great man. In part, Macbeth's decline results from flaws within his own character. But he is also subject to a host of supernatural phenomena which seem to limit the scope of his independence: the Witches' prophecies, the air-drawn daggers, unnatural dreams, terrifying omens, cannibal horses, day-time darkness, storms and hidden stars.

The human element, however, is provided by the relationship between Macbeth and his lady. They are bound by the strength of their love, and their understanding of and support for each other, but their attempt to achieve a mutual ambition destroys them and without each other they fall into despair and die. The withering of this relationship reflects the gradual disintegration of the social and political world in Scotland and of the kingdom's relationship with its new king, as well as the disintegration of Macbeth as an individual. By tracing the meetings between the couple, therefore, we gain a greater insight into the meanings of the play and into the workings of the tormented heart and mind, for the protagonists live the greater part of their lives through their imaginations. It is in the mind, perhaps above all, that their tragedies are enacted and thus, as these disintegrate, their deaths become inevitable.

From the moment of receiving Macbeth's letter until Duncan's murder, Lady Macbeth is ruled by her imagination, aware of the present but living in the future:

> Glamis thou art, and Cawdor, and shalt be
> What thou art promised.
>
> (I.5.13–14)

She is already planning how to overcome the humane sides of Macbeth's nature by pouring her spirits into his ear. In her terrifyingly, unnatural prayer — 'Come, you spirits ...' (I.5.38–52) — she imagines the actual wounds she would make were she to carry out the murder herself:

> That my keen knife see not the wound it makes
>
> (I.5.50)

And when Macbeth arrives, she admits that she has been 'transported':

>   ... beyond
> This ignorant present, and I feel now
> The future in the instant.
>
> (I.5.54–6)

Undaunted by Macbeth's brief words, she seems already to have the entire plan organised: 'Leave all the rest to me.' (I.5.71)

Macbeth more expediently works out, in his mind, the consequences of:

> Bloody instructions, which being taught return
> To plague the inventor
>
> (I.7.9–10)

He ponders the immorality of murder, but his wife's analysis of his character (I.5.14–23) has already shown us how well she knows her man. The fearful nature of his deeds on the battlefield, reported earlier by the bleeding captain and Ross, show what potential for violence he has, but we have seen him introduced in the early scenes as 'brave', 'valiant' and 'worthy'; Duncan himself calls him 'noble' and he has crushed Cawdor's rebellion loyally; his irresolution before the murder is prompted by moral arguments:

> He's here in double trust:
> First, as I am his kinsman and his subject,
> Strong both against the deed; then, as his host
>
> (I.7.12–14)

And Lady Macbeth fears his 'nature':

> It is too full o'the milk of human-kindness
> To catch the nearest way
>
> (I.5.15–16)

Macbeth is also subject to the fear conjured up by his own imagination. His immediate response to the Witches, for example, suggests that he has already contemplated gaining the crown, yet his initial reaction is not the excitement one might expect:

> Good sir, why do you start, and seem to fear
> Things that do sound so fair?
>
> (I.3.50–51)

He cannot even name Duncan or the idea of murder:

> . . . that suggestion
> Whose horrid image doth unfix my hair.
>
> (I.3.133–134)

Lady Macbeth thus realises that though Macbeth has the potential for 'merciless' violence, she must persuade him against his will and conscience and the moral and human leanings of his nature.

It is too glib to say that Lady Macbeth is simply 'fiend-like'. It is not, for example, she who puts the idea of murder into Macbeth's mind. That 'horrid suggestion' was the fruit of Macbeth's own imagination and it was he who told her to ponder deeply the Witches' prophecies — 'Lay it to thy heart' (I.5.12). What Lady Macbeth does is to give him the support he needs, the strength and courage to perform the deed. Her methods are perhaps devious but she only uses her own powerful imagination to gain power over his in order to help him attain their mutual desire. Indeed, she is only acting as a faithful partner in thus supporting him and it is their mutual support for and instinctive understanding of one another that makes them a remarkable couple.

It is clear from Macbeth's eagerness to acquaint his wife with the prophecies so that she 'mightest not lose the dues of rejoicing' (I.5.10), that he loves his wife. He calls her his 'dearest partner of greatness', he talks of 'what greatness is promised *thee*' (I.5.9,11) and from the moment the murder is committed, apart from an interlude at the banquet, it is he who tries to protect her. Knowing this, Lady Macbeth begins her taunts by questioning his love for her, persuasively turning his own words back on him ('dressed' I.7.36, for his 'worn' I.7.34):

> Was the hope drunk
> Wherein you dressed yourself? Hath it slept since?
> And wakes it now to look so green and pale
> At what it did so freely? From this time
> Such I account thy love.

(I.7.35–39)

'Green and pale' suggest cowardice and so next she assaults his manliness, questioning his sexuality, his honour and his reputation:

> Art thou afeard
> To be the same in thine own act and valour
> As thou art in desire? Wouldst thou . . .
> . . . live a coward . . .?

(I.7.39–41, 43)

She clearly recognises that his 'desire' matches hers.

Macbeth counters her taunts with conceit and a defence of his honour:

> I dare do all that may become a man;
> Who dares do more is none

(I.7.46–47)

But again his wife turns his words against him, the term 'beast' contrasting insultingly with 'man':

> What beast was't then
> That made you break this enterprise to me?
> When you durst to it, then you were a man;
> And to be more than what you were, you would
> Be so much more the man. Nor time nor place

```
    Did then adhere . . .
                        . . . their fitness now
    Does unmake you.
```

(I.7.47–54)

'Unmake' is an ironic pun on 'unman', against which she contrasts the strength of her own femininity to humiliate him further. She ends with an emotional challenge that she knows he cannot resist and which is thus the climax of this scene. She moves in imagination from looking backward ('I have given suck') to the beastly imagining of braining her baby. Her utterance is designed both to contrast her dependability and self-control (she would fight her strongest instincts, those of a mother, without emotion, rather than go back on her word) with his vacillation and temptation to break an oath ('had I sworn so as you/ Have', lines 58–59) and to remind him of his lack of heirs, thus again challenging his sexuality. Macbeth argues no further and his next words show his agreement. He needs only to be shown that they can act with impunity. His wife is sufficiently resourceful, however, and explains how false appearances will cover their tracks and provides him with a clear, simple plan. Her practical resourcefulness allows her to take command at this point: he need only perform the act.

One cannot simply place Lady Macbeth in the Morality tradition, as Macbeth's bad angel. Unless his letter had prompted her to read between the lines, this scene suggests that Macbeth had himself first raised the question of murder — 'What . . ./. . . made you break this enterprise to me?' and 'had I so sworn as you/ Have done to this'. It seems a little too easy to say that this is simply persuasive hyperbole or Shakespeare's poetic licence and anyway she has succeeded in convincing him too quickly, within a few seconds. Her words are clever and manipulative but it takes her only thirty-six lines to wind his acceptance and certainly the remainder of the play would not support the suggestion that Macbeth was weak-willed. He seems now both convinced and in command — 'Away, and mock the time with fairest show' (I.7.81) — and the couple are united in thought and desire.

Macbeth began as a great man and his continuing hesitation is designed to show that he is not without moral fibre. He is therefore aware of the upheaval in the social and moral order that is threatened. He is conscious always of the immorality of his act, haunted by his conscience, tortured both by his imagination, which produces the hallucination of the dagger or the voice that cries 'Sleep no more', and later by remorse: 'Wake Duncan with thy knocking! I would thou couldst!' (II.2.74). Indeed, all the murders are committed either off-stage or by someone other than Macbeth so as not entirely to alienate the audience from him, and each is followed by a scene showing the Macbeths as victims too of the crimes they have engineered.

As Macbeth commits the first murder, therefore, we see Lady Macbeth, not in command but a prey to her own imagination, first in fear of the present — 'Alack, I am afraid they have awaked' (II.2.9) — and then in digging up affections from the past:

> Had he not resembled
> My father as he slept, I had done't.
>
> (II.2.12–13)

When Macbeth re-enters with the bloody daggers she calls him 'My husband' for the only time in the play and each looks to the other for comfort and support. Macbeth is frightened and remorseful and Lady Macbeth recovers her composure first, having not yet seen the body:

> MACBETH   I am afraid to think what I have done;
>   Look on't again I dare not.
> LADY M   Infirm of purpose!
>   Give me the daggers.
>
> (II.2.51–53)

Momentarily, Macbeth is mastered by his imaginative fear:

> How is't with me when every noise appals me?
> What hands are here! Ha — they pluck out mine eyes!
>
> (II.2.58–59)

and Lady Macbeth leads him off. But she is only composed because she has not yet had time to think on what she has seen and it is she who voices a real subconscious fear:

>   These deeds must not be thought
>   After these ways; so, it will make us mad
>
> (II.2.33–34)

And her 'A little water clears us of this deed' (line 67) comes in hindsight as an ironic rejoinder to Macbeth's:

>   Will all great Neptune's ocean wash this blood
>   Clean from my hand?
>
> (II.2.60–61)

For all the images of this Act — hands, blood, time, hell, darkness, courage, fear, power, the father — ultimately crowd into her imagination and do indeed contrive her madness.

After the brief Porter scene, Macbeth re-enters both composed and entirely in command. His wife appears calm but she utters only a few words. She stands silent whilst her husband explains the killing of the grooms and puts on all the semblance of affronted loyalty. We cannot tell whether her swoon is real or feigned but just as her being the first character to enter alone hinted at her future isolation from humanity and society, so her swooning isolates her now from her husband's thought and action because she is removed from the scene, leaving him to act alone. When they are next seen together, Macbeth is king. He addresses no word to her as he plans the next murder and she is dismissed with the lords without a word to herself: 'We will keep ourself till supper-time alone' (III.1.43).

It is part of their personal tragedy that neither Macbeth nor Lady Macbeth foresaw the results of evil on themselves or the state. They failed to realise that one murder would lead inevitably to others and to suffering and degradation, for their victims, the state, and ultimately themselves:

>   To be thus is nothing;
>   But to be safely thus!
>
> (III.1.47–48)

The disease in the state would be mirrored in their own minds and within their own relationship.

This relationship depended on mutual trust, instinctive understanding and practical resourcefulness. Act III, however,

[margin note: M'beth alone]

stresses Lady Macbeth's loneliness and gradual isolation as she has to send for her husband to talk with her and admits that possession has brought only unhappiness:

> Naught's had, all's spent
> Where our desire is got without content.
>
> (III.2.4–5)

When Macbeth arrives, she tries to comfort and support him again and Macbeth seems about to confide in her — 'O full of scorpions is my mind, dear wife!' (line 36) — but he senses instinctively that it is she who feels helpless, he who must comfort her, protecting her from these mental scorpions:

> There's comfort yet! They are assailable.
> Then be thou jocund.
>
> (III.2.39–40)

She has become dependent on him and ends not with resolution but with a question: 'What's to be done?' (line 44). Macbeth's jovial, tender attempt to protect her from further involvement — 'Be innocent of the knowledge, dearest chuck' (line 45) — recognises her mental fragility but pushes her further from his life. They leave together, but silently, and he is now leading her.

The banquet scene is the climax of their disintegrating relationship as well as of Macbeth's attempt to impose order and health on the state, for it contrasts with the welcome banquet for Duncan in I.7, a scene of peace and harmony. The banquet is itself a symbol of order but here Macbeth's response to the ghostly hallucination brings 'most admired disorder' (III.4.109). As Lady Macbeth bids the nobles welcome, the First Murderer appears and those who entered on the words 'You know your own degrees, sit down' (III.4.1), in a semblance of order, leave on the words:

> Stand not upon the order of your going;
> But go at once.
>
> (III.4.118–119)

This disorder in the state is again mirrored in the relationship of husband and wife. They begin by sitting apart and Lady Macbeth cannot see the Ghost; she no longer knows her husband's mind. She does use her practical cunning again to try to restore order and cover for her husband — unmasked by his tortured imagination — employing the same taunts as before:

> Are you a man? . . .
>
>   . . . O, these flaws and starts,
> Imposters to true fear, would well become
> A woman's story . . .
>
>   . . . What, quite unmanned in folly?
>
>   (III.4.57, 62–64, 72)

This time, however, they are ineffectual, he makes no attempt to answer them and she fails to pursue them when the guests depart. She seems to have nothing left to say and he leaves her out of his future plans:

>   . . . I will send.
>   . . . I will tomorrow —
> And betimes I will — to the Weird Sisters.
>   . . . for now I am bent to know
> By the worst means the worst . . .
>   . . . I am in blood
> Stepped in so far, that, should I wade no more,
> Returning were as tedious as go o'er.
> Strange things I have in head, that will to hand
>
>   (III.4.129–138)

The speech is remarkable not only for its imagery and faltering rhythm, suggesting Macbeth's increasing despair, but for being spoken entirely in the first person. The royal 'we' has disappeared as has any thought of involving Lady Macbeth. The scene does end, however, on a note of intimacy:

> LADY M   You lack the season of all natures, sleep.
> MACBETH   Come, we'll to sleep
>
>   (III.4.140–141)

But the final image is one of destruction, the couple isolated amongst the ruins of their feast, symbolising the destruction of order in the state and the mind. They never speak together again.

When we next see Lady Macbeth she has become over-powered by her imagination. Her mind is diseased — 'A great perturbation in nature' (V.1.9) — as all the secrets of her conscious and unconscious mind crowd together, her barely articulate utterings, now reduced to prose fragments, suggesting a mind tormented beyond endurance. The anxiety she had voiced in Act II ('It will make us mad') is realised here in the climax of Shakespeare's study of her psychology. The Doctor and Gentlewoman act as a symbol of the norm against which Lady Macbeth's disorder can be contrasted. The Gentlewoman also exemplifies loyalty and duty — 'I will not report after her' (V.1.14) — significantly reappearing only as the royal deaths approach, for only then will renewal be possible.

Lady Macbeth's reference to hell and its darkness ('Hell is murky', line 35) suggests that the taper she carries represents her search for spiritual light and recalls her earlier 'Come thick night,/ And pall thee in the dunnest smoke of hell' (I.5.48–49). The memories of all the past blood-letting are chronologically confused in her subconscious but she remembers even the time of the murder in which she was directly involved: 'One: two: why then, 'tis time to do't' (V.1.34–35). In her mind she links the murder of the Macduffs with that of Duncan and perhaps a memory of Macbeth's fit at the banquet:

> The Thane of Fife had a wife ... No more o' that, my lord ...
> You mar all with this starting.
>
> (V.1.41–43)

She begins with a child's jingle and we recall that she had earlier compared Duncan to her father; Banquo's sons, it is prophesied, will succeed and the Macbeths are without heirs; she recalls Macbeth's fear after Duncan's murder and the 'flaws and starts' at the banquet have now indeed 'become a woman's story'. But the ideas mingle in her mind. She has also become obsessive, typical of psychological disturbance. The Gentlewoman tells us:

> It is an accustomed action with her to seem thus washing her hands. I have known her continue in this a quarter of an hour
>
> (V.1.28–30)

She is obsessed by blood and this provides her with two new horrors, unacknowledged previously, though clearly hidden in her subconscious: 'who would have thought the old man to have had so much blood in him' (lines 38–39) — it was she who had returned to the scene of the crime — and 'the smell of the blood' (line 48). As they rise to plague her conscious mind, the weight is so great that she can only summarise her torture in one long inarticulate moan: 'Oh! Oh! Oh!' (line 49). As Macbeth had feared from the first, their 'bloody instructions' have returned 'to plague the inventor'. The echoes from the past are tragically ironic here, as is the completeness of her isolation and her poignant expressions of need for her husband. The Gentlewoman tells us that the sleep-walking has started 'since his majesty went into the field' (V.1.4) and as she hears again the knocking at the gate, she asks him to lead her — 'come, give me your hand' (line 63) — to bed, reversing the details of the real occasion. Her despair will clearly lead to 'self-abuse' and suicide.

However, just as she disintegrates without her husband, so Macbeth is next seen on the verge of despair. Lady Macbeth has just informed us that he is still beset with nightmares — 'I tell you yet again, Banquo's buried; he cannot come out on's grave' (V.1.59–60) — and some say he is mad. Certainly he vacillates constantly from one passionate outburst to another: he is defiant, angry, self-pitying, then 'sick at heart' (V.3.19). He too is surrounded by metaphors of disease — his 'distempered cause', his 'pestered senses', the 'sickly weal' full of 'weeds' — and disorder. Just as Lady Macbeth calls for his presence, so Macbeth is poignantly aware of such losses 'As honour, love, obedience, troops of friends' (V.3.25), all the promise of the coronation banquet. When his wife's death is announced, life becomes meaningless. 'Sound and fury' become insignificant, life is reduced to an 'hour', 'a tale/ Told by an idiot' (V.5.25–28), and everything that had seemed so important before — ambition, hopes, desires, fear, bravery — is reduced to 'nothing'. He has violated the values that give meaning to life and sees himself a poor and quickly forgotten player on the stage of life. Though he leaps into action again as the Messenger arrives, rushing off to die a hero, from this moment, he begins 'to be aweary of the sun' (line 49) and is only looking to the end.

Obviously, the couple's crimes are unforgivable: from the start they have upset the natural order, creating a world which shattered the images that surrounded Duncan — 'loved', 'wooingly', 'procreant cradle', 'breed and haunt', 'temple-haunting' (I.6) — crimes 'against the use of nature', invoking 'murdering ministers' who 'wait on nature's mischief'. Nevertheless, Macbeth wanted to restore order and heal his 'sickly weal'. His murder of Banquo was an attempt to make his state perfect, the banquet an attempt to reimpose an order where society could be in harmony with nature, bound by love and friendship, ordered by law and duty. Indeed, his Lords do call, 'Our duties and the pledge!' (III.4.91), but the unnatural Ghost enters as Macbeth toasts, 'love and health to all!' (line 86) and is seen as soon as the Lords speak. For there is no retreat either from evil or from the consequential psychological disturbances, disturbances which mirror those in the state.

Exploring the Macbeths' relationship clarifies the upheaval in the kingdom, its relationship with the king, the causes of Macbeth's fall and disintegration, and allows us insight into the effects of conscience and remorse on the human mind; but it also lets us recognise the personal tragedy of the Macbeths, and their deaths come as a welcome escape, both for them and us, from unendurable self-knowledge. The English king can heal, magically, with his own hands; here, the Doctor says, 'This disease is beyond my practice' (V.1.55). He cannot cure it; they cannot live with it. This is why, when Malcolm dismisses them at the end of the play as simply 'this dead butcher and his fiend-like queen', we cannot help but feel, having suffered with them, that as a summary, this is totally inadequate.

AFTERTHOUGHTS

1

This essay opens by describing *Macbeth* as a 'classical tragedy'. On what grounds does Mills make this claim? How does this compare with the point of view expressed by Holderness in the next essay (page 64)?

2

Mills refers to Macbeth's attempts to 'protect' his wife (page 51). What evidence can you provide to support this view of his behaviour?

3

Consider the suggestion (page 53) that we are less alienated from Macbeth than we would be if we saw him actually commit murder on stage. Do you agree?

4

Can you see any dangers in analysing characters in a play as though they were real people?

Graham Holderness

*Graham Holderness is Head of the
Drama Department at the Roehampton
Institute of Higher Education, and has
published numerous books and critical
articles.*

ESSAY

'Come in, equivocator': tragic ambivalence in *Macbeth*

The fact that the Porter in *Macbeth* is a drunken clown should
not disguise from us the significance of the words he uses. When
he jokes about 'equivocation' (II.3.8–11) — which means not
simply lying, but affirming or swearing to the truth of two
opposite or incompatible statements — he foreshadows his
master's use of the same term later in the play, when Macbeth
begins:

> To doubt the equivocation of the fiend
> That lies like truth.

> (V.5.42–44)

'Equivocation' links the play directly to the contemporary
political world of its original genesis, the period of the
Gunpowder Plot and other kinds of opposition to James I's
government, by Catholics who regarded double-speaking, even
on oath, as a legitimate form of resistance to tyranny. But the
concept of equivocation is more than a topical allusion welding
the play to Jacobean politics: it can also be recognised as the

fundamental 'deep structure' of the play itself, which is based on a principle of 'even-handed' ambivalence. *Macbeth* can be said to 'equivocate' with its dangerous material: to palter with its audience in a double sense, to swear to the reality of its experience in both the scales, and to lie like truth.

It is a commonplace that *Macbeth* is a play of conflict and opposition, not only in terms of the political power struggles that constitute its plot, but in terms of its dramatic structure, its imaginative universe, its ethical configurations, its patterns of imagery. The play is particularly known for its memorable expressions of the experience of moral perplexity and confusion:

> This supernatural soliciting
> Cannot be ill, cannot be good. If ill,
> Why hath it given me earnest of success
> Commencing in a truth? I am Thane of Cawdor.
> If good, why do I yield to that suggestion
> Whose horrid image doth unfix my hair,
> And make my seated heart knock at my ribs
> Against the use of nature? Present fears
> Are less than horrible imaginings.
> My thought, whose murder yet is but fantastical,
> Shakes so my single state of man
> That function is smothered in surmise,
> And nothing is but what is not.

> (I.3.129–141)

Macbeth articulates the experience of temptation in a pattern of sickening see-saw rhythms — 'Cannot be . . . cannot be'; 'If ill . . ./ If good'; 'Why hath it given me . . .?/ why did I yield'; 'nothing is but what is not'. His speech composes a peculiarly dialectical poetry, which seems to excite the imagination by drawing it through a dizzying spiral of antitheses towards a condition of emotional and moral bewilderment. But the traditional view of the play holds that this powerful expression of ambivalence is always safely contained within the firmly delineated parameters of a stable and agreed system of beliefs and values. Most criticism of the play operates a process of naturalisation, wherein what is strange becomes familiarised, what is disturbing becomes reassuring, what is subversive becomes a confirmation of orthodox political, moral, and aesthetic values.

These are the three principal areas over which the critical emasculation of the play has been conducted, and I will discuss each in turn.

Conventional wisdom affirms that *Macbeth* is a statement of political orthodoxy, both in terms of its presentation of the sovereignty of King Duncan, and in terms of its function as a courtly compliment to King James. The 'royal play' of *Macbeth* is supposed to present the old kingdom of Scotland as a stable and firmly legitimated hierarchical commonwealth, governed by universally agreed principles of authority and subordination, which Macbeth's act of regicide violates and overturns. The celebration of monarchist values was then offered to King James as a cultural endorsement of his own legitimacy and power. I will argue on the contrary that the political world of the play presents no such celebration or confirmation of royal sovereignty, either in feudal Scotland or in Jacobean England.

The moral universe of the play has traditionally been regarded as an ethical mirror of the political hierarchy: the security of a society depends on the preservation of values such as loyalty and trust, and when these are betrayed the commonwealth itself collapses into chaos and brutality. An orthodox moralistic reading of the play has to assume a fixed moral framework from which Macbeth's action can be seen as a deviation; and to further assume that the play can guarantee from its audience a preconditioned response to its ethical propositions. We are obliged to recognise and commend the virtues of honesty, loyalty, friendship, trust; and to diagnose and abhor the vices of duplicity, betrayal, enmity, faith-breach. In much critical discussion of the play its moral dimension is resolved into the transparent simplicity of a Morality-play battle between good and evil — an ethical discourse more appropriate to the latest Steven Spielberg movie or to the political rhetoric of Ronald Reagan than to the sophisticated insights we have been taught to expect from a Shakespearean tragedy. I will argue on the contrary that the play equivocates with its morality as well as its politics: that its characteristic effect is to render heroic what it criminalises, to lend glamour and excitement to the very things it warns against, and to induce a strange kind of respect in us for those impulses and actions we are taught by the play's morality-fable to fear, reject and shun.

Both these arguments, the political and the moral, are often bound together by certain ideas about how *Macbeth* functions as a tragedy. We know that the Elizabethans had mixed ideas about what tragedy was, and that they drew their practice from previous models of tragic writing, such as Seneca, rather than from a clear grasp of any aesthetic theory. Despite this warning proviso, much criticism of the play has assumed that Aristotle's theory of tragedy can be applied in more or less detail to a play like *Macbeth*. The Aristotelian model of tragedy offers a particular concept of the tragic hero, a formalistic recipe for the artistic structure of a tragedy, and a view of how tragedy operates upon its audience. In the light of this theory Macbeth becomes the noble hero with a single tragic flaw — 'ambition'; the action of the play can be seen as the rhythmic arousal of expectations to a sudden reversal and fall; and the ideological effect of the play can be seen as the provocation and subsequent 'purgation' (*catharsis*) of the emotions it arouses in the audience. In these terms the powerful ambivalence of Macbeth's experience can only be a temporary stage in a process of clarification: it may arouse 'pity', but its true significance crystallises out of the play's action as an awful warning against this or any other attempt to challenge the supreme laws of nature or the dominant authority of the gods. Tragedy for Aristotle was really a form of cultural oppression, a means of ideological coercion by which the audience was invited to sympathise with the tragic hero in his challenging of law, morality or fate; and then required to cleanse that sympathy through an awed contemplation of the terrible consequences of the challenge. The audience is meant to leave the theatre with all its immoral, antisocial and politically dissident impulses safely cauterised or quelled. Modern critics have used Aristotle to prove that *Macbeth* follows the same pattern: that the play induces a pitying sympathy for the tragic hero, which then resolves into a quiescent acceptance of the 'human condition' he has striven to transform. I will argue on the contrary that the tragedy of *Macbeth* does not exemplify Aristotelian theory: the play does not end in catharsis, and does not work to moderate and pacify the emotions it arouses.

We often take Duncan's word as an accurate description of the kingdom he governs. His kingly language creates the powerful and persuasive image of a society which is ordered like a well-conducted family, wherein the various members enjoy equality of distinction despite the differences in their status and function. The patriarchal kingdom is constructed from 'natural' bondings like those between parents and children: so the hierarchical organisation of society can be seen as an organic and indissoluble biological unit. Macbeth himself expresses his relationship to Duncan in precisely these terms when he offers his lord the tribute of his victories over Macdonwald and Sweno:

> MACBETH   The service and the loyalty I owe,
> In doing it, pays itself. Your highness' part
> Is to receive our duties; and our duties
> Are to your throne and state, children and servants,
> Which do but what they should by doing everything
> Safe towards your love and honour.
> DUNCAN   Welcome hither.
> I have begun to plant thee, and will labour
> To make thee full of growing.
>
> (I.4.23–30)

The formal reciprocal exchanges of service for patronage, loyalty for love, are couched in a language of limpid simplicity which seems not so much to naturalise a set of social relationships, as to remind us of what is self-evidently natural. But we know already from the opening scenes of the play that this language is neither an adequate nor even an accurate description of Duncan's Scotland. This, however, is:

> CAPTAIN   The merciless Macdonwald —
> Worthy to be a rebel . . .
> And fortune on his damnèd quarrel smiling
> Showed like a rebel's whore. But all's too weak:
> For brave Macbeth — well he deserves that name —
> Disdaining fortune, with his brandished steel,
> Which smoked with bloody execution,
> Like valour's minion carvèd out his passage
> Till he faced the slave —
> Which ne'er shook hands nor bade farewell to him
> Till he unseamed him from the nave to the chops,
> And fixed his head upon our battlements,

DUNCAN O valiant cousin! Worthy gentleman!

(I.2.9–10, 14–24)

The inadequacy of Duncan's comment, which translates a description of savage butchery into a decorously chivalric gesture of courtly compliment, testifies to a radical uncertainty at the heart of the play: since the very language with which the King seeks to unify his kingdom involves a systematic denial of its constitutive reality. In modern terms we would call Duncan's world-picture 'ideological': it depends on some degree of falsification, distortion or omission of the true facts about a society. The 'commonwealth' of Scotland which Duncan dignifies and legitimates with his vocabulary of nature and family, has already been revealed to us as an unstable and violent society, vulnerable to internal rebellion as well as external invasion, and relying for its protection on the unleashing and control of brutal, blood-soaked savagery. Duncan governs his thanes through his graceful and measured language of loyalty and gratitude, service and love; but he rules Scotland through the barbaric violence of those same professional warriors.

The kingdom of Scotland in *Macbeth* is historically imag-ined as a feudal kingdom in which the central authority is the weakest point in a precarious structure of tensions. Duncan rules not simply by grace or love, but by his capacity to restrain and let slip the enormous violence concentrated in his men of blood. The moment of his supreme power, having suppressed rebellion and repelled foreign assault, is paradoxically the moment of his greatest weakness: and it is clearly in recognition of this contradiction that he chooses this moment to declare Malcolm as his successor:

> Sons, kinsmen, thanes,
> And you whose places are the nearest, know
> We will establish our estate upon
> Our eldest, Malcolm, whom we name hereafter
> The Prince of Cumberland. . .

(I.4.36–40)

This ceremony of nomination and investiture indicates an awareness within the play (and by inference, on the part of the dramatist) of the elective system of monarchy which historically existed in feudal Scotland. This was not a dynastic monarchy in which the eldest son inherited, but a system whose legitimate procedures could equally have brought other worthy dignitaries, such as Macbeth or Banquo, to the throne.

The political realm of *Macbeth* is dramatised as a precarious and vulnerable configuration of tensions, already shaken to its foundations before the play begins. The internal contradictions of feudal society arise from the 'centrifugal' nature of its organisation — physical power (military power) is vested in those who serve rather than those who rule — but also from the contradictory pressures of its system of values. Honour, the feudal version of self-respect, has to be fought for in confrontation with the strongest challengers. But the largest and therefore most provocative focus of power rests with the very authority which has the power to grant or deny the commendations of honour, the king. The biggest challenge, therefore, that Macbeth can face is that of killing the king: even though to do so involves murdering the weakest and most vulnerable of individuals.

If the play's political universe is presented not as a simple confrontation of oppositions like sovereignty and treason, legitimacy and rebellion, authority and subversion; but rather as the embodiment of a contradictory historical society which cherishes at its heart the violence and uncertainty which will eventually destroy it, then no simple pattern of moral antitheses will be effective in analysing the ethical structure of *Macbeth*. If a society bestows its highest commendations on acts of desperate courage and sacrificial violence, it will need correspondingly powerful sanctions with which to restrain its most powerful members from turning their violence inwards and striking at the heart of the commonwealth. Feudal societies certainly display such sanctions, and Macbeth feels them as strongly binding:

> He's here in double trust:
> First, as I am his kinsman and his subject,
> Strong both against the deed; then, as his host,
> Who should against his murderer shut the door,
> Not bear the knife myself.

(I.7.12–16)

The objections Macbeth considers are not universal moral principles but ethical scruples derived from the values of feudal society, in which crimes against kin or against a superior, or violations of the laws of hospitality, bear a particularly strong taboo. But in contemplating regicide Macbeth is challenging more than the conventions of a particular society, as the subsequent imagery of that same soliloquy can testify. When his imagination attempts to realise the essentially *moral* quality of the crime he is meditating, it appears as an image of fragile and vulnerable innocence:

> And Pity, like a naked new-born babe,
> Striding the blast . . .

(I.7.21–22)

At this point the warlord's imagination momentarily retreats from the battlefields and castles that are the dominant images of feudal culture, and draws closer to that realm of family and domestic responsibilities occupied by his wife, who similarly envisaged the daring of their crime as the violation of helpless innocence:

> I have given suck, and know
> How tender 'tis to love the babe that milks me;
> I would while it was smiling in my face
> Have plucked my nipple from his boneless gums,
> And dashed the brains out, had I so sworn as you
> Have done to this.

(I.7.54–59)

The voluntary self-exposure to peril of Duncan, the old man entrusting himself to the hospitability and protection of his most powerful subject, is recurrently embodied in such images of *family* violence (now all too familiar to us), where the powers established to protect weakness find themselves sorely tempted to violate the vulnerable innocence entrusted to their charge. Lady Macbeth is aware that the duties of hospitality bind her as strongly to protect Duncan as the laws of nature enjoin upon her the defence of her child; both are connected in her confession that 'Had he not resembled/ My father as he slept, I had done't' (II.2.12–13). But in both cases the power entrusted to the protector generates the desire to violate the weak and helpless. Just as Duncan's patriarchal kingdom needs violence as well as loyalty to defend it against both internal and external threats; so the socio-biological unit of the patriarchal family surrounds itself with a defensive violence that can turn too easily inwards to menace those it is designed to protect. As Macbeth stalks towards Duncan, through the silence of his own house, with the appetite of a rapist ('With Tarquin's ravishing strides', II.1.55) he displays all the characteristics of the patriarchal 'abuser' of family values.

What I have called the 'equivocation' of *Macbeth* resides in its powerful realisation, not just of moral and social taboos, but of the criminalised desires and forbidden delights involved in breaking them: the play is, in Freud's terms, the return of everything civilised values are obliged to repress. I am certainly not suggesting that the play does anything so simple as to invert moral categories, or to embrace and validate the demonised; it could hardly be read as a recommendation of practices such as baby-battering or regicide. But in the process of releasing such fantasies of sacrificial violence and the satisfaction of proscribed desires, the play brings powerfully into focus those historical institutions, codes of custom and cultural practices which form one of the infrastructures of the long history of human exploitation.

Neither does the play ultimately dispel, moderate or purge the violent delights it dramatises: criminal desire is aroused and accounted for, but not pacified. To fulfil the requirements of Aristotelian tragedy, the play would have to show a moral order disrupted and ultimately healed. Macbeth violates a social contract by enacting a characteristic historical experience (rebellion and treason) of his society. But where the rebellion of Macdonwald served only to provoke and legitimise the defensive violence on which Duncan's state was built, Macbeth's action discloses the contradictory reality of Duncan's kingdom: demystifies it, strips it of its cultural superstructure, and exposes it as a naked system of pure power. When Macbeth says, after the murder of Duncan, that:

> . . . from this instant
> There's nothing serious in mortality

(II.3.89–90)

he may be dissimulating an artificial grief, but the sterility of his subsequent history may suggest that he has in fact been successful in destroying the moral and political world which constituted his poetic experience to that point; the blow with which he despatched Duncan really was, for him, the be-all and the end-all. Contrary to many critical interpretations, Malcolm does not restore the original order of Duncan's kingdom to its pristine unity. The government he establishes is transformed both in political terms — his personal retainers ('thanes') become administrative officers ('earls') — and in terms of the emotional and moral relationship between king and subject. Where Duncan bound his subjects by contracts of reciprocal indebtedness, Malcolm proposes to make himself 'even' with them. Where Duncan invited himself to Macbeth's castle of Inverness, in order to stimulate the civilised exchanged courtesies of mutual hospitality, Malcolm — rendered wary and suspicious by recent events — invites his retainers to see him crowned at Scone. Duncan's system of trust and loyalty is replaced by a remote and vigilant cautiousness, exercised with the defensive calculation of a king who will not expose himself to the protection of those whose power he relies on.

If the moral order is not restored in anything like its original form, then the tragic experience of the play cannot be integrated into the Aristotelian model: the destructive fury it unleashes is not assimilated into any pattern of reassurance or consolation. *Macbeth* marks not only the death of a king, the death of a heroic age, and the death of a moral and political system: it also represents a stage in the death of tragedy.

AFTERTHOUGHTS

1

What do you understand by the phrase 'critical emasculation' (page 63)? How appropriate do you find it?

2

Compare Holderness's view that Macbeth is *not* a tragedy in 'the Aristotelian model' (page 64) with Mills's opening statement in the previous essay (page 48). What is your own view?

3

Holderness rejects the idea that *Macbeth* is 'a courtly compliment' to King James (page 63). Consider his claims in the light of the case put forward in Watts's essay (pages 102–109). Which argument do you find more convincing?

4

What do you understand by the last ten words of this essay?

Peter Reynolds

*Peter Reynolds is Lecturer in Drama at
the Roehampton Institute of Higher
Education, and author of* Text into
Performance (*Penguin, 1985*)

ESSAY

The banquet scene (III.4): a dramatic analysis

> When you are at thy table with thy friends,
> Merry in heart and filled with swelling wine,
> I'll come in midst of all thy pride and mirth,
> Invisible to all men but thyself,
> And whisper such a sad tale in thine ear
> Shall make thee let the cup fall from thy hand,
> And stand as mute and pale as death itself.
>
> > (Beaumont and Fletcher, *Knight of the Burning Pestle* —
> > performed in 1607)

Recognising how and why Shakespeare organises the incidents and events in his dramatic text is a very important part of trying to understand how meaning is manufactured in performance. The order in which the audience sees the action unfolding is carefully contrived: certain events are scenically juxtaposed in order to make dramatic effects and meaning. In this essay I am going to focus in particular on Act III, scene 4, the banquet scene, but I shall also be paying attention to the action that immediately precedes it (III.iii) and to a subsequent scene (V.1) that is very much linked to what happens in III.4.

When *Macbeth* was first performed by the King's Men in

1606, it was almost certainly an audience in the Globe theatre on Bankside which was lucky enough to see it. The Globe, of course, was a theatre open to the elements, and performances there took place in daylight. Therefore, if it needed to be established that the action on stage was taking place at night, this had to be achieved through the words and gestures of the actors, and by the use of specific stage properties, such as torches. There are plenty of scenes in other plays by Shakespeare and his contemporaries that contain scenes which take place at night, but few plays of this period require so much of their action to occur under cover of darkness as does *Macbeth*. The three scenes which form the basis of this dramatic analysis are connected not least because all take place at night. The audience are prepared for the stage-time of the first of the three by Macbeth himself, when, at the end of III.2 he calls on night to be his ally:

> Come, seeling night,
> Scarf up the tender eye of pitiful day,
> And with thy bloody and invisible hand
> Cancel and tear to pieces that great bond
> Which keeps me pale. Light thickens
> And the crow makes wing to the rooky wood;
> Good things of day begin to droop and drowse,
> Whiles night's black agents to their preys do rouse.
>
> (III.2.46–53)

III.3 is a short scene of violent, chaotic, and bloody action. Murderers — night's black agents — (often played in performance by actors recognisable as those who also take the parts of the three Witches), ambush Banquo and Fleance. The latter escapes. *Macbeth* is a very violent play. It includes not only this killing, but infanticide (IV.2) and regicide (II.2). We do not see the actual killing of Duncan. Shakespeare spares us that because he wants us to concentrate not upon the act itself, but upon the significance of it, and the subsequent reaction of Macbeth and his wife. But this brutal killing, and other even more violent actions (the stabbing of Lady Macduff's young son), *are* shown to us. The effect is that we see clearly, and are therefore made to *feel*, the nature of Macbeth's power, and the price paid by others for his ambition.

With torches and a spoken reference at line 5 ('The west yet glimmers with some streaks of day'), Shakespeare makes a particular point of signalling that the action in III.3 is taking place in semi-darkness. Establishing through these conventions that it is dark facilitated the credibility of the plot, since the darkness covers Fleance's escape. The main function of darkness, however, is metaphoric. These killers are acting on behalf of the new King of Scotland whose deeds must be done in darkness and in secret. Duncan was killed at night as he slept, and here the darkness covering the gross act of Banquo's murder is itself symbolic of the dark reign of Macbeth, underpinned as it is by assassinations and intrigue.

The action of the following scene (III.4) also takes place at night, and though it appears to be a total contrast to what has immediately preceded it, there are continual reminders in the action which take the audience (and Macbeth) out of the glittering world of state to a crude world in which men are slaughtered. The scene is set for a state banquet at which all those of rank and distinction in Scotland (except Banquo) are present. It is reasonable to surmise that the occasion is formal: the meal is the first opportunity for the new king and his queen to entertain the nobility of Scotland, and thus, through the shared fellowship of the meal, symbolically to unite the kingdom under its new king. In performance, costumes could perhaps be chosen to emphasise both the nature of the occasion, and the rank of those wearing them. The entry of the characters should be formal, perhaps accompanied by music, each entering according to the precedence to which his rank entitles him.

Macbeth's first words tell us that the seating at table was also, as convention dictated on ceremonial occasions, according to the etiquette of state:

You know your own degrees, sit down.

(III.4.1)

There is an ironic undertone to this speech, for while all the invited guests do indeed know their own degrees, Macbeth knows his to be illegitimate. All the guests are then seated. It is possible that, in the first performances of this play, the seats of the King and Queen were distinguished in some way from the others, perhaps by a ceremonial canopy. Certainly they would have been seated in prominent positions at the table. However,

Macbeth does not immediately sit down. In fact, he is on his feet for the whole of this scene, and is never seen as being united with or heading his countrymen. As the Lords are presumably settling into their seats, he moves around the table in order to:

> . . . mingle with society
> And play the humble host.

(III.4.3–4)

But as we know, Macbeth grossly abused his role of host when he 'entertained' Duncan at his house in order to murder him. Moreover, as the preceding scene makes clear, this man indeed 'plays' the humble host rather than showing his true murderous self. Because he moves around, perhaps greeting his guests, the most important seat at the table is vacant. The symbolism of this is powerful, for Macbeth is not the legitimate King of Scotland, and is therefore unfit to preside at a state occasion.

Lady Macbeth remains seated and, together with the rest of the company, waits to begin eating. Before Macbeth can join them, and the meal commence, the potential for a harmonious image is shattered when Macbeth's attention (and that of the audience) is drawn to the presence of a figure standing apart from the company, whose face is smeared with blood. The sight of the 'bloody man' serves to trigger the audience's visual memory, connecting them not only to the previous scene, but to a whole series of bloody images left in the wake of the preceding action: the bloody hands of Macbeth after the killing of Duncan, the killing of Banquo, and the first terrible image of blood encountered by the court of Duncan after the Witches have left the stage (I.1) and the startled King cries out:

> What bloody man is that?

(I.2.1)

With the entrance of the figure of the Murderer, the audience sees both the spectacle of a state banquet and a lone, blood-smeared figure: a grossly incongruous and even grotesque juxtaposition of images. The dramatic consequence of this is that, even now, when Macbeth should be revelling in his newly acquired power, his preoccupation is not with his country's leaders and nobles, but with its dregs, through whose agency he attempts to sustain his authority.

Macbeth's speech, as he moves quickly to confront the uninvited guest is in contrast to that he has so recently employed upon his other guests. From:

> Be large in mirth. Anon, we'll drink a measure
> The table round

(III.4.11–12)

he moves immediately to:

> There's blood upon thy face!

(III.4.13)

The audience watches simultaneously the guests and the Queen, seated at the table laden with food and drink, and Macbeth, who is deeply engaged with the murderer of Banquo. He praises his villainy warmly:

> Thou art the best o'the cut-throats.

(III.4.16)

Anyone staging this scene, either in the theatre or in the imagination, has to decide what the seated players are doing whilst Macbeth and the Murderer are deep in conversation. It would seem important to the meaning of the scene as a whole that they *not* begin to eat or drink. Protocol dictates that they wait for the King. If they are seen to be waiting, perhaps rather awkwardly passing the time in conversation with one another, it shows the audience that this event, which ought to symbolise Macbeth's legitimacy, is never concluded; instead of a triumphant demonstration of the new king's hospitality and generosity, the evening degenerates into a fiasco. Order is transformed into disorder. The food remains uneaten, the wine not drunk.

After the exit of the Murderer, the King's mind is already distracted from the ceremony he so confidently began minutes before. The failure to dispose of Fleance has fractured the temporary elation he experienced when hearing the news of the death of Banquo. Murder, not the ceremony and pleasures of kingship, is his preoccupation now:

> . . . I am cabined, cribbed, confined, bound in
> To saucy doubts and fears.

(III.4.23–24)

Lady Macbeth has to call him back to his role of host (and king):

> My *royal* lord,
> You do not give the cheer.
>
> (III.4.31–32 — author's italics)

Lennox invites Macbeth to sit, and join in the company and make the table harmonious. But before he can do so, Banquo's ghost enters and sits in his place, disrupting the spectacle. Those around the table cannot, of course, see the figure. But Macbeth and the audience can. The image of blood on the face of the Murderer has now developed into the image of a murdered man covered in blood:

> . . . never shake
> Thy gory locks at me.
>
> (III.4.49–50)

The response of Macbeth to the apparition understandably perplexes and further unsettles the Lords. Ross suggests to the others that the meal cannot continue:

> Gentlemen, rise. His highness is not well.

But Lady Macbeth quickly intervenes with a contrary instruction:

> Sit, worthy friends.

For the second time in the scene she has seen her role as being the one who attempts to hold together the unity of the occasion. The Lords obviously don't know how to react to this extraordinary interruption of a familiar state ritual. Lady Macbeth has again to insist:

> Pray you, keep seat

before the company reluctantly comply. Leaving their monarch still standing and isolated from the rest of the company, she gives an instruction to the men to:

> Feed, and regard him not

whilst she presumably also leaves the table to confront her husband. We now have the banquet with neither host nor hostess present. In such circumstances eating the meal would have been unthinkable, and the Lords are left stranded, unable to continue the ritual without the main players, and unsure of what course of action to take.

Lady Macbeth's anger and frustration with her husband comes because she thinks that he is imagining that the figure of Duncan is present. She has no knowledge of the killing of Banquo and attacks Macbeth's behaviour by comparing it to that prior to the act of regicide:

> O proper stuff!
> This is the very painting of your fear.
> This is the air-drawn dagger which you said
> Led you to Duncan.
>
> (III.4.59–62)

It is apparently the increasingly obvious fascination and horror of the guests that compels Macbeth eventually to listen to the promptings of his wife and return to table. He calls for wine, and is about to drink a toast when Banquo's ghost re-enters. The timing of the entrance coincides with the toast from King to subjects, and the chorus that returns their sovereign's good wishes is, seemingly and inexplicably, followed by an insult:

> Avaunt, and quit my sight!
>
> (III.4.92)

The guests soon realise that Macbeth is not addressing them, but still have no clear idea of who or what is causing this behaviour. Unlike the first appearance of the Ghost, there is no recovering the situation after his second showing. When their curiosity spills over into interrogation, Lady Macbeth is quick to insist, not that they remain seated, but that they go, and go quickly:

> At once, good night.
> Stand not upon the order of your going;
> But go at once.
>
> (III.4.117–119)

This banquet that began so formally with due regard paid to status and appropriate behaviour, ends in chaos and disarray as the order symbolised in the etiquette of state is disregarded in the hurried exit from the room. Macbeth has disgraced himself both in front of those whose superior he now affects to be, and also in front of the servants, the attendants at the meal whose lives are governed by such as those gathered round this table. Aside from the evidence of his involvement in something distinctly unsavoury, the assembled nobility of Scotland might well leave the table with considerable misgivings as to the fitness of this man to hold the highest office in the land.

The ending of the scene has Macbeth looking towards a meeting with the three Witches, and to the next murder. Lady Macbeth, once his partner in ambition, is now distanced from him. She is ignorant of the web he is weaving, a web which will eventually entrap them both. The only way in which she can now respond is to suggest that what Macbeth needs is sleep:

> You lack the season of all natures, sleep.
>
> (III.4.140)

The scene ends with Macbeth leading his wife off-stage in search of comforting sleep. But calm and trouble-free rest are not to be enjoyed by either of this couple. The 'sleep that sometimes shutteth sorrow's eyes' is denied them. They cannot escape the guilt of what they have done.

The fact that the murder of Duncan has imprisoned Macbeth and his wife rather than liberating them is particularly powerfully revealed in performance by the scene in which Lady Macbeth next appears: Act V, scene 1. The audience soon learns that she too lacks 'the season of all natures', for this is the so-called sleep-walking scene.

Before the audience sees Lady Macbeth, they are prepared for her arrival by the commentary of the Doctor and Gentlewoman. Their conversation informs us that the sleep-walking is following an established pattern: it is not a one-off event. The enactment of sleep-walking was not a common occurrence on the Elizabethan stage, and Shakespeare uses the presence of the two minor, but dramatically significant characters to ensure instant recognition of the signals given out by the actress playing Lady Macbeth for what they are intended to mean. When the actress enters, she is immediately identified by the Gentlewoman (remember that the last time she was seen she was probably wearing a costume which clearly showed her in the role of queen; now she appears in a nightgown):

> Lo you! Here she comes. This is her very guise
>
> (V.1.19)

This use of a very specific kind of garment (not of course a flimsy shift, but a robe, probably worn over other clothing) is an important indicator in performance: it heightens the contrast between the appearance of Lady Macbeth on a very public occasion (the banquet) and the private role she now inadvertently displays before the Doctor and Gentlewoman. It also points to the new vulnerability of Lady Macbeth as evidenced by the unintentional but helpless exposure of her feelings of guilt and remorse. The nightgown symbolises the stripping away of the public outer shell — so hard and effective in the banquet scene — to reveal what has happened since to the woman beneath it. It also establishes a link with the murder of Duncan: those characters who are awakened immediately after his death are presumably seen to enter the stage in their nightgowns, for they are subsequently told to 'put on manly readiness'. Above all, this scene registers the tremendous change in Lady Macbeth, from confident and assertive queen to a desperate, pitiful and isolated woman, close to suicide.

Finally, what also links this scene to the banquet and to the murders of both Duncan and Banquo, is the night-time location. The bloody career of Macbeth, and his wife's involvement in it, is a history best confined to dark places where the truth cannot so easily be seen. The forces of darkness and light are at war in this play. Now, towards its end, Lady Macbeth carries with her a lighted taper. Indeed, as the Gentlewoman remarks:

> She has light by her *continually*

> (V.1.22–23 — author's italics)

The taper represents a little light of conscience in an otherwise dark and lost soul. But it is a vulnerable flame, soon to be extinguished for ever. She, and her husband, will soon be confined for ever to night without end. As Macbeth says, in his final great soliloquy:

> Out, out, brief candle!
> Life's but a walking shadow; a poor player
> That struts and frets his hour upon the stage
> And then is heard no more. It is a tale
> Told by an idiot, full of sound and fury,
> Signifying nothing.

> (V.5.23–28)

AFTERTHOUGHTS

1

Can a performance of a scene ever be 'wrong'?

2

Should our knowledge of Jacobean stage conventions (page 73) influence how we stage *Macbeth* today?

3

Reynolds draws attention on page 75 to '*play* the humble host' (III.4.4). What other images drawn from the world of acting do you find in the play as a whole?

4

The RSC production described in the essay by Siddall that follows (page 82) is available as a video recording. Watch how the banquet scene is presented, and consider to what extent the director shares Reynolds's view of its significance.

Stephen Siddall

*Stephen Siddall is Head of English at
the Leys School, Cambridge.*

ESSAY

Ceremony in *Macbeth*

In 1976 the Royal Shakespeare Company presented a highly
successful *Macbeth* in the almost oppressively intimate
enclosure of the Warehouse Theatre. Perhaps there is nothing
very original nowadays in putting the great tragedies in such
surroundings rather than in a large theatre where design and
staging can match the plays' grandeur. Approaches to Shakespeare have become more flexible in recent years; directors
range widely in whether they try to recapture the playwright's
social and intellectual assumptions in 1600, or to present more
private experiences for the fragmented society of the 1980s.
Should one try to judge what Shakespeare 'intended' — and
inform that judgement with scholarship about his plays and
audiences? Or is it better to acknowledge that the play lives only
at the time of its performance, and to focus on those aspects
which seem relevant to each particular decade?

    Macbeth is an interesting case. In one sense it can appeal
powerfully to an audience living after Freud, Jung and Kafka;
it contains few public scenes and explores penetratingly a nightmare world of blur and negation which the hero has knowingly
stepped into. It may be seen as a private and domestic tragedy
about a man and his wife whose lives fragment and who become
alienated both from their world and from each other. The
enclosure of Trevor Nunn's production for the RSC gave focus

to this individual suffering, but the director and company also acknowledged that *Macbeth* is an early-seventeenth-century play about a successful general who becomes king and whose life therefore has a massive public dimension. It is the public context which causes the potential problem because it obliges the director to dramatise the hero's world as well as the hero himself; the cultural conditions of this world may date and future audiences may find it hard to project themselves imaginatively into them. In contrast, the private tragedies of the common man may seem more universally valid. The RSC production faced this difficulty and chose not to patronise their audience; they did not assume that people can feel and understand only what is close to their own lives. One of the great strengths of this production was to find new ways of presenting old beliefs about kingship, the social order and their religious dimension. We react to tyranny and fragmentation in Macbeth's regime partly because we are given a vision of its opposite too — the glimpses of trust, harmony and a type of sacerdotal kingship, expressed through images of fertility and grace. Perhaps even more strikingly, these are dramatised through moments of ceremony, all of which proclaim the proper bonds that hold a society intact. For example, King Duncan responds to Macbeth not only as a high-achieving individual, but also as part of the social order. His deeds and proper ambitions are acknowledged and absorbed. Their naturalness is further shown by contrast with the former Thane of Cawdor, who moved outside the bounds of loyal duty and then deeply regretted his defection.

There is clear development in these early scenes. Duncan's first appearance is characterised by haste, danger, the tenuousness of success and a great deal of blood-thirsty description. We may visualise him as presiding over a small band of vulnerable supporters, at some distance from the battle, making sense of partial reports, and all hoping for survival. His next appearance — scene 4 — indicates a growing security as the heroes, Macbeth and Banquo, formerly distant, are greeted and rewarded. They have stepped from the brink of chaos back into the social order, and it must feel natural to all present that Duncan shades this half-private and personal greeting into the first royal ceremony of the play. He invests his son as Prince of Cumberland, so ensuring the succession, strengthening the community and extending the king's gift 'to all deservers'. For an audience watching, there is personal warmth and public statement in this ceremony, but it is undercut by the irony of the lurching emotions in Macbeth himself — he is bound to interpret the King's benevolence as a threat to himself and his intentions. This undercutting will be true of every ceremonial occasion in the play and will give an unintended force to Lady Macbeth's instruction, 'Look like the innocent flower,/ But be the serpent under't' (I.5.63–64). Even the play's first five minutes lead us to expect such contrasts. The Witches occupy these moments with a few lines of their own more oblique ceremonial in which their curious questions about time and place focus on Macbeth himself, the one human being mentioned in the scene. The context of this mention gives him the equivocal colouring of both hero and victim. In the next scene, the more specific celebration of his virtues as military hero does little to remove the unease. He has achieved remarkable feats for Scotland and his king, but it is dimly evident that such violence could exist outside the common good as well as — here — within it.

When Duncan invests Malcolm in I.4, Shakespeare brings to an end the first movement of the play, the story of a successful battle against military threat. These early scenes are matched by the events of Act V, another successful battle (or crusade) against Macbeth's tyranny within Scotland and the even more internal moral disease in himself and his wife. The play is thus framed by events and descriptions of violence. In between, much of the action describes the nightmare of the mind, but is punctuated by three scenes of symbolic ceremony: I.7 to welcome Duncan at Macbeth's castle; III.4 to celebrate Macbeth's kingship and the supposed unity of the realm; IV.1 where the Witches preside and Macbeth, the 'great king', as they name him, is their guest, as Duncan was at Macbeth's feast. In the first two, a wholesome ideal is clear and stated, but undercut by hypocrisy: for the last, Macbeth leaves the public arena, attends a private parody of his own ceremonial occasion, where there is deference, entertainment and an array of 'guests' who will inhabit his and Scotland's future.

'The sauce to meat is ceremony' (III.4.35) — by this Lady Macbeth means that the food is less important than the rituals and the sense of sharing at a particular occasion, which thus comes to symbolise the virtues which the participants hold dear. All communities, through their traditions, have created ceremonies; these are planned to be outward embodiments of abstract positives, which both are felt deeply inside each individual, and also (in a religious sense) enable members of the community to make contact with powers beyond their tangible human experiences. The ceremonies in *Macbeth* have two major sources. One is the ancient war-like culture of the Anglo-Saxon epics, in which masculine virtues are celebrated in the lord's mead-hall. The other is specifically Christian and is evident through such powerful images as the Last Supper and the chalice which in I.7 Macbeth speaks of poisoning and which may be seen as recurring in horribly parodic form as the cauldron the Witches fill with poisoned entrails. There is Christian significance too in Shakespeare's two priest-kings. In Duncan he mingles the virtues of the good private man with the public significance of the saint. Note how Macbeth speaks of him in I.7 when anticipating the sense of universal horror which will burst forth after the murder. King Edward the Confessor is a faint offstage figure when mentioned in Act IV, but he is sheltering Malcolm, perhaps educating him to kingship and playing the role of second father to him. The English Doctor speaks of the King coming forth to conduct a healing ceremony for 'wretched souls/ That stay his cure' (IV.3.141–142). He hangs 'a golden stamp about their necks' (IV.3.153), he offers holy prayers, and his mystical skill is handed down the ages to future kings. Such ceremonies announce that the king's role is to heal, release and bless. Macbeth's public occasions, by contrast, are mere mockeries, and the scenes more appropriate to his state are dark and alienating. In fact, the contrast is most strikingly expressed at one of the play's grimmest moments: in Act II Shakespeare prophesies release for Scotland when Macduff beats on the castle gate, which the Porter in his drunkenness has imagined to be the entrance to hell. The ominous sound continues for some sixty lines, but its significance beyond the immediately dramatic moment is to remind the audience of Christ's ceremonial presence at hell-gate after his crucifixion. In *The Harrowing of Hell*, an often-performed Miracle play, Christ strikes at the gate and compels Lucifer to release the souls of the patriarchs and prophets. As Christ leads the tormented souls into the light, so

Macduff, (after enduring great pain himself) will enter the castle for the second time, kill the tyrant, and proclaim to Malcolm that 'the time is free' (V.6.94). Shakespeare's powerful allusion here takes us outside the action of his play, so that an 'offstage' Christian ceremony can deepen the meaning of what we experience onstage.

In fact, much that is important about this very intense play occurs offstage. The first ceremonial banquet is an obvious case, and some of its impact on the audience is the result of what is *not* shown. Firstly, Macbeth is not present to greet his king; it is Lady Macbeth, very soon after her instruction on how to 'beguile the time', who gives the performance. Her words on duty and gratitude are similar to Macbeth's on service in scene 4. Both speeches are 'mouth-honour', they are intended to deceive, but their hypocrisy permits a clear statement of the theories behind all honest ceremonial duty. Shakespeare, then, omits the scene which we might think it obvious to show. Instead of presenting the banquet, he dramatises a conflict in the mind of the truant host. This decision has two striking advantages: firstly, it throws particular focus on the play's central scene, III.4, the banquet which he *does* present onstage; secondly, it allows (in the I.7 soliloquy) a developing perception in Macbeth's mind to take him beyond the analysis of the present moment, to a vision of cosmic horror and then down into the mocking anticlimax of 'vaulting ambition' and the hero's collapse into victim. *Off*stage we assume the traditional ceremonies of welcome, feast and necessary hierarchies; onstage is the anguished host and soon Lady Macbeth, bitter and frustrated. Duncan retires without the attendant courtesies of his host — nonetheless he displays generous appreciation to the household and sends a diamond to his 'most kind hostess'.

At the second banquet, Macbeth is both host and king. However, there is great irony in the fact that, despite all his intentions, he is again absent — in any significant sense — from his own feast. He has spent much of Act III concentrating on Banquo, at first urging him not to miss the occasion, and then ensuring — via the Murderers — that he shall. The irony has a distinctly comic flavour when, in objecting to Banquo's ghostly presence, he protests that:

> The times has been
> That, when the brains were out, the man would die,
> And there an end. But now they rise again
> With twenty mortal murders on their crowns,
> And push us from our stools.

(III.4.77–81)

Macbeth can't occupy his own stool, and his queen 'keeps her state', not, we may assume, through a felt dignity and decorum, but through the sense of apartness from Macbeth which has been growing throughout Act III.

All ceremonies have their appropriate rules, and in this one Macbeth states his intention that order shall be observed: 'You know your own degrees' (line 1). By the time the guests depart, much has occurred to shatter decorum, and Lady Macbeth urges them to leave as a disordered rabble:

> Stand not upon the order of your going;
> But go at once.

(III.4.118–119)

The staging of this moment in Trevor Nunn's production gave wonderful focus to the change: Lady Macbeth was cradling her broken husband, while the departing guests, trying to observe a now empty ritual, began, one by one, to kiss his drooping hand. It was the prospect of a long succession of these unfelt gestures that made her shriek these final lines at them.

The difference between what the occasion should be and what it becomes gives the banquet scene its important comic value. The cup of fellowship or communion may be passed round, Macbeth drinks 'to the general joy o'the whole table' (line 88), and twice challenges his deepening fears by naming Banquo in order to regret his absence. His soliloquy in III.1 about Banquo had referred to the 'rancours in the vessel' (line 66) of his peace and stated a determination to challenge his fate. Fate's grimly comical reply is to present him twice with Banquo, the first time to occupy the king's stool, so reminding him who is to inherit the throne.

The role of the woman at such a ceremony is conspicuous, and Shakespeare uses the accepted separateness of the noble woman in a male society to highlight the special type of alienation that is growing in this scene. On the face of it, Macbeth's reference to her keeping 'her state' may be describing proper decorum, though in III.2, a strange and intense prelude to the banquet, we were made aware of the strain and emptiness that she feels beneath the ceremonial surface. Some good productions of this scene dress her in heavy jewel-crusted robes and when Diana Rigg played the part for the National Theatre, she became more and more of a spiritless, painted doll — thus making visual the play's recurrent image of clothing that is inappropriate for its occupant. By contrast, Macbeth, in the interests of male conviviality, tries to become one of his thanes, and selects a place 'i'th'midst' as though the seat simply happened to be available. For the first thirty lines the stage picture will be divided into three: the Lords, Macbeth and the Murderer, with Lady Macbeth apart. Her anxiety for the public occasion then forces her into a rather strained speech defining the purpose of the feast, but she has no clear knowledge of Macbeth's problems about Banquo and has to make assumptions about his mental state by observing his erratic behaviour. She then has to allay the suspicions of their guests — an increasingly vain ambition — and try to recapture some of her Act I force. Scorn for his cowardice now has no effect — the separation between them is too great. The strain in maintaining vestiges of decorum has exhausted them both, hence the long, slow brooding in the scene's final moments when they are alone. The 'admired disorder' of this scene has been so extreme that the play contains no further moments of Macbeth in his public role. When he takes charge in Act V, he acts not so much as a leader as an erratic caged beast, terrifying those who dare to bring him messages. All steadiness and order now lie with the opposition: Malcolm makes cool and competent decisions and his crusade moves closer and closer to its fulfilment.

The third ceremony is given by the Witches. They have anticipated Macbeth's secret purposes and have prepared their cauldron with its fragments of horror in order to welcome him. In one sense they are his masters, in that their prophecies have fed the temptations to which they know he will succumb. But in another sense they are his servants, like the liveried players who perform for the Jacobean lord in his great hall. They provide entertainment in the form of visions and a prophetic pageant; when these distress their guest, they feign anxiety and charm him with a dance:

> That this great king may kindly say
> Our duties did his welcome pay.

(IV.1.130–131)

Their manner is of tribute, flattery and mock-graceful perform-ance. Their language is contrived in the form of rhyming couplets that can express both riddling uncertainties that confuse and mislead their victim, and also the banal naivety of children's games. In spite of the play's horror, directors should not shy away nervously from eliciting audience laughter in these scenes. Shakespeare has envisaged the Witches with a type of comedy because evil is absurd as well as destructive: the Witches and their masters are mocking the folly of a great hero who has become their fool. One means of mockery is to pretend deference in speeches that are sometimes patterned into cer-emonial triads. At the first meeting on the heath they 'all-hail' Macbeth, they give a simpler threefold greeting to Banquo and then puzzle both with the three paradoxes that follow ('Lesser than Macbeth, and greater' (I.3.64) etc.). In Act IV they summon three apparitions, which both sustain and threaten him, and then they summon Banquo's ghost for its third appearance to show the future monarchy. In particular, they give a special warning about Macduff, who, as it happens, is the third good man to stand in Macbeth's way. The content of their speeches is designed to baffle, but the presentation gives the certainty of planned performance, which itself is undercut by their dress, bearing and general ugliness. The result is parody, the appro-priate destination of the play's major ceremonies. And their hovel or cave is strewn with fragments, much like the life of the man they have fixed on for their special sport.

Act V brings retribution, and Macduff deals with the tyrant much as Macbeth did with the rebel Macdonwald. The play ends with a brief celebration of Malcolm's success, in which he offers rewards, and announces a new era of earls replacing thanes. The tone, however, is not Duncan's and it is hard to see in Malcolm the grace and warmth of his father, even though we may safely assume that his government will be more watchful. Perhaps a production that is faithful to the feel of these last moments should not aim for triumphant ceremony to proclaim order restored (which in the dramatic context might seem rather glib). The feeling is more of exhaustion and relief in equal measure — with the dominant visual image being the bleeding fragments of Macbeth's corpse.

AFTERTHOUGHTS

1

What is your answer to the two questions posed at the end of the opening paragraph of this essay?

2

The RSC production described in the opening paragraph is available as a video recording. Look at the way in which the banquet scene (III.4) is directed, and consider to what extent this presentation seems in line with (a) Siddall's remarks in this essay (pages 86–88) and (b) Reynolds's analysis in the previous essay (pages 72–80).

3

Siddall refers to the 'important comic value' of the banquet scene (page 87). Do you agree that comedy is a significant element of this scene?

4

What does Siddall himself see as the essential 'feel' of the last moments of *Macbeth* (final paragraph)? Do you agree with him?

Andrew Gibson

Andrew Gibson is Lecturer in English Literature at Royal Holloway and Bedford New College, University of London.

ESSAY

Malcolm, Macduff and the structure of *Macbeth*

Shakespeare's tragedies depend for their effect on more than just the central character or his characteristics, be they strengths or 'flaws'. A Shakespearean tragedy isn't just a play about a particular kind of individual who meets with a particular kind of fate. It always involves a certain sort of structure, a set of relationships between the protagonist and the characters who surround him in the play. The protagonist is always different from others, and in some ways often superior to them. It may be a question of rank and status, of course. It may be the fact that he has imagination, or a different and more interesting imagination. It may be that he thinks or feels differently, and in more complex ways. The difference is always very much a matter of language. The hero invariably speaks a kind of poetry that others simply aren't granted. The important point, though, is that at all events tragedy feeds off a sense of difference, disparity, relative value.

The tragedies, then, involve us in very complex responses. But they are responses that are always being determined and guided by comparisons and contrasts. This is particularly true of *Macbeth*, and the kind of complexity I've just referred to is particularly noticeable in that play. I want to concentrate on the end of *Macbeth*. The endings of the tragedies usually depend on contrasts in very important ways. There's the contrast, for instance, between the tumult before the climax, and the return to order after it. There's the contrast between the difficulties and struggles of the tragic hero, and the (often victorious) calm and resolution of those who follow him, and close the play. The issue of the ending is particularly important in *Macbeth*. For we may be tempted to see the contrast, here, as merely a contrast between tyranny and disorder, on the one hand, and the justice and right that finally prevail, on the other. The endings of Shakespeare's tragedies normally arouse complicated feelings. But the ending of *Macbeth* might seem only to excite a sense of relief, like a fairy tale or certain kinds of novel. Good tragedy, though, should ask a bit more of us than that and, in point of fact, *Macbeth* does. But we need to take a careful look, not just at the very end of the play, but at the characters featured there, and at what the rest of the play has told us about them. In particular, we need to look at Malcolm and Macduff.

Malcolm credits Macduff with a basic integrity, and we shouldn't doubt it. Its ingredients may nonetheless seem rather less than engaging. The obvious point, to start with, is Macduff's comparative lack of intelligence. The play-acting in Malcolm's deception of Macduff in Act IV, scene 3, for instance, is really quite transparent. But Macduff doesn't see through it. That some of Malcolm's claims are just windy pretence is self-evident (lines 91–99, for instance). But Macduff doesn't notice their hyperbole — he simply isn't sharp enough. Indeed, in this scene, he's so slow-witted that Malcolm effectively persuades him to accept almost as much evil from himself, as potential or future king, as he has had to bear from his present king, Macbeth. Macduff also ends up agreeing to turn a blind eye to sins which, as he says himself, are often 'The sword of our slain kings' (IV.3.87) and 'The untimely emptying of the happy throne' (IV.3.68). In other words, he's accepting sins which would very likely mean a swift end to Malcolm's kingship, and a return to disorder. Macduff thus ends up caught in ironic self-contradiction. If he's determined to prefer Malcolm to Macbeth, however, one of the reasons is that his image of Macbeth isn't like the real Macbeth at all. Macduff's Macbeth is a crude, simplistic, melodramatic conception, a 'devilish' figure (IV.3.117). Conversely,

Macduff's Duncan is 'a most sainted king' (IV.3.109), and Duncan's queen is a paragon who 'Oftener upon her knees than on her feet,/ Died every day she lived' (IV.3.110–111). One of the most striking paradoxes in *Macbeth* is that the minor characters' world often seems, in one sense, to be as much a world of phantoms and superstitions as Macbeth's does. Whereas Macbeth conjures the 'horrible shadow' of Banquo out of thin air, for instance (III.4.105), Macduff, in his own mind, creates an image of Macbeth that has as little reality as a phantom. Macduff's notion of Macbeth as fiendish is as far removed from the real Macbeth as Banquo's ghost is from Banquo in the flesh. That shows, again, how limited Macduff's mind is, just as his self-contradictions did.

Macduff's simplicity is also apparent in his values: the national interest, on the one hand, and manliness, on the other. He stresses the theme of Scotland and its sufferings from the beginning of IV.3 (lines 4–8, for instance). Macduff is clearly genuinely and sincerely concerned about the state of the nation. He's also genuinely committed to the manly and soldierly way of doing things. He dismisses Malcolm's initial suggestion that they might 'weep' their 'sad bosoms' empty together (IV.3.1–2), preferring 'rather' to 'Hold fast the mortal sword' (IV.3.3–4). The lines are important, in particular, because, in IV.2 Lady Macduff has been regretting her husband's want of 'the natural touch' (IV.2.9) of tenderness and affection. She has also bitterly recognised the apparent impotence of 'womanly' expedients (IV.2.78). Macduff himself will later refuse to 'play the woman' by weeping for his dead family (IV.3.229). He prizes the no-nonsense attitudes of 'Industrious soldiership' (V.4.16). He feels they're most likely to be actually effective. Macduff is always talking about swords. He's determined to express himself through his sword above all and, in the end, he does so. In V.6 he will finally declare to Macbeth that 'I have no words;/ My voice is in my sword' (lines 45–46).

This only enhances our sense of his limitations — at least, in the context of a play like this. His concern for Scotland, for instance, if genuine, is always basically abstract. Macduff's lament for the 'sorrows' of the 'new widows' and 'orphans' is really only rhetoric (IV.3.5). We're the more aware of this because IV.2 has confronted us with the flesh-and-blood fact of the wife and child that Macduff himself has left behind. His concern for a 'nation miserable' (IV.3.103) is urgent but general. Macduff never calls any (painfully) specific examples to mind. To use his own words, his preoccupation is with 'the general cause' rather than the 'fee-grief/ Due to some single breast' (IV.3.196–197). This might sound rather selfless and noble. Coupled with his stress on masculine hardness and martial valour, it's actually a sign of his emotional narrowness. He has only a limited ability to feel for real human beings. The point about Lady Macduff's criticism of her husband (IV.2.6–13) is not just that she means it, but that she's right. Ross sees Macduff's desertion of wife and children as 'noble, wise, judicious' (IV.2.16). That may be so. But it's nonetheless a sign that Macduff genuinely 'wants the natural touch' (IV.2.9). It's noticeable that his son talks about him with a curious detachment, which suggests distance, and an emotional bond that is basically frail. In any case, when Ross defends Macduff against his wife's accusations, he may defend him as noble and wise and judicious, but that rather misses the point. Ross doesn't protest that Macduff is affectionate or loving. The capacity for affection isn't substantially there in Macduff, and his response to the death of his family seems — at least partly — to illustrate the point. It's bluff and soldierly. In saying that he 'cannot but remember' his family, Macduff seems almost to be apologising for his grief (IV.3.221–222). He speedily turns to thoughts of revenge in battle. Certainly, Macduff later converts his grief to fury in the field. But the trouble with grief turned into vengeful rage is that you can't be sure how much of it was really grief in the first place.

One might object, of course, that Macduff is a good man of principle, that he sacrifices his own interests to eventual peace and justice. The ends justify the means. Perhaps. But that can't stop us having qualms about what Macduff has to be to help achieve those ends. The same is true in the case of Malcolm. Malcolm is certainly cleverer than Macduff. But his powers of insight are nonetheless limited. His deception of Macduff in IV.3 not only makes him look like a faintly tawdry, calculating figure. It's unnecessary from the start. Stolid Macduff is quite obviously no Machiavel. It's very hard to imagine him as out to trick Malcolm on Macbeth's behalf. Malcolm's 'black scruples' seem more boyishly inept than anything else (IV.3.116). In fact, there's more than a touch of boyish fatuity to Malcolm. He likes making rhetorical declarations, for instance, in which there's very little substance. When Malcolm suggests that he and Macduff 'seek out some desolate shade' to weep together, he sounds silly and self-indulgent, like Orsino at the beginning of *Twelfth Night*. Similarly, it's surprising to find that, only twelve lines after referring to Macbeth as 'devilish', Malcolm is telling Macduff that he wouldn't betray 'The devil to his fellow' himself (IV.3.129). The little contradiction is striking. It seems devised to show how little Malcolm thinks about what he says, how little brain there is in his bombast.

Like Macduff, Malcolm is content to think of Macbeth in terms of trite stereotypes. Macbeth is a devil, or a 'butcher' with a 'fiend-like queen' (V.6.108). Like Macduff, again, Malcolm is wedded to the abstraction of his 'country'. Scotland's metaphorical 'weeping' and 'bleeding' appear to disturb him more than real wounds or tears (IV.3.40–41). He, too, is a prizer of things 'manly' (IV.3.234). His most energetic response to Macduff's loss comes in his urging Macduff to 'Dispute it like a man' (IV.3.219). Malcolm is able swiftly to detach himself from the stuff of Macduff's grief. He is apparently neither much shocked by the grief himself, nor moved to real sympathy. He makes a short and rather feeble attempt to persuade Macduff to 'Give sorrow words' (IV.3.209). Then he turns to arguing for 'revenge' (IV.3.214), and for the conversion of grief 'to anger' (IV.3.227–228). Malcolm seems even less capable of the 'womanly' response than Macduff. Significantly, Ross connects him with the idea of turning women into soldiers (IV.3.187). Like Macduff himself, Malcolm hardly registers the feelings of the particular individual. When Malcolm deceives and then undeceives him, Macduff mutters, in some bafflement, that 'Such welcome and unwelcome things at once/ 'Tis hard to reconcile' (IV.3.138–139). But Malcolm cannot begin to understand Macduff's responses, as his own incredulous question proves (IV.3.137). Like Macduff's, his feelings are tied to abstractions, not concrete individuals.

This also tends to be true of the characters with whom Malcolm and Macduff are most closely associated. They are simple, decisive men, who believe in clarity and certainty.

Unlike Macbeth's, theirs is a daylight world. There is no doubt in it, and no room for doubt. It's a drum-beating, tub-thumping world, full of concern for 'manhood'. Seyward's army, we're told, for instance, is full of youths out to 'Protest their first of manhood' (V.2.11). If the side that is ultimately victorious in the play sometimes seems rather short on sensitivity and humanity, the lack is most crudely evident in the general of the English forces, old Seyward himself. The thought of the deaths of numbers of his men, for example, merely prompts him to note that 'Some must go off' (V.6.75). 'Go off' was a theatrical phrase, and meant exit from a stage. The metaphor, here, enhances our sense of the way Seyward cheapens human life. His reaction to the news of his son's death is still more remarkable. He checks that his son wasn't running from the enemy, like a coward (V.6.86). Then he calls it a 'fair' death (V.6.88), decides that his son is 'God's soldier' now (V.6.86), and dismisses the memory of him with some flat alliteration, a weak pun (V.6.87) and a paltry rhyme: 'He's worth no more:/ They say he parted well, and paid his score' (V.6.90–91). It is here, if anywhere, that the forces of right in the play seem not only trivial and emotionally stunted, but feeble-witted to boot. What is striking is that all these latter qualities are thus connected with the reassertion of order. The victors' allegiance is clearly to order. Lennox even has a 'file', a list 'Of all the gentry' in the army (V.2.8–9). Malcolm and his allies see themselves as 'purges' for sickness, (V.2.27–28), and associate themselves with discipline and 'the belt of rule' (V.2.16). Not surprisingly, in Malcolm's final speech — the last one in the play — the emphasis falls on regulation and system. Malcolm promptly attends to the question of rank and status (the 'thanes and kinsmen' are quickly made 'earls', V.6.101–102). He promises to reward his friends (V.6.100), and says he will perform everything 'in measure' (V.6.112). The sense of 'measure' is very much there in Malcolm's speech itself. Much of what we have previously seen, however, of Malcolm, Macduff and their confederates suggests that 'measure' — however necessary — must also look, here, suspiciously like an impoverishment in humanity.

As the play progresses, Macbeth himself stands increasingly opposed to this group. Eventually, of course, the opposition becomes the literal clash of opposed forces on the battlefield. But the structural opposition in the play itself involves far more than mere literal enmity. The characters in the 'group' in question tend to be simple, if not simple-minded. Macbeth is obviously complex. The others share particular convictions and certainties. Macbeth is a passionate doubter. Macbeth's is the world of 'Thoughts speculative' and 'unsure' to which Seyward pointedly contrasts his own world (of warfare) in which 'strokes' will arbitrate 'certain issue' (V.4.20). Macbeth is seldom content with simplistic conceptions of anything. Malcolm and Macduff are quite content with a simplistic conception — for instance, of Macbeth himself. They repeatedly slide away from concrete particulars into abstraction. It's a mark of their lack of imagination. Macbeth himself has a powerful imagination, of course. It means that he tends to 'give body' to things abstract and non-existent, like the 'dagger' he sees before him in II.1 (line 33), or Banquo's ghost. Macbeth is like the others in being preoccupied with ideas of manliness. Indeed, his discussion with Lady Macbeth about whether or not to murder Duncan partly revolves around the issue of manliness (I.7.45–54), and Lady Macbeth is capable of taunting him with not being manly enough. She herself competes in the 'manliness' stakes, rhetorically begging the spirits, in I.5 to 'stop up the access and passage of remorse' (line 44) and 'unsex' her (line 39). Macbeth tells her, admiringly, that her 'undaunted mettle' should 'compose/ Nothing but males' (I.7.73–74). The play tends to present notions of manliness as a disease infecting a whole society. But if it has infected Macbeth as well as others, his imagination and his qualms are also capable of taking him in different directions. In the early part of the play, Macbeth steels himself to a complete 'manliness' that is actually far more foreign to his true nature than to Macduff's, let alone Seyward's. Later on, his circling, probing mind compulsively 'unbends' his own 'noble strength' (II.2.45), as though, in a stricken world, he were trying, in a distorted way, to reach back to something of authentic value. But, in this particular world, for Macbeth to 'unman' himself means that he must inevitably court defeat and disaster.

Of course, we can't make very large claims for Macbeth's powers of affection and compassion. But to feel confidence in and sympathy with Malcolm, Macduff and what they represent, we need to feel that they are Macbeth's superiors in this respect. By and large we don't. A kind of atrophy of the heart seems characteristic of the society as a whole, and it's in Macbeth himself that we're likely to notice anything slightly different. In II.2, for instance, Macbeth responds to the deaths of his own victims with an agonised intensity that is entirely absent (for example) from Seyward's view of his son's death. Similarly, Macbeth's guilt-ridden reaction to Macduff on the battlefield is actually far more powerful than Macduff's own reaction to the death of his family (V.6.43–45). It's significant that Macbeth is the only character in the play who can actually produce a vivid and convincing image of pity (I.7.21–22).

Perhaps the most important point, however, is that, whilst Malcolm, Macduff and their allies are associated with order and system, Macbeth is associated with disorder. Disorder is the consequence of his actions. His brooding, criminal, conscience-stricken mind is itself plunged in disorder. But, above all, his imagination is a disordering force, equipped with a power to reshape the world, to turn it upside down. Macbeth's predicament is in large part due to the fact that, as Lady Macbeth says, he considers things too 'deeply' (II.2.30). Malcolm and Macduff hardly consider them at all. Macbeth's imagination is repeatedly fascinated by images of disorder (as in IV.1.49–60). Malcolm, on the contrary, simply has no imagination. He is at best equipped with 'modest wisdom' (IV.3.119), prudence, a concern for his 'own safeties' (IV.3.30). Macbeth's is a world in which 'the equivocation of the fiend' can lie 'like truth' (V.5.43–44). It's a world of strange and sometimes portentous transformations. In Malcolm's comparatively shrivelled world, 'equivocations' are a way of being politic. He uses false appearances, and practises deception until he's sure of victory. It's no accident that the pattern of Malcolm's trick with the 'leavy screens' (V.6.1) so exactly mirrors the pattern of the trick he plays on Macduff in IV.3. Both are decisive indications of his nature, particularly in contrast to Macbeth's.

Macbeth is an unusually disturbing and challenging play. On the one hand, it links evil with large imaginative resources and emotional powers. On the other hand, it associates the victorious forces of right with dullness, mediocrity, insensitivity and emotional boorishness. Macbeth and the others simply do not share the same world. Macbeth's mind and temperament charge everything with intensity. By contrast, Malcolm and Macduff are, at best, plain, humdrum men. Emotionally and imaginatively, the gap between the two worlds is absolute. But morally, matters are of course very different. The moral gap is by no means as absolute as it might appear. But it's obviously there. There is no question who we'd rather be ruled by. Better sterile order than savage anarchy, however compelling the poetry that its perpetrator speaks.

So we're left with complex feelings at the end of *Macbeth*. In all of Shakespeare's tragedies, there's a sense of relief as peace is restored. But, after the loss of the tragic hero, peace is something of an anticlimax. It feels flat, and so do those who arrange it. In *Macbeth* in particular (unlike *Hamlet*), we feel we're returning to the right kind of order and justice. But we also feel that we can't really respect the representatives of order and justice (as we can, to some extent, in *King Lear*). In some ways the world of *Macbeth* hasn't changed much at the end. It's almost as bleak as it has almost always been. It's largely devoid of warmth and humanity, and full of soldierly types — bluff, cool, efficient, manly and limited. They may have beaten Macbeth. But they do little to counteract the bleak power of the poetry that he's speaking towards the end of the play. In fact, *Macbeth* is a play that's fiercely charged with passionately negative feeling. The ending doesn't work against that negativity. It's more likely to seem in harmony with it. Otherwise, it's an ending that tempts us to identify with the morally unacceptable. In other words, in *Macbeth*, Shakespeare takes an almost malign delight in trapping us in a dilemma. He absolutely refuses to let us reconcile the values of imagination, feeling and poetry with those of the good and right. He leaves us with an insoluble paradox.

AFTERTHOUGHTS

In the second paragraph of this essay Gibson suggests one possible parallel between *Macbeth* and a fairy tale. Do you see any others?

2

What arguments does Gibson put forward to justify his claim that Macduff lacks intelligence and sensitivity (pages 93–95)? Do you agree?

3

What ideas about 'manliness' and its importance in the play are presented in this essay?

4

Do you agree with Gibson's conclusion that *Macbeth* 'leaves us with an insoluble paradox'?

Cedric Watts

Cedric Watts is Professor of English at Sussex University, and author of numerous scholarly publications.

ESSAY

Macbeth as royalist propaganda

Macbeth is concise; clear and strong in structure; vigorous in its characterisations; eloquent in its poetry; and rich in interlinked themes. It is markedly less problematic than *Hamlet*, or *Troilus and Cressida*, or *King Lear*. But it seems to me that if it is less problematic, that is because it suppresses some awkward questions and steers us towards some predictable answers. The reason for these suppressions and these predictabilities is obvious: Shakespeare was flattering the monarchy of James I. *Macbeth* has long been regarded as one of the very greatest of Shakespeare's tragedies. Nevertheless, powerful though it is, its element of flattery entails so evident a limitation of Shakespeare's questioning intelligence that, in my view, the play lacks the searching and problematic features which preserve the appeal, for modern audiences, of *Hamlet, Troilus and Cressida, King Lear*, and the interlinked Roman plays *Julius Caesar* and *Antony and Cleopatra*. Again, the tetralogy, or history plays from *Richard II* to *Henry V*, displays the engaging complexity that stems from a full range of sceptical intelligence around the topics of kingship, usurpation, warfare, honour and 'the body politic'. In *Macbeth*, although the matter in hand is presented with great eloquence and clarity, the clarity is demonstrably related to the exclusion of shrewd questions which Shakespeare has been praised for raising in those other plays.

In 1603 King James VI of Scotland became James I of England; thus the two realms were united under one head of state. In the year of his accession, Shakespeare's company of players, the Chamberlain's Men, were formally taken into James's service and thereby became 'the King's Men' (the actor-sharers being entitled 'Grooms of the Chamber'). The King took a close interest in the drama, and between 1603 and 1616 the company performed 175 times at court, and far more frequently than they had done during Elizabeth's reign. During this period, playwrights and actors had many enemies, for the more puritanical members of the middle classes regarded the theatres as centres of immorality; and when the Puritans eventually gained power, in 1642, one of their first actions was to close down the theatres. King James provided a protecting hand for the players; but his protection was also a constraint (some material and some ideas would be risky and might offend him); and this constraint is clearly illustrated by *Macbeth*.

The play is generally thought to have been written in the period 1603–1606, soon after the royal accession. James was a Scot, so *Macbeth* deals with Scottish history. James had united two realms, so the play offers a precedent for this: we see how the wicked Macbeth is overthrown by an alliance of virtuous Scots and Englishmen blessed by the English king. Furthermore, the union of kingdoms is prophesied by the supernatural powers to a horrified Macbeth:

> What! will the line stretch out to the crack of doom?
> Another yet? A seventh? I'll see no more!
> And yet the eighth appears, who bears a glass
> Which shows me many more. And some I see
> That two-fold balls and treble sceptres carry,
> Horrible sight! Now, I see 'tis true,
> For the blood-boltered Banquo smiles upon me,
> And points at them for his.

(IV.1.116–123)

The 'two-fold balls' are usually interpreted as the orbs, one held by James at his Scottish coronation, the other held by him at his English coronation; and there are 'treble sceptres' because

James held one sceptre at the former ceremony and two at the latter. The 'eighth' monarch was James himself; but here Shakespeare was rewriting history, excluding from his count Mary Queen of Scots, the Roman Catholic who had plotted against the Protestant Queen Elizabeth. James was descended from Banquo, so in the play Banquo is presented as conscientious, brave and altruistic: even as he is brutally assassinated, his concern is for his son's safety ('Fly, good Fleance, fly, fly, fly!').

Like some of the ancient tragedies by Aeschylus, *Macbeth* constitutes, in part, a patriotic aetiological legend. An 'aetiological' legend offers an explanation of the origin of some surviving custom or institution; and, in Shakespeare as in Aeschylus, the explanation is given a flatteringly patriotic bias. James I revived the ancient custom of 'touching' to cure 'the king's evil'; victims of scrofula would queue to be touched by the King's hand, believing that his touch had supernatural power to effect a cure. *Macbeth* (IV.3.140–159) reminds audiences that this custom was established by Edward the Confessor, and the Doctor assures Malcolm that the procedure does indeed heal the sick and must be a sign that the King's hand has been lent sanctity by heaven.

Another flattering endorsement of the King's beliefs is provided by the three Witches and Hecat. James's book *Daemonologie* had been published in 1597; in it, the King argued that witches really existed and wielded hellish powers, and that they should therefore be extirpated. According to the Bible, God had declared: 'Thou shalt not suffer a witch to live' (Exodus 22:18). A year after James's accession, Parliament passed an act increasing the penalties for witchcraft, and in the first twelve years of his reign many unfortunate women were denounced as witches and were burnt to death. *Macbeth* undoubtedly helped to generate the climate of opinion in which such barbarous punishments were inflicted: the 'Weird Sisters' of the play are patently repulsive and malevolent, and owe their allegiance to Hecat. Hecate was the tutelary goddess of classical and medieval witchcraft. The play's grotesque endorsement of such superstition is clearly one of its most regressive and disappointing features. Shakespeare is often praised for his humanity, for his subversion of stereotypes, and for his anticipation of the ideas and attitudes of later ages; his *Hamlet*, for instance, seems an intellectually liberated play if we recall the ways in which it dramatises a questioning and sensitive intelligence. Yet *Macbeth*, though written after *Hamlet*, frankly and vigorously endorses some reactionary and lethal attitudes. We may try to 'modernise' the text in our imaginations by attempting to consider the Weird Sisters as symbols or projections of Macbeth's dark ambitions and desires; but such an attempt goes against the grain of the text, which specifies very distinctly the physical objectivity of those loathsome hags — even their unnaturally bearded chins are specified. They embarrassingly refuse to be 'interpreted away'.

In one respect, *Macbeth* may at first seem to defy the political orthodoxy of the times. Leading political spokesmen of the Tudor era had emphasised that rebellion against a monarch was sinful, and that even if a monarch proves to be a tyrant, his punishment should be left to God; it's not the subjects' duty to rise up against their ruler. James himself, in *The Trew Law of Free Monarchies*, lent eloquent support to this orthodoxy, citing the Bible to uphold the following conclusion:

> The wickednesse therefore of the King can neuer make them that are ordained to be iudged by him, to become his Iudges.[1]

Yet the play invites approval of a successful rebellion against King Macbeth. We also are shown, however, that this is a 'special case' — a justifiable exception to the general rule. Macbeth is repeatedly associated with supernatural evil (the Weird Sisters, Hecat) and with 'unnatural' corruption. His enemies are very systematically associated with supernatural virtue (the 'King's touch'; Malcolm's assurances to Macduff that he, Malcolm, is of unstained purity) and with the restoration of 'natural' order.

A literary work deserves the pejorative term 'propaganda' if it evidently falsifies the historical record in order to advocate a given political position. Shakespeare's main source for *Macbeth* was undoubtedly Holinshed's *Chronicles of Scotland*.

---

[1] *The Trew Law of Free Monarchies*, in C H McIlwain (ed.), *The Political Works of James I* (New York, 1965), p.66.

If we consider the changes that Shakespeare made to Holinshed, it is difficult to escape the conclusion that *Macbeth* has a clear propagandistic intent. To begin with, the Weird Sisters in Holinshed are markedly less repulsive than those in the play. The *Chronicles* describe them as:

> three women in strange and wild apparell, resembling creatures of elder world ... [T]he common opinion was, that these women were either the weird sisters, that is (as ye would say) the goddesses of destinie, or else some nymphs or feiries, indued with knowledge of prophesie by their necromanticall science, bicause everie thing came to passe as they had spoken.[2]

It's Shakespeare, not Holinshed, who provides those loathsome physical details which make the play's Weird Sisters far less like 'goddesses of destinie' and far more like revolting hags. Into their cauldron go:

> Liver of blaspheming Jew,
> Gall of goat, and slips of yew
> Slivered in the moon's eclipse,
> Nose of Turk, and Tartar's lips,
> Finger of birth-strangled babe,
> Ditch-delivered by a drab,
> Make the gruel thick and slab.

(IV.1.26–32)

What happens here is that Shakespeare (incidentally impeding the cause of racial tolerance) is helping to generate a stereotype of hideous witchcraft which would endure for centuries in literature, in the popular imagination, and eventually in the cinema.

Secondly, Holinshed's *Chronicles* depict the reign of Duncan as worse, and the reign of Macbeth as better, than we can infer from the play. Though Duncan's reign was plagued by rebellions, that was (according to Holinshed) partly his own fault: for years he had been a weak and negligent ruler.

---

[2] *Narrative and Dramatic Sources of Shakespeare*, G Bullough (ed.), Vol. VII (London, 1973), pp.494–495.

[A]fter it was perceived how negligent he was in punishing offendors, manie misruled persons tooke occasion thereof to trouble the peace and quiet state of the common-wealth.[3]

Macbeth ('Makbeth' in the source-chronicle) rightly rebukes the King for 'ouermuch slacknesse in punishing offendors'. True, Makbeth slays Duncan and gains the throne; but thereafter, for ten years, his reign is strong and wise:

> [H]e set his whole intention to mainteine iustice, and to punish all enormities and abuses, which had chanced through the feeble and slouthfull administration of Duncane.[4]

Shakespeare has clearly transformed the source-material so as to make Duncan seem more worthy and Macbeth far more tyrannical. Furthermore, Banquo's role is significantly changed. In Holinshed, Banquo is Macbeth's accomplice in the murder of Duncan and the seizure of power:

> At length therefore, communicating his purposed intent with his trustie friends, amongst whome Banquho was the chiefest, upon confidence of their promised aid, [Makbeth] slue the king at Enverns, or (as some say) at Botgosuane, in the sixt year of his reigne. Then having a companie about him of such as he had made privie to his enterprise, he caused himselfe to be proclaimed king . . .[5]

As James I was a descendant of Banquo, Shakespeare prudently changed the story so as to eliminate the matter of Banquo's complicity in political assassination. Given that James's life was threatened by the 'Gunpowder Plot' of 1605, this was timely prudence. (The allusions to equivocation, at II.3.8–11, and to the hanging of traitors, at IV.2.47–53, may allude to the trial of Father Garnet for his part in the plot.)

Of course, Macbeth intermittently evokes our sympathy; the play would not be a tragedy if we did not recognise the waste of his abilities and sense the loss of his human potentialities.

---

[3] Ibid., p.488.
[4] Ibid., p.497.
[5] Ibid., p.496.

The reasons for our sympathy are clear enough. First, he is ensnared by the Weird Sisters, who temptingly reflect his ambitious inclinations and misleadingly promise success; later they raise false hopes of his invulnerability in battle. Again, Macbeth's conscience revolts against the killing of Duncan, and Lady Macbeth has to impel him to the deed. Next, though he gains the throne, he loses his peace of mind; his success proves hollow; he, like his queen, is beset by nightmares. So, though we do not morally approve of his conduct, we are led to imaginative lenience towards him: he remains credible as a tormented (and finally courageous) human being. Nevertheless, this convincing treatment of the suffering of Macbeth and his wife has its obvious political function: potential usurpers are warned that usurpation may be punished not only from without (by the arrival of an avenging army) but also from within (by the torments of conscience). In short, the structural strength of the play can clearly be related to a very predictable ideological bias. *Macbeth* is, of course, far more than a doctrinaire political play, for much that it says about guilt, disillusion and the corruption of potentialities by ambition can be related to many circumstances other than the narrowly political. For instance, on hearing of his wife's death, Macbeth says:

> Tomorrow, and tomorrow, and tomorrow,
> Creeps in this petty pace from day to day
> To the last syllable of recorded time;
> And all our yesterdays have lighted fools
> The way to dusty death. Out, out, brief candle!
> Life's but a walking shadow, a poor player
> That struts and frets his hour upon the stage
> And then is heard no more. It is a tale
> Told by an idiot, full of sound and fury,
> Signifying nothing.

(V.1.19–28)

When he says that, we don't simply register the political fact that a usurper is now punished by the loss of his wife and by a sense of weary futility. We also recognise that Shakespeare has given enduringly memorable expression to what many people, intermittently, have felt. It certainly isn't the whole truth about life, but it sums up superbly the view of life that anyone can have from time to time, in periods of weariness, depression and disillusionment.

When all such credit has been given, the fact remains that Shakespeare's adaptation of Holinshed shows that, in order to flatter the monarchy of James I, the play suppresses some sophisticated and sceptical questioning which was well within Shakespeare's imaginative range. His great tetralogy of history plays (*Richard II*, the two parts of *Henry IV*, and *Henry V*) reminds us that even a charismatically successful reign may be established by usurpation and regicide, that political motives may be a very subtle mixture of egotism and altruism, and that the concept of a monarchy which is both Christian and martial is at least paradoxical, if not radically contradictory. *Macbeth* was written later than that tetralogy; but in some respects it marks a retreat. Shakespeare may have bowed a little too obsequiously before the new monarch of two kingdoms.

If William Shakespeare had possessed the independence or courage to follow more closely Holinshed's account, he could have written a *Macbeth* in which the Weird Sisters were more mysterious and ambiguous, Duncan was lax and fallible, Banquo tainted by corruption, and Macbeth a ruler capable (initially at least) of just and responsible leadership. I speculate that the result might have been a more complex, realistic and engaging play than the powerfully eloquent work of political mystification which we have now inherited.

AFTERTHOUGHTS

1

Compare Watts's argument in this essay that Shakespeare 'was flattering the monarchy of James I' with the conflicting view presented by Holderness (pages 63–67). Which argument do you find the more convincing?

2

How far should our knowledge of Jacobean politics affect our response to *Macbeth* in the twentieth century?

3

Do you agree with Watts's definition of 'propaganda' (page 105) and his belief that it is wrong for a work of literature to be 'propagandist'?

4

Consider the final sentence of this essay. How legitimate is it for us to speculate on what 'might have been'?

John Cunningham
John Cunningham currently divides his
time between writing and travel. He is
the author of numerous critical studies.

ESSAY

'The Scottish Play':
hero and villain

Actors consider *Macbeth* to be so 'unlucky' that many of them
will never allow it to be named, but refer to it as in the title
above: Peter O'Toole, when playing the leading role, always
called it 'Harry Lauder', after a once famous Scottish comedian.
No other play of the three dozen Shakespeare wrote has such
a reputation for disaster, so it may be worth asking why this
should be so. The usual explanation given is that much of the
play is performed in gloomy, underlit settings and it ends with
some vigorous hand-to-hand fighting, always a likely source of
calamity on stage. Yet other plays have underlit episodes and
many of his history plays — to which group this, in a way,
belongs — involve fighting and 'killing' in their later scenes,
when the tired actors may be at risk.

A more likely reason for its unpopularity amongst
performers is that it is rarely a successful play in the theatre.
Twentieth-century actors seldom become famous for their presentation of Macbeth — if they do it well, people praise them for
succeeding despite the difficulty of the role. The crux of the
difficulty is nothing to do with lighting or fighting, but the
nature of the main character: the hero of *Macbeth* is also the
villain, and it seems almost impossible to reconcile the two roles

in a way that will satisfy a modern audience. Other major roles show flawed characters, perhaps — Hamlet with his warped depressive's view of the world, Othello with his hypersensitive jealousy — but none pursues a deliberate course of evil as Macbeth does. Richard III does so, but he *is* a villain — and we might remind ourselves that, in the eighteenth century for example, a number of great actors were famous for their performances of Richard *and* of Macbeth. Perhaps an earlier age did not see the paradox, the villain/hero, quite as we do?

The word 'tragedy' like the word 'hero' is capable of several definitions, including the popular one which covers any sort of calamity from a chip pan on fire to a Test cricketer with a sprained wrist via airline crashes and massacres in remote countries. Calamity is, indeed, central to the way we all think of this word. The classical definition of it was given by Aristotle two thousand years before Shakespeare wrote his play. Roughly summarised, Aristotle said that a tragedy must show the sudden downfall of a great man in a position of high prosperity. It should arouse pity and terror in the audience — pity because they should be able to relate to the hero, terror at the power of the gods before which we are so impotent — and should help to cleanse them a little of the arrogance that mankind has always suffered from — the proud assumption that he is the master of his fate; he, in short, is God.

Though this definition may seem austere and academic to a modern student, it is a sound one: a disaster is most impressive when it strikes someone of great stature at the pinnacle of success; it can leave us feeling a little more humble than we were before we saw or read it — can cut us down to size for a while, at least. But this will only work if we can relate ourselves in some way to the hero, and an impossibly virtuous character alienates an audience, becomes some kind of Superman. To prevent this, Aristotle suggested that the hero should have some kind of human weakness, and, early in the present century, this 'flaw', as it is usually called, was worked into an elaborate theory of tragedy which was so influential that it still affects most people who study the genre — and it certainly offers a convenient 'explanation' of *Macbeth*. The human weakness of the hero becomes 'the tragic flaw' — the root of the entire development of the play. So Othello's 'flaw' is jealousy, Hamlet's indecision and so on. Macbeth, of course, suffers from ambition. It is a neat explanation for which Macbeth's own speeches about his ambition seem to provide good evidence, but it is not a lot of use to an actor trying to make sense of a complex role to an audience, and that has always been and always must be the most important criterion in any interpretation of such a play, intended, as it was, only to be acted, not studied.

Modern theatrical directors have not lacked ideas to try to make the play effective. Macbeth, we are told, meets the Witches when he is suffering from 'battle fatigue', the Second World War term for what used (more bluntly) to be called shell-shock. So the military aspect of the man — certainly an important one — is heavily emphasised, and it does not take long to move from this view of the play to our vision of a military society: a Fascist Macbeth is perfectly playable, though surely he is wildly different from any noted Fascist leader of our century? Our horror of military rule is matched by our concern for the deprived, and the Witches can be played as neglected old ladies, desperately poor, whose part therefore becomes a social statement. Such performances strike the viewer more by their ingenuity than by any insight they give into the central puzzle, but a brief glance at these ideas will begin to give us a notion of how very hard it is to interpret any of this play in our times. The death of young Macduff may still disturb (though it is *very* hard to act it — no small boy can make a convincing job of 'He has killed me, mother') but we, like Macbeth, have 'supped full with horrors' and have read of, seen perhaps in a documentary film, awfulness on such a scale that the casual butchering of a precocious lad seems trivial: we know too well how autocratic powers maintain themselves by systematic reigns of terror and the catalogue of suffering that Ross gives at the end of Act IV fails to shock us. We don't believe in witches. If we revere the monarchy it is in a very different way from what folk felt about it in 1605. Perhaps we don't really believe in evil — few of us, to be sure, believe in hell. To our blasé minds, both heroism and evil seem naive, simplistic: all heroes, we suspect, are looking for their fifteeen minutes of fame complete with television inter-view, all evils are social or 'psychological'. No wonder 'the Scottish Play' gives actors such a hard time.

At least, students may console themselves by recalling that

this is about the shortest play Shakespeare wrote — yet producers often feel they must shorten it further. The text is probably short because it was censored politically. Today the director will often cut out the scene where Macbeth sees the show of kings and the passage in IV.3 where Malcolm talks about the King of England curing diseased people who flock to him: these episodes refer specifically to James I (effectively patron of Shakespeare's company), to his ancestry and interest in the divine authority and power of kingship. They make little sense to a modern audience.

Yet even when we try to strip away such 'difficult' passages as this we are left with the central problem more strikingly obvious than ever: there is no hero. Macbeth starts to 'fall' as soon as the play begins; Malcolm makes a late run — he has just one good scene, the one that takes place in England, to build himself up a little in the eyes of the audience — and we are expected to join in the general junketing at the end when the patriotic hero of Act I has somehow become a 'dead butcher'. How is the actor — how are we the readers — to make any coherent sense of this?

We might begin our search for an answer with Aristotle's analysis in mind. It is at once apparent that Macbeth is a great man and that he is at the height of his success in life at the *beginning* of the play. The injured soldier from the battlefield speaks of his courage in the highest terms and Duncan is full of praise for him as for Banquo (a tactful balance, as Banquo was an ancestor of James I, early in whose reign the play was written). The first stage in his downfall is often said to be when he meets the Witches, who suggest a great future for him. This is to ignore a very important speech. When Banquo and Angus bring him the news that the first prophecy has, in fact, come true — that he *is* Thane of Cawdor — he shares his thoughts with the audience in a long 'aside' (I.3.129 onwards). If the vision he has had is good, as it has certainly foretold something good, a well-deserved reward, he asks:

> . . . why do I yield to that suggestion
> Whose horrid image doth unfix my hair,
> And make my seated heart knock at my ribs
> Against the use of nature? . . .

My thought, whose murder yet is but fantastical,
Shakes so my single state of man . . .

(I.3.133–139)

What suggestion? The Witches made no suggestions at all, but simply addressed him by three titles, the third being 'King hereafter'. *They* say nothing of 'murder' and Macbeth specifically speaks of 'my thought' as the origin of the 'fantastical' (that is, imagined only) murder. The Witches have merely triggered off a thought that he was already disposed to have, perhaps? Yet in the course of Act I, scene 7 we learn more about his previous thoughts. Lady Macbeth says:

Nor time nor place
Did then adhere, and yet you would make both

(I.7.51–52)

— referring to the occasion when Macbeth first spoke to her of 'this enterprise', that is the murder of Duncan. This has to be a reference to plans before the play began, before he had ever seen the Witches. When he does meet them, they merely confirm him in an idea he already had. On this view of him, Macbeth is a total villain, false from the start, and it is possible in performance to represent him so. Yet such an interpretation does not succeed well with audiences. A total villain is not very interesting, and Shakespeare rarely offers us one. In *Hamlet*, for example, Claudius is saved from being a pantomime wicked uncle by the torments of guilt he suffers, yet guilt is something Macbeth seems hardly to feel at all: at the end of the play he regrets that his age is friendless, that is all, and his wife's death elicts merely the comment that she died at the wrong moment.

Lady Macbeth, indeed, gives us another way of looking at him. Clearly she understands his nature well, and in her first scene (I.5) she gives us a pithy account of her husband. One phrase in particular may strike any listener: '. . . wouldst not play false,/ And yet wouldst wrongly win' (I.5.19–20). Few of us can face this truth about ourselves. We would all like to have things we should not have, and would accept them if somehow, without quite committing a crime ourselves, we could have the millions in the Swiss bank account that many modern villains probably have and enjoy. Are we to see Macbeth as some kind of universal man, a figure who symbolises our liability to temptation and is actually tempted? This seems rather to diminish him to something less than a hero *or* a villain: to make him just a fallible mortal who happens to be offered an extraordinary prize, of which he has dreamed.

This scene — surely a key episode in the play — has given rise to a different view, emphasising the role of Lady Macbeth rather than of her husband. She says that she will pour *her* spirits into his ear, chastise him with the valour or *her* tongue. Macbeth appears to some interpreters as a man basically good but lured or forced into evil by an unscrupulous wife — in other words, Macbeth is the hero, Lady Macbeth the villain. Productions based on this supposition run grave danger of the hero appearing to be a mere hen-pecked husband, but there is quite a strong case to be made here: in the scene during the banquet given for Duncan (I.7) Macbeth appears as having wholly resolved to go no further with the plot, and giving a very precise account of the reasons for ('vaulting ambition') and against.

The speech (I.7.1–28) deserves and will receive further examination because it shows us a lot about Macbeth, but the important thing to the Lady-as-villain school of thought is that, at the end of his closely argued case for going no further, his wife is able completely to change his mind for him. Yet to see her as his evil genius presents difficulties later on, when it is very clear that she is no party to his misdeeds: 'Be innocent of the knowledge, dearest chuck' he says (III.2.45), having conceived and plotted the murder of Banquo entirely on his own, as he apparently carries out his campaign of terror throughout Scotland later on. The Lady's villainy runs out almost as soon as Duncan has been murdered, where she has had the wit to tell her husband to get suitably dressed but the lack of foresight to think that merely washing off the blood will wash away the guilt. Her subsequent unhappiness, loneliness and suicide make her a fascinating character, and perhaps one of the reasons for the play's ill reputation is that the 'heroine' so much overshadows the hero — unless he has found a really effective way to play his part.

This brings us to other ways of interpreting him. In a

popular edition of the complete works, C J Sisson speaks of 'complex issues in the mind of a poet-warrior', thus succinctly expressing a widely held view of the central character. Macbeth has some fine speeches and they are, of course, poetry because Shakespeare wrote in verse. It is silly to praise Macbeth for his poetry — though critics have done so — when we should be praising the author. Shakespeare wishes us to see how Macbeth thinks and feels, and to see it as vividly as possible, so of course he gives him eloquent, sometimes beautiful, verse. Even so, he is easily misunderstood. To take the most famous example, the 'Tomorrow, and tomorrow, and tomorrow' of Act V, scene 5 (lines 19–28), we can readily see that it is a passage with perfect cadences to express despair, and with skilfully developed images — 'day to day' linking with 'all our yesterdays', 'lighted' with the 'brief candle', and that, possibly, with the 'poor player' since extras were called 'shadows'. But what it actually *says*, as at least one critic believes, is that Macbeth is off his head: at the time of the play's composition, no sane man believed that the world had no meaning at all. That is to deny God, to deny everything. A nihilist hero is himself nothing, and the play must fail if there is a blank at the heart of it. At best the speech is a statement of total despair, a condition that interests us very briefly because it leads nowhere.

The poetic eloquence of this speech may actually *hinder* the modern reader from perceiving its meaning: this is not true of two of Macbeth's soliloquies, the one to which we have already referred, in the last scene of Act I, and the famous 'river of blood' image (Act III.4.135–137) — nominally spoken to Lady Macbeth, but really his own thoughts shared with the audience, for by this stage in the play his wife knows almost nothing of what he is up to.

The first speech (I.7.1–28), as we have said earlier, is important both for the light it throws on his divided nature, and thus his role in the play, and for the help it can give the modern reader or viewer in understanding the nature of his action to the full. We are accustomed now to think of famous figures as being at risk — presidents and popes, ministers and judges have been victims of murderous attacks, highly publicised. The murder of one sweet old gentleman may not seem to us a very great matter. In this speech Macbeth with agonised care sums up all the reasons why it would be infamous of him to kill Duncan: the King is his relative as well as his monarch; he is a guest of the castle whom the laws of hospitality protect; he has been a good king — above all lacking in the corruption which power so often brings — 'So clear in his great office'. Macbeth, with the ruthless insight into his own nature that is so special to him, says he has only 'vaulting ambition' to urge him on. To us ambition is a virtue, to the Elizabethans it was a sin, for it suggested a kind of impatience against God who had called you to your station in life. Thus the only reason for the murder is a bad one. The reasons against it: it is a crime against kinship; against kingship, itself a triple sin for it is a crime not only against the man who is killed, but against the society which he heads and against God, under whose power the anointed ruler holds sway; against the laws of hospitality; against natural justice which says that Duncan is a good man and therefore should be protected, not destroyed. This analysis, which the original audience would have grasped without elaboration as the concepts were familiar, helps us to realise the enormity of the offence which Macbeth commits: more interestingly it helps us to see into his mind. He is absolutely clear about the nature of the act he contemplates and rejects it. His reason for changing his mind we shall consider in a moment.

The 'river of blood' image, like the passage we have just considered, helps us in two ways: once again it shows his very clear perception of the nature of his deeds and the position in which he stands; but it also offers an explanation of *why* he continues on his dreadful course. The whole play may be seen as a working-out of the metaphor. Once you start on a wrong course of action it is almost impossible to go back — indeed, *how* could Macbeth 'return'? He cannot bring Duncan back to life, or give up his kingdom to Malcolm — who would execute him no doubt — or call Banquo from the grave. He may, in fact, be seen as a man who is the victim of the logic of power-politics: do one ill deed, and you have to do more, until you find you have to tyrannise the whole world and retain your power by terror — including the murder of the children of dissidents. So have dictators always done.

If this is our view of the man — a hero who makes one false step and then cannot retrace it — the reason *why* he takes that step becomes very important, so we now return to the passage in Act I where he decides to stop before it is too late. The conventional explanation of the change is that his wife, so much stronger than he is we are told, persuades him. His wife is his inferior in reasoning: as soon as the murder is done, Macbeth knows it can never be undone, that the blood will remain on his hands; his wife believes that 'a little water clears us of this deed'. But she has a shrewdness that gives her power. We have seen that, in the episode where she receives her husband's letter, she shows a very good knowledge of the kind of man he is. Thus she knows exactly what taunt will stir Macbeth beyond endurance, and applies it: he cannot bear to be called a coward, so that is what she calls him.

If we are to consider Macbeth as in some sense heroic, we might start with this, for the play begins and ends with it. In the earliest part of the play there is constant reference to Macbeth's great courage on the battlefield. In the last section, though he sees clearly (as usual) how all the odds are against him — the prophecies of his death all fulfilled — he calls upon what he has always had: 'Yet I will try the last,' he says, and engages Macduff with sword and shield. Physical courage never deserts him — his horror at the ghost of Banquo is moral, the spectre of his own guilt appals him — and in the last Act it is very noticeable indeed how brisk he is, even as premonitions of the end crowd in on him.

Perhaps the way he dies illustrates Shakespeare's own awareness of the problem we have been examining. If Macbeth is a great man, in particular a very brave one, and if we are, late in the play, reminded of this fact rather energetically, our sympathy might go more to him than the conclusion of the play requires. So, it may be argued, he is killed offstage in order that we may not see him bravely fighting against odds which have been loaded by destiny itself. More probably, in my view, he is killed offstage so that his head can be brought on. This is not an easy moment to stage nowadays, for a very good reason: most of us have never seen a severed head. Elizabethan audiences might well have done, for they turned out in enormous crowds to see executions, and the very gruesome ritual of death for high treason was highly popular. At the end of the calculated savagery the executioner cut off and held up the head for all to see. In the earlier part of the business, the disembowelling, the executioner got his hands and arms covered in blood — hence the 'hangman's hands' that Macbeth speaks of immediately after killing Duncan (II.2.27). These images would have had a powerful effect on the audience, which is now lost.

If the final image of Act V is of a traitor justly punished and giving way for true leadership and restoration of a sick country, it is not the image of the whole Act. If we compare what we see in the previous Act, our perplexity increases. The bulk of Act IV is taken up with the extent of Macbeth's evil. In the first scene he is shown threatening omens by the Witches, but these seem only to confirm him in his course. In the second scene we actually see acted out a piece of calculated terrorism, the murder of women and children by jeering, brutal agents. The third, set in England, gives us a long catalogue of the appalling state of Scotland under his rule, where no one is safe; political murder so common, people are not even curious about it; and good men are at highest risk. This is villainy at its most extreme, and conscious villainy at that, deliberate, remorseless.

Yet in much of Act V there seems to be an attempt to re-create the heroic soldier of Act I, even if he fights in a wrong cause, with an additional touch to catch our sympathy. When Macbeth says:

> . . . my way of life
> Is fallen into the sere, the yellow leaf;
> And that which should accompany old age,
> As honour, love, obedience, troops of friends,
> I must not look to have . . .

(V.3.22–26)

we can almost feel sorry for him in his loneliness, an aspect of his life intensified a moment later when the Doctor brings news of his wife — and then tells the audience that he wants to desert as others are doing. Of the courage that still fills Macbeth, aware as he is of his own hopelessness and the reasons for it, we have already spoken. Surely there is something of a hero left?

Perhaps our way through this, whether we act or study the play, is to follow the course, step by step, which leads from the 'valour's minion . . . worthy gentleman' of the second scene to the 'dead butcher' of the end. We *do* begin with a great man, he *is* at the height of his achievement, fortune *does* seem to smile on him, even if he has the capacity to think of evil — we all have, after all. Pride *is* his undoing — pride in his valour, the pride that lets him think he can succeed against all the odds, can interpret his own destiny as given by the Witches in his own way. His downfall, it may be argued, is in two stages: the first fall is when he changes his mind about killing Duncan, which leads inevitably to other evil and ends in total tyranny; the second is his actual death at the hands of a man he has wronged in the service of a ruler he has usurped. He does indeed become the villain, but he never quite loses our sympathy because, at every stage, he is so painfully aware of what he is doing, and because of the element of 'inevitability' referred to earlier. After a single wrong move carried out in full awareness of its evil, he is in a way no longer the murderer but the victim of that remorseless power of destiny which should, as Aristotle said, arouse our pity and our terror.

AFTERTHOUGHTS

1

Cunningham claims that 'a Fascist *Macbeth* is perfectly play-able' (page 113). How and why might such a production be devised?

2

How reasonable is it, in your opinion, for a modern theatre director to make cuts in a Shakespeare play (see paragraph 1, page 114)?

3

How useful do you find the term 'poet-warrior' (page 116) as a key to Macbeth's character?

4

Do you agree with Cunningham's conclusions at the close of this essay?

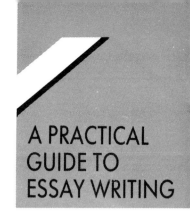

A PRACTICAL GUIDE TO ESSAY WRITING

INTRODUCTION

First, a word of warning. Good essays are the product of a creative engagement with literature. So never try to restrict your studies to what you think will be 'useful in the exam'. Ironically, you will restrict your grade potential if you do.

This doesn't mean, of course, that you should ignore the basic skills of essay writing. When you read critics, make a conscious effort to notice *how* they communicate their ideas. The guidelines that follow offer advice of a more explicit kind. But they are no substitute for practical experience. It is never easy to express ideas with clarity and precision. But the more often you tackle the problems involved and experiment to find your own voice, the more fluent you will become. So practise writing essays as often as possible.

HOW TO PLAN
AN ESSAY

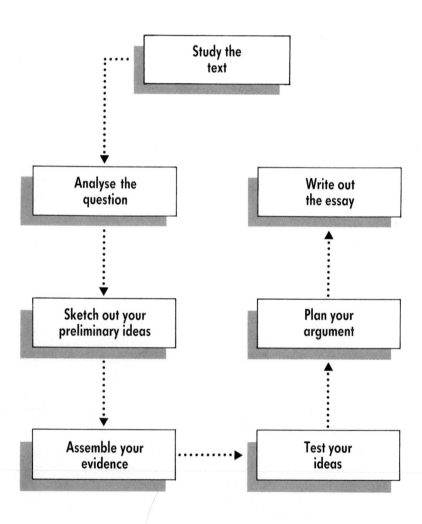

Study the
text

Analyse the
question

Write out
the essay

Sketch out your
preliminary ideas

Plan your
argument

Assemble your
evidence

Test your
ideas

Study the text

The first step in writing a good essay is to get to know the set text well. Never write about a text until you are fully familiar with it. Even a discussion of the opening chapter of a novel, for example, should be informed by an understanding of the book as a whole. Literary texts, however, are by their very nature complex and on a first reading you are bound to miss many significant features. Re-read the book with care, if possible more than once. Look up any unfamiliar words in a good dictionary and if the text you are studying was written more than a few decades ago, consult the *Oxford English Dictionary* to find out whether the meanings of any terms have shifted in the intervening period.

Good books are difficult to put down when you first read them. But a more leisurely second or third reading gives you the opportunity to make notes on those features you find significant. An index of characters and events is often useful, particularly when studying novels with a complex plot or time scheme. The main aim, however, should be to record your *responses* to the text. By all means note, for example, striking images. But be sure to add *why* you think them striking. Similarly, record any thoughts you may have on interesting comparisons with other texts, puzzling points of characterisation, even what you take to be aesthetic blemishes. The important thing is to annotate fully and adventurously. The most seemingly idiosyncratic comment may later lead to a crucial area of discussion which you would otherwise have overlooked. It helps to have a working copy of the text in which to mark up key passages and jot down marginal comments (although obviously these practices are taboo when working with library, borrowed or valuable copies!). But keep a fuller set of notes as well and organise these under appropriate headings.

Literature does not exist in an aesthetic vacuum, however, and you should try to find out as much as possible about the context of its production and reception. It is particularly important to read other works by the same author and writings by contemporaries. At this early stage, you may want to restrict your secondary reading to those standard reference works, such as biographies, which are widely available in public libraries. In the long run, however, it pays to read as wide a range of critical studies as possible.

Some students, and tutors, worry that such studies may stifle the development of any truly personal response. But this won't happen if you are alert to the danger and read critically. After all, you wouldn't passively accept what a stranger told you in conversation. The fact that a critic's views are in print does not necessarily make them any more authoritative (as a glance at the review pages of the *TLS* and *London Review of Books* will reveal). So question the views you find: 'Does this critic's interpretation agree with mine and where do we part company?' 'Can it be right to try and restrict this text's meanings to those found by its author or first audience?' 'Doesn't this passage treat a theatrical text as though it were a novel?' Often it is views which you reject which prove most valuable since they challenge you to articulate your own position with greater clarity. Be sure to keep careful notes on what the critic wrote, and your *reactions* to what the critic wrote.

Analyse the question

You cannot begin to answer a question until you understand what task it is you have been asked to perform. Recast the question in your own words and reconstruct the line of reasoning which lies behind it. Where there is a choice of topics, try to choose the one for which you are best prepared. It would, for example, be unwise to tackle 'How far do you agree that in *Paradise Lost* Milton transformed the epic models he inherited from ancient Greece and Rome?' without a working knowledge of Homer and Virgil (or *Paradise Lost* for that matter!). If you do not already know the works of these authors, the question should spur you on to read more widely — or discourage you from attempting it at all. The scope of an essay, however, is not always so obvious and you must remain alert to the implied demands of each question. How could you possibly 'Consider the view that *Wuthering Heights* transcends the conventions of the Gothic novel' without reference to at least some of those works which, the question suggests, have *not* transcended Gothic conventions?

When you have decided on a topic, analyse the terms of the question itself. Sometimes these self-evidently require careful definition: *tragedy* and *irony*, for example, are notoriously difficult concepts to pin down and you will probably need to consult a good dictionary of literary terms. Don't ignore, however, those seemingly innocuous phrases which often smuggle in significant assumptions. 'Does Macbeth lack the nobility of the true tragic hero?' obviously invites you to discuss nobility and the nature of the tragic hero. But what of 'lack' and 'true' — do they suggest that the play would be improved had Shakespeare depicted Macbeth in a different manner? or that tragedy is superior to other forms of drama? Remember that you are not expected meekly to agree with the assumptions implicit in the question. Some questions are deliberately provocative in order to stimulate an engaged response. Don't be afraid to take up the challenge.

Sketch out your preliminary ideas

'Which comes first, the evidence or the answer?' is one of those chicken and egg questions. How can you form a view without inspecting the evidence? But how can you know which evidence is relevant without some idea of what it is you are looking for? In practice the mind reviews evidence and formulates preliminary theories or hypotheses at one and the same time, although for the sake of clarity we have separated out the processes. Remember that these early ideas are only there to get you started. You *expect* to modify them in the light of the evidence you uncover. Your initial hypothesis may be an instinctive 'gut-reaction'. Or you may find that you prefer to 'sleep on the problem', allowing ideas to gell over a period of time. Don't worry in either case. The mind is quite capable of processing a vast amount of accumulated evidence, the product of previous reading and thought, and reaching sophisticated intuitive judgements. Eventually, however, you are going to have to think carefully through any ideas you arrive at by such intuitive processes. Are they logical? Do they take account of all the relevant factors? Do they fully answer the question set? Are there any obvious reasons to qualify or abandon them?

Assemble your evidence

Now is the time to return to the text and re-read it with the question and your working hypothesis firmly in mind. Many of the notes you have already made are likely to be useful, but assess the precise relevance of this material and make notes on any new evidence you discover. The important thing is to cast your net widely and take into account points which tend to undermine your case as well as those that support it. As always, ensure that your notes are full, accurate, and reflect your own critical judgements.

You may well need to go outside the text if you are to do full justice to the question. If you think that the 'Oedipus complex' may be relevant to an answer on *Hamlet* then read Freud and a balanced selection of those critics who have discussed the appropriateness of applying psychoanalytical theories to the interpretation of literature. Their views can most easily be tracked down by consulting the annotated bibliographies held by most major libraries (and don't be afraid to ask a librarian for help in finding and using these). Remember that you go to works of criticism not only to obtain information but to stimulate you into clarifying your own position. And that since life is short and many critical studies are long, judicious use of a book's index and/or contents list is not to be scorned. You can save yourself a great deal of future labour if you carefully record full bibliographic details at this stage.

Once you have collected the evidence, organise it coherently. Sort the detailed points into related groups and identify the quotations which support these. You must also assess the relative importance of each point, for in an essay of limited length it is essential to establish a firm set of priorities, exploring some ideas in depth while discarding or subordinating others.

Test your ideas

As we stressed earlier, a hypothesis is only a proposal, and one that you fully expect to modify. Review it with the evidence before you. Do you really still believe in it? It would be surprising if you did not want to modify it in some way. If you cannot see any problems, others may. Try discussing your ideas with friends and relatives. Raise them in class discussions. Your tutor is certain to welcome your initiative. The critical process is essentially collaborative and there is absolutely no reason why you should not listen to and benefit from the views of others. Similarly, you should feel free to test your ideas against the theories put forward in academic journals and books. But do not just borrow what you find. Critically analyse the views on offer and, where appropriate, integrate them into your own pattern of thought. You must, of course, give full acknowledgement to the sources of such views.

Do not despair if you find you have to abandon or modify significantly your initial position. The fact that you are prepared to do so is a mark of intellectual integrity. Dogmatism is never an academic virtue and many of the best essays explore the *process* of scholarly enquiry rather than simply record its results.

Plan your argument

Once you have more or less decided on your attitude to the question (for an answer is never really 'finalised') you have to present your case in the most persuasive manner. In order to do this you must avoid meandering from point to point and instead produce an organised argument — a structured flow of ideas and supporting evidence, leading logically to a conclusion which fully answers the question. Never begin to write until you have produced an outline of your argument.

You may find it easiest to begin by sketching out its main stage as a flow chart or some other form of visual presentation. But eventually you should produce a list of paragraph topics. The paragraph is the conventional written demarcation for a unit of thought and you can outline an argument quite simply by briefly summarising the substance of each paragraph and then checking that these points (you may remember your English teacher referring to them as topic sentences) really do follow a coherent order. Later you will be able to elaborate on each topic, illustrating and qualifying it as you go along. But you will find this far easier to do if you possess from the outset a clear map of where you are heading.

All questions require some form of an argument. Even so-called 'descriptive' questions *imply* the need for an argument. An adequate answer to the request to 'Outline the role of Iago in *Othello*' would do far more than simply list his appearances on stage. It would at the very least attempt to provide some *explanation* for his actions — is he, for example, a representative stage 'Machiavel'? an example of pure evil, 'motiveless malignity'? or a realistic study of a tormented personality reacting to identifiable social and psychological pressures?

Your conclusion ought to address the terms of the question. It may seem obvious, but 'how far do you agree', 'evaluate', 'consider', 'discuss', etc, are *not* interchangeable formulas and your conclusion must take account of the precise wording of the question. If asked 'How far do you agree?', the concluding paragraph of your essay really should state whether you are in complete agreement, total disagreement, or, more likely, partial agreement. Each preceding paragraph should have a clear justification for its existence and help to clarify the reasoning which underlies your conclusion. If you find that a paragraph serves no good purpose (perhaps merely summarising the plot), do not hesitate to discard it.

The arrangement of the paragraphs, the overall strategy of the argument, can vary. One possible pattern is dialectical: present the arguments in favour of one point of view (**thesis**); then turn to counter-arguments or to a rival interpretation (**antithesis**); finally evaluate the competing claims and arrive at your own conclusion (**synthesis**). You may, on the other hand, feel so convinced of the merits of one particular case that you wish to devote your entire essay to arguing that viewpoint persuasively (although it is always desirable to indicate, however briefly, that you are aware of alternative, if flawed, positions). As the essays contained in this volume demonstrate, there are many other possible strategies. Try to adopt the one which will most comfortably accommodate the demands of the question and allow you to express your thoughts with the greatest possible clarity.

Be careful, however, not to apply abstract formulas in a mechanical manner. It is true that you should be careful to define your terms. It is *not* true that every essay should begin with 'The dictionary defines x as ...'. In fact, definitions are often best left until an appropriate moment for their introduction arrives. Similarly every essay should have a beginning, middle and end. But it does not follow that in your opening paragraph you should announce an intention to write an essay, or that in your concluding paragraph you need to signal an imminent desire to put down your pen. The old adages are often useful reminders of what constitutes good practice, but they must be interpreted intelligently.

Write out the essay

Once you have developed a coherent argument you should aim to communicate it in the most effective manner possible. Make certain you clearly identify yourself, and the question you are answering. Ideally, type your answer, or at least ensure your handwriting is legible and that you leave sufficient space for your tutor's comments. Careless presentation merely distracts from the force of your argument. Errors of grammar, syntax and spelling are far more serious. At best they are an irritating blemish, particularly in the work of a student who should be sensitive to the nuances of language. At worst, they seriously confuse the sense of your argument. If you are aware that you have stylistic problems of this kind, ask your tutor for advice at the earliest opportunity. Everyone, however, is liable to commit the occasional howler. The only remedy is to give yourself plenty of time in which to proof-read your manuscript (often reading it aloud is helpful) before submitting it.

Language, however, is not only an instrument of communication; it is also an instrument of thought. If you want to think clearly and precisely you should strive for a clear, precise prose style. Keep your sentences short and direct. Use modern, straightforward English wherever possible. Avoid repetition, clichés and wordiness. Beware of generalisations, simplifications, and overstatements. Orwell analysed the relationship between stylistic vice and muddled thought in his essay 'Politics and the English Language' (1946) — it remains essential reading (and is still readily available in volume 4 of the Penguin *Collected Essays, Journalism and Letters*). Generalisations, for example, are always dangerous. They are rarely true and tend to suppress the individuality of the texts in question. A remark such as 'Keats always employs sensuous language in his poetry' is not only fatuous (what, after all, does it mean? is *every* word he wrote equally 'sensuous'?) but tends to obscure interesting distinctions which could otherwise be made between, say, the descriptions in the 'Ode on a Grecian Urn' and those in 'To Autumn'.

The intelligent use of quotations can help you make your points with greater clarity. Don't sprinkle them throughout your essay without good reason. There is no need, for example, to use them to support uncontentious statements of fact. 'Macbeth murdered Duncan' does not require textual evidence (unless you wish to dispute Thurber's brilliant parody, 'The Great Macbeth Murder Mystery', which reveals Lady Macbeth's father as the culprit!). Quotations should be included, however, when they are necessary to support your case. The proposition that Macbeth's imaginative powers wither after he has killed his king would certainly require extensive quotation: you would almost certainly want to analyse key passages from both before and after the murder (perhaps his first and last soliloquies?). The key word here is 'analyse'. Quotations cannot make your points on their own. It is up to you to demonstrate their relevance and clearly explain to your readers *why* you want them to focus on the passage you have selected.

Most of the academic conventions which govern the presentation of essays are set out briefly in the style sheet below. The question of gender, however, requires fuller discussion. More than half the population of the world is female. Yet many writers still refer to an undifferentiated *man*kind. Or write of the author and *his* public. We do not think that this convention has much to recommend it. At the very least, it runs the risk of introducing unintended sexist attitudes. And at times leads to such patent absurdities as 'Cleopatra's final speech asserts *man*'s true nobility'. With a little thought, you can normally find ways of expressing yourself which do not suggest that the typical author, critic or reader is male. Often you can simply use plural forms, which is probably a more elegant solution than relying on such awkward formulations as 's/he' or 'he and she'. You should also try to avoid distinguishing between male and female authors on the basis of forenames. Why *Jane* Austen and not *George* Byron? Refer to all authors by their last names

Playing his joker: Showing off his prize after *That Peter Kay Thing* wins 'Best New Comedy' at the British Comedy Awards in December 2000.

In the club: As nightclub owner Don Tonay, with Steve Coogan as Tony Wilson, in Manchester music movie *24 Hour Party People*.

Her indoors: Peter and his wife Susan arrive at the London Palladium for the 2003 BAFTA Television Awards.

Friends United: At Manchester United's annual UNICEF charity dinner with Susan, *Coronation Street*'s Sally Lindsay and Justin 'Young Kenny' Moorhouse.

Put big light on: Switching on the Christmas lights in Bolton, 2003.

The dynamic duo: Filming *Phoenix Nights* spin-off *Max And Paddy's Road To Nowhere* in Bolton, June 2004, with Paddy McGuiness.

Teenage kicks: Peter as *Phoenix Nights'* Brian Potter at the Teenage Cancer Trust Comedy Night at the Royal Albert Hall, London, in April 2005.

Boltonian rhapsody: Peter sends Hyde Park radio ga-ga as warm-up to Queen in July 2005.

Little and large: *Little Britain*'s David Walliams and Peter backstage at Live8, London, in July 2005.

Salutes you, Sir: Peter hails the crowd after mass 'Amarillo' sing-a-long at Live8.

Meat and potato pie piper: Peter mimes playing the panpipes at the Live8 concert in Edinburgh.

Channel fir: Appearing on the *The Paul O'Grady Show Christmas Special* with Barbara Windsor in 2005.

With the band: Peter Kay joins the Kaiser Chiefs at the 2006 Brit Awards.

Chapter Six

Give Me Three Rings When You Get In

'Money can't buy you love, but it can get you some really good chocolate ginger biscuits.'

Dylan Moran

'All you have in comedy, in general, is just going with your instincts. You can only hope that other people think that what you think is funny is funny.'

Will Ferrell

In December 1998 Peter Kay began writing his as yet untitled debut series for Channel 4. He had a rough outline for all six shows and knew that all the episodes would stand alone but that some of the characters would interconnect. As with 'The Services', all would be fly-on-the-wall documentaries shot with a hand-held camera to capture that authentic docu-soap feel. And, importantly, all six would be set in and around Bolton.

It was an ambitious project that would need six separate locations, six huge casts and six unique scripts, but Peter Kay's attitude was to see it as a challenge. 'I want to stretch myself,' he said at the time. 'My logic is, I might only get one crack at this TV lark so I'm climbing on big time.'

The process was an arduous one, not because Peter struggled for material but because he had too much of it. Lots of scenes had to be completely cut from the script. Among them was a brilliant interview with Peter's psychotic ice-cream man Mr Softy which reveals that he'd enjoyed more of a romance with his vans than with any women. 'I had my fair share as the years passed on,' says Mr Softy in Peter's script. 'They got bigger and harder to handle. I had a crack at Pamela and then Madam Georgia, then I fell for Christabel, she was the big love of my life, she was everything to me, we were inseparable, we were together for seven years, I was in bits when she died, it was on the A6 outside House of Rajas.'

Characters who have enjoyed little luck with the opposite sex were to become a recurring trait over the years for Peter Kay, from Brian Potter to Max to Keith Lard – women are a foreign country yet to be explored for every one of them. As borne out by his sentimental gifts for his first girlfriend Catherine Hurst, Peter himself is an old-fashioned romantic. The pair were engaged a year into their relationship and did not live together until they were married.

Having agreed the storylines for the new series, Peter would write ideas then send them on computer disks to his co-writers, Dave Spikey and Neil Anthony, who would then post them back with their suggestions, changes and ideas along with some ideas of their own. Additionally, he'd try out some of the gags in his live shows and, judging on the audience response, would weave them into the plots or spike them – hapless pop duo Park Avenue were born from a routine about the kind of trashy acts you see in Blackpool cabaret clubs. Next, Peter would edit the whole lot down and bash out final scripts on his PC in his bedroom. This was before any of them had access to the Internet, which would have speeded up the process somewhat. Incredibly, throughout the six-month period of writing Peter, Dave and Neil met up together only once – in a pub near the hospital where Dave worked.

'It were a bit like Bernie Taupin and Elton John,' joked Peter, who also says that he did everything he could to avoid actually sitting down to write the shows – not just alpha-betising his CD collection but also splitting it into genres and subgenres.

A pleasurable part of the development was what Peter called 'field trips'. Peter and Dave would visit a variety of businesses as background research for the series. At one working men's club in Daubhill, they stifled laughter as they watched a committee being briefed on the latest advance-ments in urinal block technology and immediately wrote what they witnessed into the script.

Meanwhile producer Sandie Kirk hit on the idea of Peter taking a video camera to Southport Film Fair to try and find some characters who would inspire him. A year later, in the run-up to the show being screened, Peter explained Kirk's technique: 'Normally people would get suspicious, but at a film fair they were more easy-going, as they were used to people pointing cameras. Afterwards I would point out people we saw and say, "I want that moustache, I want that hairstyle." The actual characters are from people I know, or I'd steal voices from people we interviewed when we did research for the series.'

One of the first episodes to be written was the final show of the series, 'Lonely at the Top', which cleverly rounded off the characters we'd meet in the very first episode. '"Lonely at the Top" was Neil's idea,' Peter reveals. 'He wanted to take a look at what the recent trend of TV documentaries had done to the members of the public who had become the stars. The media had made them into celebrities for the simple reason that they had appeared on TV – Mo from *Driving School*, Jeremy from *Airport* and, most successfully of all, Jane McDonald. We decided to use Park Avenue from the first episode of the series, "In the Club", and look at what would happen to them as a result of that first episode being broad-cast. It was a clever idea, turning the whole thing on its head and highlighting what we and the media do to these so-called celebrities.'

In late December 1998, Peter found himself doing a series of 'Turkey and Tinsel' Christmas-meal shows every evening for a week at the Porthouse Hotel in Birmingham and staying at the hotel every night. It wasn't the most glamorous of engagements, but it paid well. 'I had borrowed a laptop and gave myself a challenge, that for the duration of the week I had to write the episode. I managed to do it.'

He also completely rewrote one episode at the eleventh hour. Utah, the coach driver, and Mathew, the drama student from 'The Services', were set to reappear in an episode called 'The Trip', which concentrated on the adventures of an A-level school drama field trip to the theatre where they were due to take part in a drama workshop. On the way Utah's coach breaks down and after a lot of wasted time he decides that it's too late to go to join the other group at the theatre, so they end up going to Knowsley Safari Park instead. Ever the perfectionist, Peter decided that the episode wasn't strong enough and transformed the coach party into the story of two girls from Birmingham travelling to a show in Manchester (keeping Utah as the driver), while Mathew was transferred from a budding actor in a drama workshop to a budding actor working as a steward in the MEN Arena.

The series had lots of working titles – *Six of One and Half a Dozen of the Other*, *Peter Kay's Friends in the North*, *Peter Kay's Midget Gems*, *Pack of Six*. Desperate to name the series, Peter was at the house of his close friend Danny Dignan (the producer who had landed him the *Parkinson* warm-up-man job) discussing possible titles into the early hours of the morning. Then, in a moment of revelation, Dignan said, 'Whatever you call it, people will still go into work the next day and say, "Did you see that Peter Kay thing last night?" ' So, *That Peter Kay Thing* it was.

'Tragically,' says Peter, 'we had a lot of media arsehole types getting the complete wrong end of the stick and assuming it was "That Peter Kay THANG". We had to put them right on that, of course.'

The scripts were finished in March 1999, but still had to be trimmed down and rewritten ready for filming. Travelling down to a meeting at Channel 4 in London, Peter later claimed he was physically sick on the train because he knew he'd be spending the entire day 'arguing and defending the scripts' with Sandie Kirk, executive producer Ivan Douglass and director Andrew Gillman. Peter won the arguments and ended up with the scripts he wanted. He knew he was right; indeed, as an actor on the set of 'The Ice Cream Man Cometh' episode would later tell him, 'It's you that's f***in' the goose, they're just holding its neck.' Worryingly, this pearl of wisdom came from an extra dressed as a policeman! There were, though, some regrets about changes he felt forced into, and one in particular that would rankle for years to come. About the multiple parts he was due to appear in, Peter wrote on his official website that he had reservations about being labelled 'the new Steve Coogan': 'But after much deliberation I thought f*** 'em, there's enough room for everybody, and if it wasn't going to be him then it would be Dick Emery or Peter Sellers. Journalists will always pigeon-hole you somewhere, as sadly some of them are lazy bastards after free meals and weekends in Jersey.'

With the scripts rewritten and the series given a title, *That Peter Kay Thing* began filming in May 1999.

As with 'The Services', the production team working on the 'Eyes Down' episode had tremendous difficulties finding a bingo hall willing to let them film inside because of the tremendous trend of prime-time docu-dramas dishing the dirt on ordinary professions and basically revealing what we all knew already: nobody knows what they're doing, least of all the people in charge. Eventually they managed to persuade the Apollo Bingo Hall in Blackpool to let the cameras in, Peter even charming the manager and staff into appearing in the show. Unpaid extras were essential to Peter's idea, and gave it an air of authenticity he felt he couldn't achieve with actors. When they were shooting 'Eyes Down' they even provided some of the funniest lines – not that they realised it. Ivan Douglass hit on the idea of asking the old ladies what they thought of Tom Jones and George Clooney and filmed their responses, but for the show it was as if they were swooning over Peter's misogynistic bingo caller – 'Wigan's famous for two things, rugby players and beautiful women. What position do you play, Sheila?'

The MEN opened its doors, too. It had been less than a year since he'd stopped working for them and, proud of an ex-steward made good, they were more than happy to give Peter access all areas, even though they knew he would more than likely be making a mockery of the place in an episode that would follow the life in a day of the venue. The managers of the bingo hall and the arena, believed producer Sandie Kirk, gave their trust because of what she described as 'Kay's gift' – that although his comedy is hysterical and subversive, as with Victoria Wood before him, it is done with respect. 'We all recognise those people,' she says of his characters. 'His comedy is gentle, but gentle with bite.'

Nowhere is this better demonstrated than in the opening episode of *That Peter Kay Thing*, 'In the Club', which was shot at the Farnworth and District Veterans Club, a local social club heavily populated by the over-sixties. Like all the subject matter of *That Peter Kay Thing*, Peter is drawn to working men's clubs because they connect to his personal past (he attended countless parties and wedding receptions in them) and because he is fascinated and amused by disappearing institutions.

'It's nostalgia,' Kay has admitted. 'I used to go as a kid. I loved the names of the acts and the pictures of them pinned up outside. I used to ask if I could have them to put on my wall. I love the fact that outside it's car alarms going off and razor wire, and inside it's like Vegas. The nightlife always fascinated me. The acts, butcher by day – Elvis by night. The escapism of it all, of these people trapped by a mortgage and family by day, living out their fantasies by night.'

In 1999 he told a reporter visiting the set of 'In the Club': 'I'm interested in the sort of jobs that won't make it to the next millennium – ice-cream men, paper boys – and following people as they try to hang on to the past. Look at ice-cream men. No one wants to stand queuing for a cornet in the rain when you can go down the shop and get a Ben and Jerry's. And ice-cream men don't make any money so they resort to anything to get by.'

At the Farnworth Veterans Club the visit of the film crew was the biggest event to happen in the area since the opening of the Lidl superstore – although some of the older members could recall James Mason recording a scene from the movie *Spring and Port Wine* on the canal at Nob End. As well as requiring the members of the club to appear as themselves in the episode, Kay also booked several real cabaret acts to appear in the Talent Trek competition, including a limbo dancer from Southampton, local singer Marie Perrigo and Oldham's very own one-man band, Billy Bedlam.

'It was great fun,' says Billy, who appeared on the show in his clown suit and blowing a tune through a shower tube. 'Everyone treated it like a real talent show and we all had four minutes each to do our act. There were lots of bits that they cut out. In my scene Dave Spikey grabbed my bass drum and started marching around the hall with it. Peter was a bit less friendly than he'd been in the past,' claims Billy Bedlam. 'But that was understandable; he had a lot on his plate. You could tell it was very much his show, that he was in charge.'

In fact Peter's desperation to get everything just right in the series drove many of the crew potty. His obsession was such that when he was filming 'The Arena' episode he spent 40 minutes arguing with the stylist over whether or not his character's hair had sufficient curls on top. The art of delegation was not a strong point, courtesy of his years of stand-up, where there was no one to tell him what to do, but it was a trait that went much further back than that. At school, his friend Michael Atherton remembers that 'he wanted to hold the camera and be in front of it as well'. Peter, though, held the vision of the series in his head, and having studied films and TV for years he had an in-built sense of how things should be done. For example, he knew how to capture the absurd in the ordinary without veering too far into the unbelievable.

'I often have to pull back because the screen enlarges everything anyway,' he said during filming. 'Some people say that Mike Leigh's characters are not believable, but I know those people. It's just that he will put six great characters in a room and it becomes a caricature – it's too much on screen at the same time.'

He also saw *That Peter Kay Thing* as maybe his sole chance on TV, and he wasn't prepared to let go – even if that meant arguing with people about hair. In a typical illustration of his latent Catholic guilt, imagining the world is going to come crashing down around you the moment something good happens to you, he was fatalistic about his chances of success and shrugged, 'If I fail, I'll go and work on the bins; at least I've given it a go.'

Despite his controlling nature and worries about a project that was very much his 'baby', the team of Gillman, Kirk and Kay worked well, with director Andrew Gillman even having a part in an additional scene in 'The Ice Cream Man Cometh' which replicated – albeit above a takeaway called Kebabylon – a famous scene from Martin Scorsese's *Taxi Driver*.

After each show was completed Peter would go down to London for the post-production editing, where he would stop overnight at the house of his friend from *The Royle Family* Craig Cash. Cash's keen ear for comedy and knowledge of the machinations of television production were crucial to this final stage of the series. Each night the pair would review unedited tapes and Cash would offer suggestions. One of them was that in order to retain the dry docu-soap feel of the shows some of the more obvious jokes should be taken out. As much as Peter appreciated his input, crucially it was the fact that he found the shows funny that Peter enjoyed the most. The pair were good mates and for some while there was talk of them writing together on various projects such as a *Royle Family* movie and a spin-off series (later to become the brilliant *Early Doors*), but neither came to fruition.

Despite the exhaustion and the fears of compromise, Peter described the experience of filming *That Peter Kay Thing* as 'overwhelming'. One of the most difficult and eye-opening scenes he filmed was as Leonard the elderly god botherer, who wheels a giant cross into Bolton's Victoria Square and begins preaching and reading from the Bible to passers-by. The film crew were a hundred yards away, above Clinton Cards, so Peter with just a small radio mic was effectively alone as he stood clutching the 10-foot cross as nonchalant shoppers passed by assuming he was another of the town's resident eccentrics.

'Leonard really opened up my eyes to some things that I never knew existed,' he said. 'I spent over an hour wandering around unrecognisable to anybody and it really affected me. I was treated so differently by the public. The majority of people treated me with contempt and looked through me rather than at me. I do realise that probably had a lot to do with me carrying a 10-foot crucifix. Or did it? I also had a few people coming up to me when I was praying and chatting to me about the word of the Lord and spreading God's good news. I never knew that so many people were actually interested or believed in anything else or needed some kind of guidance in their lives. They stood and prayed with me and sang with me. That really freaked me out, but in a good and surprising way.'

Among the life-enhancing experiences of filming there was also a near-death incident. His role as Marc Park – the Talent Trek winner who suddenly shoots to fame – entailed Peter shooting a cliché-laden seasonal pop video for Park's pretentious stab at a seasonal number one, 'Christmas 2000', with fake snow falling as he mimed the lyrics. Mucking around between shots, one of the dancers threw a snowball at Peter and a piece became lodged in his throat. Unlike real snow, it didn't melt. 'Next thing I knew, it had mixed with saliva and expanded like a tampon. I was choking and apparently turning a funny colour. There was all of a fuss and confusion, and I was outside with my head between my legs and being given oxygen. I felt like a right idiot, and what was even funnier was, my face went white and my false nose stayed tanned.'

With the series done and dusted, it was originally due to première in early November, but in a very late change of heart Channel 4 decided to move the series back to January 2000. The wait was terrible, but after all the trauma of putting *That Peter Kay Thing* together, returning to his stand-up was a welcome relief, even though he found himself beginning to stretch his itinerary beyond the limitations of a drive back to Croston Street. However, it was on home ground, at the Frog and Bucket in Manchester, where Peter made the first ill-advised decision of his career – that's if you don't count those Bermuda shorts he wore in *The Wizard of*

Oz – when, shortly before he was about to appear onstage, another one of the comics told him a sick joke he'd heard and Peter decided to incorporate it into his act.

It was DJ Mark Radcliffe's 41st birthday that evening and to celebrate he and a dozen members of staff from the BBC Manchester studios, where he recorded his Radio One show, had decided to visit the Frog and Bucket to see Peter Kay, who was headlining. Peter began in his normal fashion with a series of one-liners, but 10 minutes in discussed people making sick jokes, such as the one about Rod Hull, the puppeteer famous for his narky bird alter-ego Emu, who had died after falling from his roof trying to adjust his TV aerial: 'The funeral was great but the reception was crap.' Asking the audience, 'What's black and white and eats like a horse? A zebra', he followed it with, 'What's black and white and wants feeding?' The answer? 'Jill Dando's cat.'

It was a mistake. A big one. Jill Dando, who presented the BBC's *Crimewatch*, was a popular personality who had a few weeks earlier been murdered on the steps of her home in west London. Among the BBC party was someone who had worked with Dando, who although saying nothing at the time, was upset enough to report it to a journalist friend. The following day, back home in Bolton, someone phoned Peter to ask if he had 'any more Dando jokes'. It was a reporter from the *Sun*. Later, two more *Sun* reporters called round to his house. The next day, the story loomed large on the front page. 'Sick comic makes disgraceful joke' they bellowed, labelling him 'Podgy Pete'. It was a story nobody would ever have expected to be associated with a comedian who had such an avowed aversion to unpleasantness as Peter Kay.

'I just thought, "That's me finished now, that's it," ' he said later. 'It was ironic, really. I'd never done anything about sex or anything like that. I just didn't think.'

Although padded out with a few half-truths in the press, the story caused a nationwide backlash and Peter went into hiding. The BBC issued a statement that read: 'Clearly this was unacceptable and we apologise for the offence that has been caused and are speaking to Peter Kay about this ill-judged attempt at comedy.' A few days later, Peter spoke of his regrets to the *Bolton Evening News*, telling them it was all 'a big mistake' and 'God knows, I feel bad about it. If I could rewind it and unsay it, I would ... I apologise. I did tell the joke. I would be a liar if I said that I didn't,' he told them. 'I have never done it before. When I said it I just looked at the audience and said: "Oh, I really shouldn't have said that." '

Illustrating that comics find it harder to accept a joke that bombs than a joke you regret, he went on to claim that although the *Sun* had said the audience was shocked and fell into a stunned silence, the crowd actually laughed. 'I'm not making excuses – I just didn't come on and tell the joke straight off. It was all part of a routine I have been doing for a year about people who tell sick jokes.'

Even if the rest of Britain hated him for laughing at the untimely death of TV's golden girl, the people of Bolton supported him. Long after the national press had let go of the story, the controversy rumbled on in the *Bolton Evening News*, following a letter from an outraged reader who wrote: 'He insulted the memory of Jill Dando, with his sickening joke about her cat.' The letter writer went on to promise that she would no longer watch TV or read the *Bolton Evening News* if either featured the evil Kay. Rather than prompt more demands for the head of Peter Kay, the newspaper received a flurry of correspondence defending him, one replying: 'Try being proud of what Peter is doing (putting Bolton on the map).'

The strength of the response affected Peter deeply and only strengthened his loyalty to Bolton. Immediately after-wards, when the story first broke Peter said he felt 'ashamed, but me mum especially were great about it'. Typically, his dad said that he didn't get the joke. 'He said: "Tell me again. Wants seeding?" I said, "No, feeding!"

'When I rang up me nan to warn her, she went, "Oh my God. Oh Peter, Peter, Peter, Peter … why don't you think before you open your mouth?" And then she thought for a bit and went, "Anyway … I don't think Jill had a cat." I thought, "Well, I'll ring them up and tell them to take it off front page … Hullo, it's Podgy Pete here, take it off, she hadn't got a cat." '

The whole event does illustrate a darker side to Peter Kay. Although he is portrayed as a family-friendly comic he is not without an edge that often frays the boundaries of political correctness, and for some often cuts too close.

'It was the best of times; it was the worst of times.'
Charles Dickens, A Tale of Two Cities

Having fallen foul of the redtops with his ill-judged gags about Jill Dando and her non-existent cat, his image as an entertainer with a populist worldview was repaired when he contributed to TV's *100 Most Memorable Moments*, broadcast on Channel 4 on 11 September. Peter's appearance came at no. 97 and centred on public information films, for which Peter wrote a hilarious commentary claiming 'they were like mini-Ken Loach films when I was young. There was one that sticks in my mind,' he said. 'It's the one with a child running down a beach, a little boy, and there's a piece of broken glass, a lemonade bottle. That still upsets me now and I still can't rundown a beach. I'm 26 and I still can't run down a beach with nothing on my feet.'

He went on to remind viewers that after Dave Prowse had stopped doing the Green Cross Code adverts, saying things like 'Make sure you find a safe gap between cars' in a broad Cornish accent, he was replaced by Dr Who, Jon Pertwee, and a new acronym for children to remember as they crossed roads: SPLINK. 'SPLINK!' laughed Peter. 'Find a safe place … Pavement … by the time I'd got to P I'd been hit by a bus.'

Then, on 18 November he began his first proper headline tour, ten dates starting at the Derby Assembly Rooms and ending at the Barracuda Club, Lincoln, on 6 December. The biggest date of the tour was at the 1,600-capacity Bridgewater Hall in Manchester – an event which Peter saw as a massive leap forward from the usual venues he'd played in the city over the years.

'It obviously meant a lot to him,' says his former lecturer at Salford University, Lloyd Peters, who was in the audience that night. 'I remember him taking photos of the audience.' Nervous, and somewhat incredulous that he should be playing such a premium venue, Peter asked the audience, 'What the f*** are we doing here, eh?' before launching into a 90-minute set that featured his tried and trusted reminiscences of school trips and the pop aisle at Asda on top of new material about people nagging him to book a holiday on Ceefax – 'Booked it, packed it, f***ed off' – and people who blow their lifelines on easy questions in 'Who Wants to be a Millionaire?' – 'How many legs has a dog got? Can I phone a friend?' At Sheffield City Hall he slid, as usual, energetically across the stage on his knees in his imitation of children's giddy abandon at weddings and ended up covered in hairs shed the evening before by Elkie Brooks's golden retriever. While at the Nottingham Old Vic, *Independent* writer Brian Viner reported sitting next to two student teachers, Heidi and Mel, rolling with laughter 'as Kay starts to evoke, with devastating accuracy, the last day of school term, when you were allowed to take in Etch-a-Sketch and Kerplunk, and Mastermind with that Vietnamese lady on the front. His next routine, about school dinner ladies, is the point at which Heidi rushes to the loo,' wrote Viner. 'Later, Mel forces her to admit that she had actually wet herself laughing. "Yeah," she protests, "but only a tiny bit." '

Meanwhile, on Peter's website message board, a fan who attended the same show wrote: 'As an asthmatic, I found the performance drained me and had to catch a taxi home at the end of it all as I couldn't bloody walk!'

With people wetting themselves and wheezing home from his gigs and *That Peter Kay Thing* just weeks away from being aired on national TV, Peter's career was hitting a new peak. Then, the day after the final date of the tour at the Barracuda Club in Lincoln, he received a call from Margaret Faulkner, his father's partner since he had left his mum nearly 10 years previously. His father was dead. The cause of death was liver failure. He was a few weeks away from his 52nd birthday.

Michael Kay had played a huge part in his son's future profession – not just through the corny jokes he told, but also via his taste in comedy (he had adored Morecambe and Wise and *Only Fools and Horses*). Humour was the thing that united them, and after his dad left his mother Peter would visit him at the one-bedroom flat he shared with Margaret, where they'd stay up late into the night laughing. Later in life Peter had found the things that had irritated him as a child about his dad now amused him, and were a rich source of material. For his part, Michael was proud of his son and would boast of his achievements in the pub – sadly, he didn't get to see *That Peter Kay Thing*. Peter was due to pop round later in the week he died to show him the tapes. According to Margaret, the 50th birthday he spent with Peter in London – at the *Parkinson* show and the Comedy Store – was one of the best weekends of his life.

At the time, Peter coped as best he could, taking a few of his father's records and helping Margaret donate his clothes to a charity shop. Organising the funeral kept him occupied and helped keep his mind off his bereavement. 'Dad always said I was not funny enough to be a comedian,' he told the *Stage* a couple of weeks later. 'But he ended up the biggest fan of my work. I always asked him if he wanted to come to my gigs. I think I made him feel it would make me feel uncomfortable, but I told him I'd always love him to come. I don't know why he said no.'

Even in tragedy Peter was able to find things to amuse him, and at his father's funeral he found it hysterical when one of the mourners told him: 'I've just come out of hospital. Rectal abscess.' But then Peter Kay's comedy recorder is seldom switched off, and throughout his career he has kept a finely tuned ear out for the normal everyday things people say, which when you step back from them are actually quite strange: 'You've brought the weather with you'; 'Is it hot in here or is it me?'. Or the time when Peter's mother visited her local library and the librarian said, 'Your Peter's doing very well. Mind you, he's very quiet when he comes in here.'

Peter also really loved a friend of his who would talk about himself in the third person. 'He'll say, "Baz went out last night. Baz had a great time." And we're like, "Well hang on, you are Baz, you idiot." I find things like that very funny.'

As with everything, Baz was locked away in the Kay comedy cupboard, to be brought out many years later when he came to write *Max and Paddy's Road to Nowhere*, re-created in Max's pa's groan of 'Paddy has needs'.

Although in his grief Peter didn't realise it, on Christmas Eve he was the main attraction of Channel Five's schedule when they broadcast a show he'd recorded a few months earlier at the Comedy Store in London. It was one of a series of half-hour-long stand-up sets that Five broadcast, but this was the only one that found itself on at such an attractive prime-time spot. For many viewers it was the first time they'd experienced Peter in full flow. The show was just wonderful and an excellent demonstration of how far his act had advanced in the two-and-a-half hectic years since that gig at the Pint Pot in Salford. Of course to those who had seen his act in Nottingham or Derby or at the Birmingham Glee Club there was also the realisation that Peter's act wasn't quite as wildly improvisational as they had imagined. Over the year he'd develop the incredible feat of making people believe he was almost making it up as he was going along, that he was confiding in his audience for the first time. Then there were the brilliant sideways glances and eye-rolling looks that you'd never notice in venues the size of Bridgewater Hall, such as when he recounts the story of telling his nan that Elsie Haslam ('Do you know her?') has died.

'She said, "When?" I said, "Wednesday." ' He mimics his nan sucking her teeth. ' "I only saw her in supermarket on Tuesday." ' Pause. 'I said, "And? What does she expect? Grim Reaper pushing a trolley behind her? Come on love, get in, come on, you don't need bleach where you're going, come on. Soap-filled pads? KP choc dip? Come on, time's time." '

Most brilliantly of all, when a woman gets up on the front row to visit the toilet, he waves after her, as if she were a relative leaving after a visit: 'See ya love. Take care. All the best,' he calls. 'Give me three rings when you get in, let me know you've got home safely.'

Give me three rings when you get to t'next chapter, three rings ...

Chapter Seven

Garlic Bread?

'The British working men's club. Yesterday's dream factory. But now with each passing year there are fewer and fewer people to peddle those dreams to. The Neptune is one such club. With attendance figures dwindling and a permanent lack of funds, it continues to struggle in an effort to appeal to a younger generation with more modern tastes.'

Andrew Sachs, narration on 'In the Club',
That Peter Kay Thing

'You'll have to forgive him. He's from Barcelona.'
Basil Fawlty, Fawlty Towers

Of all the shows in *That Peter Kay Thing* it was 'In the Club' that would have the most lasting significance for his future TV career and, crucially, the decision to cast comedians instead of actors – among them Toby Foster, whom he'd met at the Raw of the Roses show; Archie Kelly, who had a brilliant act where he performed as old-time crooner Jackie 'Mr Goodtime' Valencio; and of course Peter's writing partner Dave Spikey, who auditioned for the role of club compère Jerry St Clair, even though he'd played a major part in creating him. It gave the episode a naturalness that really worked. The comics were joined by the Talent Trek competitors, most of whom were real acts on the club circuit in the Manchester area, and the real audience of the Farnworth Veterans Club who, plied with cheap drinks, treated the event like a real variety show.

'When Michelle Coffee sang "Don't Go Breaking My Heart" you can see some of them feeling sorry for her,' says Peter. 'They were amazing.'

There was some opposition from Channel 4, who were worried about the comedians' acting inexperience – something that was exacerbated by the fact that Peter also wanted to cast his schoolfriend Paddy McGuinness as the Neptune's bouncer. There were also arguments at Channel 4 over the Neptune's social secretary, Brian Potter. Did he have to be in a wheelchair?

'I remember at Salford, Peter showed me a few script ideas for TV shows,' says his former lecturer Lloyd Peters. 'And I remember one featuring a love affair between an able-bodied man and a disabled woman. I told him to be careful, but I think it spurred him on. In my opinion some of his best stuff is when he's ruffling feathers.' Feathers were ruffled but, yet again, Peter's argument – 'Why shouldn't he be disabled, there's no other disabled people on TV' – won through.

Peter also liked the idea of planting a doubt in the viewer's mind that Brian Potter was so low, such a skinflint, that he might actually be feigning his disability in order to claim benefit. Indeed, his story as to how he became para-lysed didn't exactly ring true: 'I was managing the Aquarius Club,' Potter tells the documentary cameras. 'We had a big Christmas bash, 15 quid a ticket, sell-out, everyone were there, but then tragedy. The pipes burst, water everywhere, utter chaos. People running round getting electrocuted. It was like something out of *The Poseidon Adventure*. I were terrified, me. I had to swim for the safe for the night's takings and that's when I saw it coming towards me, fruit machine pinned me to the serving hatch. I blacked out; all I can remember is this warm, bright, pulsating glow ...' As Brian delivers his speech one of the Talent Trek singers, Marie Perrigo, can be heard singing in the background: 'Walking back to happiness, whoop a oh yeah yeah.'

Peter would have preferred to leave viewers' suspicions there, but unfortunately, having won so many conflicts with Channel 4, he agreed to a closing scene, with the Neptune Club burning down. In his horror at seeing his 'dream factory' in flames, Brian Potter stands up out of his chair to bully the firefighters. 'The idea was that we gave the viewers little clues, made them wonder,' Peter Kay told me a couple of years later. 'I'm still a bit annoyed by it, to tell you the truth; it were never supposed to have gone in. I buckled to pressure.'

The opening scene of 'In the Club' sees the committee debating the entertainment for the forthcoming Christmas party, with Brian campaigning for an entertainer called Nobby Alcock. 'Now hear me out, I know he's blue but he does a smashing sideline in Punch and Judy.' When Toby Foster's character, Les, swears in response, Brian responds by saying, 'There's no need for that foul language please, I've got a photograph of my wife in the pocket.'

'It was brilliant, absolutely spot on,' says Billy Bedlam of the re-creation of a working men's club committee meeting. 'They'd be run by men who worked on the buses or in factories during the week but then when they'd get to committee meetings they'd turn into little Hitlers, arguing about whether or not they should have a cigarette machine in the corridor.'

The show was broadcast at 10.30 p.m. on Wednesday, 12 January 2000. Directly after it, Peter took part in a live web chat on <Channel4.com> and had to respond to a series of bizarre rapid-fire questions from people hiding behind pseudonyms such as Applejack, ERV200 and Banzai Barber III. 'Have you ever ridden a camel?' ('No.') 'Do your family own Kay's catalogue?' ('Yes.') 'Is playing characters just dressing up for adults?' ('That's a bit deep! Go out. Kiss a girl.') Among them, though, one barbed comment from a viewer called 'Pople' stood out. 'Why were you so crap in *The Sunday Show* and suddenly come up with something as subtle and clever as this?' ('Erm, because I was getting more money?')

It was a question the critics – who had written *The Sunday Show* off as dead the moment Dennis Pennis left anyhow – were asking too. The *Herald* reported: '*That Peter Kay Thing* went about its creator's task with seamless subtlety' and that 'Kay delivered a ton of slow-burning corkers'. Not that all the reviews were undiluted praise. In the *Observer*, TV columnist Kathryn Flett compared the programme unfavourably with *The Royle Family* and wrote, 'what you get with Kay is a near forensic obsession with the source material which unfortunately has the effect of negating most of the comedy'. Which missed the point of what Peter had achieved. However, she did compliment the use of narrator Andrew Sachs, as did Charlie Catchpole in the *Mirror*, who described his commentary as containing just enough 'authentic, energy-sapping dullness'.

Getting Sachs, the actor best known for his role as Manuel in *Fawlty Towers*, on board was a huge coup, especially as he was fresh from narrating *Parking Wars*, one of the terminally eventless docu-dramas *That Peter Kay Thing* was sending up. 'Andrew Sachs was brilliant,' says Peter, revealing that the actor had even lowered his fee to take part, having been impressed with 'The Services'. 'Although I never got to meet him. We'd just send him the scripts and he'd do them in London, then they'd send the finished tapes up to us in Bolton.'

As well as Brian Potter, for 'In the Club' Peter played three more characters: Max the doorman, Marc Park – one half of Park Avenue, a double act in the Talent Trek Final ('If you can't be the song then let the song be,' he pompously tells his singing partner) – and a reprise of Chorley FM DJ Paul LeRoy from 'The Services' as the judge of the Grand Final of

Talent Trek 99. LeRoy had no lines, except mumbling 'I'm not' when his girlfriend catches him staring at Cheryl Avenue and tells him to 'stop looking at her tits'.

As with his stand-up set, many of the storylines mirrored things that had happened to Peter in his real life, such as being disciplined at the bingo hall for time-wasting and Mathew Kelly in 'The Arena' being given the wrong name tag on his first day at work. While the speech Marc Park pretentiously gives about yoga – 'yoga: I find it stimulates my mind and my body' – is taken almost verbatim from a *South Bank Show* special on the singer Sting, Park's brother's speech about him showing off in a school play was very reminiscent of Peter's own life. 'He ruined the nativity. He was the innkeeper, he only had one line, "There's no room at the inn." He offered them en suite with full English. You can't ad-lib the Bible.'

It could have been Sister Barbara talking!

In the remaining five shows following 'In the Club' Peter would appear as a dozen other characters, many of them inspired by his part-time jobs over the years and others by the strangers he'd interviewed at Southport Film Fair. The line-up of larger-than-life personalities includes: Leonard de Thomkinson, the world's longest-serving paper boy, who was closely based on the real elderly eccentric whom Peter had befriended during his time at the Esso petrol station; Robert Edge, aka Mr Softy, inspired partially by a kid from Mount St Joseph's who'd tried to sue the school in an incident involving a Bunsen burner; Rose, a middle-aged bingo player who says, 'We never had time for sex, we were too busy having babies'; Mathew Kelly and Utah from 'The Services'; and Tom Dale the bingo caller, who charms the old women with the dabbers with lines like 'Thanks for coming tonight, was the cemetery shut?'

At first Peter was open about his inspiration, admitting

that Brian Potter was based on an amalgamation of his ex-bosses. But first Tom Henderson from the bingo hall where Peter had worked said, during an Internet interview, 'I want royalties because he used me in a piece in one of his sketches, I know he did.' And then a fire safety officer from Bolton Council, called Keith Laird, appeared in the *Bolton Evening News* claiming that Peter's character in the bingo hall episode, also a fire safety officer, and with the incredibly similar name of Keith Lard, was based on him. 'I've never met Peter Kay,' Laird told the local paper. 'But he must have seen me somewhere because there's no doubt it's me. He's got everything down to a T. The facial expressions were spot on. He kept saying it's not fire that kills, it's ignorance – I say that all the time.' He went on to claim that he had 1,300 witnesses at the council. Indeed Laird was something of a legend in Bolton, alleged to be so obsessed with fire safety that he would pack a pair of smoke alarms in his suitcase whenever he went on holiday. No doubt the similarity would have been easier for Mr Laird to take if it hadn't been for the fact that in *That Peter Kay Thing* his almost-namesake was rumoured to enjoy illicit romantic liaisons with canines. As Laird revealed to the *Bolton Evening News*: 'My new nickname is Woof-Woof. It's a good job I can see the funny side.'

As for Peter Kay, he claimed innocence: 'Honestly, the character was just made up. I never met him, even when I worked at Top Rank bingo. I can't believe it's almost the same name but then again, a Brian Potter came forward after I featured a Brian Potter character in the first show. I suppose this kind of thing is bound to happen, but I've never met him in my life. There are bound to be similarities,' he said. 'There are nine Peter Kays in the Bolton phone book.'

Once the show had been screened and his colleagues tired of barking at him, Laird went quiet. For now ...

For the people of Bolton there were also other references

in the show that only they would get. The *Bolton Evening News*, for example, is known locally as BEN; for *That Peter Kay Thing* the invented local paper is called the *Bolton Independent Leader*, BIL for short. While in the Leonard episode, the main character is fleetingly caught in conversation with a local elderly gentleman who was something of a legendary eccentric in the area because in the summer he enjoys frequenting pubs dressed in tennis whites and carrying a racquet.

Before *That Peter Kay Thing* was broadcast, Peter already had the idea of expanding the first episode and in January 2000 began mapping out a whole series following Brian Potter's new venture. The moment of realisation that this was the episode to follow up came at the mecca of old-fashioned, outdated northern clubland: Bernard Manning's World Famous Embassy Club.

Manning, in the enlightened era of the 1980s and 1990s, had found himself marginalised by the comedy establishment because of some of his racist and sexist jokes, but still managed to fill his own club three times a week. As Jonathan Margolis claims in his biography of the overweight millionaire, 'Manning was a potential working-class hero, a master of the comedy of vulgarity and insult whom Chaucer would have admired, but who ruined it all by being racist.' However, even in his own heartland he was beginning to appear past his sell-by date. Nowhere is the old-school comedian's struggle to keep up with changing trends better illustrated than in John Thomson's ironic pastiche of a fat northern comic in *The Fast Show*, Bernard Righton, whose jokes began worryingly un-PC before redeeming themselves: 'There was a Jew, a Paki and an Irishman in the pub. What a fine example of racial integration!' In 1999, more than aware that times had changed and that his father was well behind them, 39-year-old Bernard Manning Jnr (who once got sent off for Stockport County reserves when the referee asked him his name) took over the venue, renamed it the New Embassy Club and started booking acts from the new breed of Manchester comics. Headlining the opening night was Peter Kay.

'It's been turned into an alternative comedy venue,' he said. 'But it's kept the same audience Bernard would play to. I find that hilarious. That's when I realised the "In the Club" episode from the last series had potential for a series of its own.'

Once *That Peter Kay Thing* finally made it on to our screens, Peter himself loved watching them screened live – somehow it all didn't seem real unless there were adverts and other programmes around it. The series and all the accompanying publicity had helped take his mind off his father's death, but once the run was complete he felt a strange purposelessness. '*That Peter Kay Thing* has shuffled off into the distance and that's a shame,' he wrote on his website in a March 2000 message to fans. 'It all seemed to go so fast, the six episodes flew by.'

His feelings of emptiness weren't helped by some senior people at Channel 4's lukewarm reaction to the series and their reluctance to schedule a repeat run. As had been proved in recent years with *The Fast Show*, *Father Ted* and *The Royle Family*, repeats were crucial to a series' lasting success with the word of mouth from the original showing pushing up ratings when it was moved to a new slot. The show had been well received by the public and most of the press, but the peak viewing figures of just 1.6 million were relatively low. Frustration led Peter to start an Internet campaign urging fans of the show to bombard Channel 4 with requests for another chance to watch it. Upset by the lack of plans, he wrote, 'Why? It was critically acclaimed, it got viewers, it wasn't the best programme in the world, but it was a lot more charming than some of the shite that's on. Anyway, if you would like to see it repeated then write to either Katie Taylor or Kevin Lygo in the Entertainment Department at Channel 4, 124 Horseferry Road, London, SW1P 2TX. Good luck!'

Elsewhere on the site, in a question-and-answer session Peter says: 'I went to see Channel 4 the other day and surprisingly they said that they don't think the series would be repeated unless it was to promote a second series. Now whether this was an attempt at convincing me to do another series or sheer blind f***ing stupidity remains to be seen.'

Peter's official website <www.peterkay.co.uk> had been started by a pair of Peter's friends, Glenn Jones and Chris Greeney, in June 1997 as a bit of fun but as Peter's fame grew the site got more serious and in July 1998 it became a fully formed beast rather than an amateurish affair hosted on AOL's free webspace. The site had a major part in spreading the good word of Peter Kay by publishing tour dates and booking information and long before any other comedian had noticed how important this new technology could become Peter Kay was taking an active role in it with monthly messages to fans and answering reader's messages. As well as all the normal website fare, the site also included reviews of his shows, fans' jokes and some original material penned by Peter. Some of this, like his rant against public transport, veered more into the territory of irate commuter rather than quick-witted comic: 'Why are two hundred people packed into economy while there are two "business" men in first class?' he grumbled.

The website also included a couple of rough ideas for what might have been developed into future characters, such as Roy, the manager of the Majestic Cinema: 'Unfortunately, due to neglect and abuse the old girl's gradually wearing away, so much so that she's now turning into a stale decrepit hell hole. In fact only this morning my u-bend in the Gents went all to cock, but never mind.'

One development in Peter's career went unreported online, though it would be another turning point in his career. In the spring of 2000, after being recommended to him by his friends Craig Cash and Caroline Aherne, Peter left Lisa White, his manager and agent for the past two years, and appointed Phil McIntyre as his new representative. McIntyre was a huge player in the theatre industry and in addition to Cash and Aherne handled some of the biggest names in British comedy (Victoria Wood, *The Fast Show*). His involvement instantly gave Peter Kay some weight (no pun intended) at Channel 4.

Robert Popper, who was a commissioning editor at the channel at the turn of the century, says that 'If you heard Phil McIntyre's name associated with someone you would certainly take it more seriously. He's a big, big name in the industry, someone who knows what they're doing, so whatever he brings to you, you're going to listen.'

With a background in live rock concerts, McIntyre also brought experience in areas Peter Kay hadn't begun to think about, and one of the first decisions was to get a video done of Peter's live performances.

'The idea is to get paid for something you really want to do!'
                                                        Michael Palin

In February 2000, on the front page of the site, Peter Kay alerted his fans to the fact that this April he would be recording his first live video in Blackpool. Originally the two gigs were booked for the theatre on the North Pier, but then when all 1,000 tickets for the first show sold out in a couple of days and the video crew suggested it might be a bit dicey taking all the filming equipment down a pier, it was moved to the theatre at the foot of Blackpool Tower, usually the home of the resident circus.

'I wanted to do it somewhere special, rather than some faceless theatre somewhere,' he says. Early in the year he had cancelled a few dates in Liverpool, Birmingham and Preston because so much of his act was about his dad that he felt it would be uncomfortable. But when he went on holiday with Susan to Egypt in March he found himself writing more and more material about him. 'Maybe that was my way of grieving and coping with losing him,' he tells people before the Blackpool gig. 'Don't get me wrong, the material's not sad or nothing and I'm sure he'll be pretty chuffed with it.'

The new material about his father found him recalling his dad holding him in a headlock when he was a kid and yelling out to passing police cars, 'It's OK, I've got him', and witnessing cheesy cabaret shows like the singer with an American accent called Tony Colorado, about whom his dad said, 'I know him, he's from Burnley.' On top of this, because it was Blackpool there was a whole new section about foreign holidays – how you hate it when you get home without a suntan, how terrible it is having to check out of a hotel at 10 a.m. when your plane doesn't leave till midnight, not to mention how dads on holiday abroad always manage to find a place where they can eat English food and none of that foreign muck. 'Garlic bread?' he says, mimicking his dad. 'Garlic? And bread? Am I hearing you right?'

With the audience in on the joke, he calls the video *Live at the Top of the Tower* – 'How'd you all get up here in the lift?' He also films a series of small sketches and in one of them he takes a sideways pop at his comedy enemies when future *Phoenix Nights* regular Archie Kelly, dressed in his Jackie

Valencio wig, says to camera: 'He steals all my stuff, you know. "Smack Me Bitch Up", I've been doing that for years. And he swears. It's rude, it's crude and its f***ing offensive.'

The music for the *Live at the Top of the Tower* was recorded by Toni Baker, a musician from Bury (not the gay area of Manchester, by the way). Toni had been in a few bands in the 1970s and 1980s (Shabby Tiger, very big in Belgium, apparently), and following a divorce was making some extra money by giving piano lessons, advertising his services in the northwest edition of *Loot*.

'I got a call from this guy saying he'd like to play piano,' says Toni. 'So we talked for a little while about what he wanted to do and we found out we both liked the same kind of music – Billy Joel. When he told me who he was it were incredible cos I'd just watched *That Peter Kay Thing* so I said, "What? That Peter Kay that did *That Peter Kay Thing*?", which were absolutely brilliant. He came round, we had a couple of brews and had a couple of lessons, then later he came back with a keyboard and he told me what he was learning for. He said he didn't want his fiancée to know because he wanted it to be a surprise. He wanted to play "Dancing Queen" at the wedding.'

Peter and Susan had got engaged a few months earlier, Peter proposing outside Andy's Records in the town centre because it was where they'd had their first kiss. After a few weeks, and having found out about Toni's background, Peter asked Toni if he'd like to perform the music for his *Live at the Top of the Tower* video. 'He said what he'd like was three or four pieces for the opening titles in the style of [organist] Reginald Dixon but songs that you would never expect him to play. So he said he wanted "Shaft", "Sussudio", "Deeply Dippy" and "Bat Out of Hell".'

Over the course of the next couple of months Peter visited Toni every Tuesday and Wednesday afternoon but when

Susan began to suspect he was having an affair, Peter had to tell her he was having lessons. Then Peter told Toni, 'I'm going to have to knock this on the head. I'm doing a new TV series. Do you want to do the music?'

'I thought about it for about a second,' says Baker.

Despite their initial reluctance to schedule a repeat of *That Peter Kay Thing*, when Peter and his new manager Phil McIntyre visited Channel 4 to discuss Peter's idea for a new series they were instantly sold on the idea when he described it as 'Ken Loach does *Cheers*'. The docu-spoof style was binned and instead it would be a sit-com picking up from where the *That Peter Kay Thing* club episode left off, with Brian Potter trying to start again after the demise of yet another club. There would be no laughter track and the whole thing would be filmed on location in Bolton. How could they say no?

As with *That Peter Kay Thing*, the new series remained untitled deep into the writing process. To help name the series Peter turned to the regular visitors of his website, who sent in suggestions – a bit like the Peter Kay version of naming a new *Blue Peter* pet. *Out of Order, On Its Arse, The Club, Phoenix Rising, Potter Files* and *Brian Potter and the Ring of Fire* were among the suggestions, but knowing a good thing when he saw it, Peter plumped for *Phoenix Nights*. Later Channel 4 would twist it slightly to become *Peter Kay's Phoenix Nights* in order to give some continuity between *That Peter Kay Thing* and the new spin-off series from it.

Phoenix Nights was co-written by Peter Kay, Dave Spikey and Neil Fitzmaurice, with occasional remarks by Patrick McGuinness ('He's the George Harrison of the group,' said Peter). This time, as a measure of their newfound professional status, the series wasn't to be written via a complex game of Royal Mail tag but in an office where they would spend each day from nine to five together from June to August.

'You never really clock off, not when you're writing. It does take over your life and your thoughts. I would lie awake for hours thinking of lines and structure. Worrying that we'd got everything in.'

Writing together was good fun, although sometimes they'd waste an entire day giggling over an idea like Keith Lard setting fire to a bonsai tree with his lighter or a scene where Brian Potter would go to Jerry Dignan for sexual advice and all his answer would be masked by a hand dryer in the toilets except the last line 'covered in piss'.

'At the end of the day,' says Peter in the *Phoenix Nights* DVD commentary, 'you can write the best jokes in the world but nothing beats a good fart gag when it's done properly.'

Before they started writing those fart gags, though, there was serious work to be done. 'The first thing we did was research,' says Peter. 'We went out and chatted to local club owners. But I only spoke to about three because they all seemed to have the same stories. They were like, "We had Matt Monro and then we had this woman who swallowed birds." ' As with 'In the Club', Peter noted how the clubs he'd visit had a strange sadness to them and that they were becoming more rundown and derelict. 'Yet to the people running them there is no slump,' he says. 'They don't see it, just like they don't see the bit of tinsel left on the ceiling after Christmas that's still there in July.'

Getting this right was the key for Peter, who says, 'To me, it has to be rooted in some kind of reality or it isn't funny.'

With *Phoenix Nights* Peter, Dave and Neil developed a new skill. Annoyed that so many of their gags had been lost in the editing process of *That Peter Kay Thing*, they decided to layer every single scene in the new series, taking every chance for a funny line even if it was hidden as a sign on the wall or a song on the radio.

The next task was to cast the show which, apart from one

or two actors including Sian Foulkes as Paddy's love interest Mary (she's Holy Mary's daughter, whose brother is called Joseph) and Alex Lowe as the slightly unhinged mind reader Clinton Baptiste – a brilliant invention of Neil Fitzmaurice's – was to be completely made up of stand-ups. It was an incredible masterstroke and one that would be replicated in the following years in the casting of the movie *24 Hour Party People* and in the West End production of *One Flew Over the Cuckoo's Nest*.

'Stand-up comedy is acting,' Kay said. 'It is going onstage every night and making it sound real and making it sound like it's the first time you've ever done it. They make you believe they've just remembered it or it's just happened, and it's the skill of making it sound fresh. Going on and knowing verbatim every little intonation, every little "oh" and "ah" and making it sound like it is, and getting people's eyes to widen and taking a full room with you. You see a spark and you go "They're good", or "She's not", and I got all these ones over the last three or four years that I'd seen. We had about 20 or 30 or 40. Some were really good at stand-up but no good at acting – some were better actors than stand-ups!'

Among the cast who hadn't been seen in the pilot (as everyone was now referring to the *That Peter Kay Thing* episode as) were Janice Connolly, who was making a name for herself with her housewifey alter ego Barbara Nice – perfect for the saintly Holy Mary, who'd be wearing a Princess Diana sweatshirt in most of her scenes; Steve Edge, who became the new keyboardist in the house band Les Alanos; and brilliant Scouse legend Ted Robbins, transforming himself from the most charming man on Merseyside into the dastardly Den Perry. In all, 22 stand-up comedians appeared in the series, which was filmed on location at St Gregory's Club in Farnworth, Bolton, during September and October 2000.

It was around this time that the BBC began screening their *I Love the 1970s* series. It was a bit like Paul LeRoy's speech in 'The Services'. Someone at the corporation had noticed that 'every year something different happened' and came up with the idea of combining old clips with the comments of a few comedians and social experts. Each episode was presented by somebody significant to the year in question, be it David Cassidy in 1972 or Carrie 'Princess Leia' Fisher in 1977. Despite barely being out of their prams in the years being discussed, it was Peter Kay and Johnny Vegas who lit up the show.

Because it was the first year of a new century there was a huge wave of nostalgia going into the new millennium. Suddenly it didn't seem sad to wallow in the past a bit, in fact it seemed quite vital and fun. Like Friends Reunited and the relaunched Mini, the *I Love ...* series surfed this wave of re-examining our recent history.

'*I Love ...* was the child of *TV Heaven and TV Hell*, the first BBC clip show,' says author and *I Love ...* contributor Andrew Collins. 'One of the achievements was that it completely redefined the seventies as a decade of fun and innocence and plurality, of sweeping cultural change and speeded-up shifts in attitude. For most of the eighties, the seventies was "the decade that style forgot".'

It was also – when Vegas or Kay were on screen, at least – fantastically funny. Kay's finest moment was during the 1977 episode (remember, he was four years old at this point in his life). In all the rest of the shows, the talking heads said something quickfire – 'it were all crackly in my mouth' or something when talking about space dust – then we would hear from the next one 'you'd put a load in your gob at once'. There was no room for pontificating, but it was a bit annoying. However, just once in the entire series, they let one person speak uninterrupted for about four hysterical minutes. The occasion? Peter Kay's incensed rant against *Take Hart* and in particular Tony Hart's plasticine pal, Morph. 'It was a show where Tony Hart got to do all the things you weren't allowed to do in art at school,' he began. 'A lovely man, though, but I think he were off his head cos he talked to Morph. You know, a bit of plasticine ...'

He went on to recount in incredible detail a whole episode of *Take Hart* – 'Sophie sent this picture in and as you can see she's created a beach effect ... by using sand.' The piece featured an interview with Morph's animator David Sproxton, a man who to this day still lives under the misconception that people actually watched the show to catch the annoying adventures of his creation. Thankfully, Peter Kay delivered the thoughts of a nation ...

'I wish you could just get a mallet and squash him ... bye, bye Morph, eh! Mind, he'd be gone to the other side of the studio before you could get to him.'

As the series progressed into the 1980s Peter got the chance to reveal his views on Samantha Fox's ample bosoms – 'She could breastfeed a crèche, but that were it' – and recite the lyrics to Nik Kershaw's 'The Riddle' – 'There's a tree by the river ... who gives a shit?' While both Peter and Johnny Vegas confessed an infatuation with *No Limits* presenter Jenny Powell, especially her rather appalling taste in American soft rock bands like REO Speedwagon and Journey – 'That's how I got into that music,' croaks Vegas. 'If that's what Jennie's listening to that's what I'm listening to.'

The *I Love ...* programmes were the harbinger of hundreds of similar clip shows – some of which would feature Peter Kay discussing adverts or pop music. What docu-soaps were to the end of the 1990s, talking-head list shows were to the start of the 2000s – they were on all the time. *I Love ...* was the format at its peak.

If his 'Smack My Bitch Up' gag on the Blackpool video

indicated that the accusations that he borrowed material still rankled with Peter Kay, he received validation that he was pleasing some of his peers at the 2000 British Comedy Awards in December 2000, where *That Peter Kay Thing* scooped the prize for Best New TV Comedy, beating *Alistair McGowan's Big Impression* and another show that had originated from *The Comedy Lab, Trigger Happy TV*. *Trigger Happy*'s Dom Joly was regarded as the strong favourite, and when *That Peter Kay Thing* was announced as the winner by Richard E. Grant and Cerys Matthews from the Welsh rock band Catatonia, Peter Kay, Dave Spikey and Neil Fitzmaurice were shocked, none more so than Peter.

'I know people always say they are shocked when they win, but I genuinely could not believe it when they announced my name,' he says. 'I made a joke just before the announcement saying that if we won we should stand up and pretend to throw our chairs in disgust. In the end I was gobsmacked.'

Perhaps swayed by the fact that, along with Sandy Gall, Geoffrey Palmer, Ken Dodd and Miss Coal Board 1981, a photograph of himself had adorned the bedroom of Peter Kay's loveable eccentric Leonard, veteran broadcaster Dennis Norden – who was on the voting panel – had swayed the other judges with an impassioned plea.

'I didn't have a speech prepared,' says Peter. 'But I was keen to make sure I thanked the people of Bolton.' As for Dave Spikey, he said of the evening, 'It was like a dream.' Although he wasn't talking about winning an award so much as Carol Vorderman asking to have her picture taken with him.

There was no chance for Peter to get too many fancy showbiz ideas. 'No, because a week later I were doing Eccles Masonic Hall,' he says. 'The British Comedy Awards were on the Saturday, and this were Friday after. I were on after a Cher look-alike, although she looked more like Shania Twain.

The DJ said to me, "How do you want your lights?" I said, "What are me options?" He said, "On or off." I did raffle and all. It were for my fiancée Susan's Auntie Anne, to raise money for motor neurone. You can't say no to family, can you, especially your fiancée's family.'

The 2000 Comedy Awards were viewed as a triumph for the north. As well as Peter Kay, other winners that night included Victoria Wood's Lancashire *Dinnerladies*, the Manchester-based *Cold Feet*, *The Royle Family*, Salford-set movie *East is East* and Yorkshire legend Alan Bennett. *Liver Birds* and *Bread* writer Carla Lane made a speech saying that the televised awards were the 'north's finest comedy hour' and that 'with the exception of the fantastic *Only Fools and Horses*, northern comedy has always been the funniest because of the very real, everyday situations it has dealt with'. The press agreed, and in the eyes of the redtops it was no longer a case of it being grim but grin up north.

Seeking to capitalise on Peter's triumph at the Comedy Awards and the prevailing mood of north is best, anti-Margot and Jerry sentiment, Channel 4 decided to bring *Phoenix Nights* forward in their schedule to the second Sunday of the new year. Not only that but the show would have a prime-time slot, 9.30 p.m., and be repeated on Thursday evenings. It was a bold move, a sign of Channel 4's increased confidence in their rising star, and perhaps Phil McIntyre's negotiating skills. But there was a slight problem. They hadn't finished making it yet.

Each episode of the first series of *Phoenix Nights* was finally edited only one day before transmission, a ridiculously tight deadline for such a major programme. Among the last things to be added was the music, Toni Baker adding new background pieces when required, right up to the last minute. Indeed such was the rush to get the show ready that the first episode didn't have a theme tune. After watching it on the Sunday evening Peter decided that he'd like one after all and visited Baker in his Bury home.

'I wasn't going to have a theme tune to *Phoenix Nights*,' he says. 'I'll tell you the full story. I have always loved the James Bond teaser at the start of Bond films when they have a little thing beforehand then you get a bit settled and you think, "Oooh, James Bond", and I wanted that. Channel 4 weren't really keen on me doing it before each episode comes on, but I like it; I like having a little two-minute thing before it comes on. Then a friend said to me you should have a theme cos it's like that thing where you're in the kitchen making a cup of tea and someone shouts out "It's on … it's started." '

Peter likes the fact that the first show has no theme tune; it makes it special – and he would later repeat the trick in subsequent shows. But for now they needed a theme and they needed it quick. 'His brief was that he wanted something jolly but with a slight hint of menace,' says Toni, on the phone from a music shop in Manchester. 'He wanted it on a solo instrument. The parallel that he drew was with *Some Mothers Do 'Ave 'Em*, which is done on a piccolo flute. So we tried it on various instruments – guitar, piano, cello, trombone like *Hancock's Half Hour* – but it sounded too obviously comic. So, in the end, we settled for the glockenspiel – it gives you that feeling like when you're watching a horror film and it's in a child's bedroom and there's a creepy jack in the box moving in the corner.'

There was also late trouble clearing some of the music for the cover versions used in the show. 'One of the reasons music is always last-minute is that you're always waiting for tracks to be cleared,' says Toni. 'Sometimes Peter would get clearance on what he wanted, sometimes it's got to be the fourth choice. I know that he really wanted to use something by the Smiths and by Prince, but it's hard with artists like that.'

Despite the stress of the deadline, Toni Baker hails Peter as 'the easiest person I've ever worked with'. The pair would collaborate on all the music for the series, Baker coming up with ideas and Peter adding to them. 'He was looking for comedy all the way through,' he says. 'So no matter how good it is musically, it's got to suit the scene perfectly. Previously I'd worked with other musicians, and there's always someone who wants to stamp his feet. It ends up great, but the process is painful. I never have that with Peter. At the end of the day it's his gig so I'll bow down to him anyway. There's only been a couple of times when I've said "No, you can't do it like that" and he's said "Give it a go". And when I see it on the TV he's always been right. He's got the vision of what the cameras see. It's like having another ear. He knows what he wants and 99 per cent of the time I know how to achieve it.'

Over time it would transpire that not everyone was as happy to work alongside the Bolton boy made good. For now, though, it was more a case of 'top of the world, Ma, top of the world'.

Chapter Eight
Can You Hear Me Now?

'In the rich chocolate box of life, the top layer's gone and somebody's nicked the orange cream from the bottom.'

Bob (Rodney Bewes), The Likely Lads

'Sometimes you want to go where everybody knows your name.'

Theme tune to Cheers

It wasn't only Dennis Norden whom Peter Kay could count among his growing flock of celebrity worshippers – darts player Jocky Wilson, snooker legend Tony Knowles and DJ Chris Moyles were all confirmed fans of the Bolton funny man. With *Live at the Top of the Tower* out on video, Peter also saw himself become a tour-bus favourite of dozens of rock acts, whose arduous trips around the world sampling free lager were enlightened by watching TV on the road. Peter's musical followers included Texas, Eric Clapton, Doves, Fatboy Slim and Starsailor. There was, though, one exception to this expanding list of musical Kay disciples: Liam Gallagher of Oasis.

Talking to the *Observer Music Monthly* in June 2005, his brother, Noel, explained why. 'Liam hasn't got a sense of humour, f***ing full stop,' he says. 'Like with Peter Kay. If you're a northern guy about our age, all the reference points are spot on – you can't not like him. We were on the tour bus one night and somebody put a Peter Kay DVD on and I thought: "This is going to be a disaster." There's a few Mancs in our crew and everyone was laughing their heads off. And Liam's just sat there going: "He's a f***ing shit, f***ing fat idiot." So he gets up to go to the bog and someone goes: "Why doesn't he like Peter Kay?" Because he'd been to the NME Awards when Liam won a trophy for being hero of the year – and Liam wouldn't go up and collect it ...'

The night was 6 February 2001. Not wishing to see the reluctant Liam go without his prize, Peter clambered down from the stage and waded through the tables of rock stars until he got to Liam Gallagher who, despite the fact that he wouldn't feel the benefit when he went outside, was wearing a vast white fur coat. Peter brought his trophy over to him and went, "Ere you are, lad.' And then, as he walked off, he said: 'Me mam's been looking for that coat.' 'F***ing uproar!' says Noel. 'I was laughing like f***.'

The first episode of *Phoenix Nights* was broadcast on Sunday, 14 January 2001. Within the first five minutes it was obvious to everyone watching that the show was destined to rank alongside the likes of *Rising Damp*, *Porridge* and *Father Ted* as a comedy classic on UK TV. And the main reason is Brian Potter – played by Peter Kay in grey wig and a disturbing assortment of brown and beige cardigans – the disabled club secretary. Our first glimpse of Potter comes as he trundles over the brow of a hill on his shopmobile, Bolton glimmering in the sunlight beyond him, to a soundtrack of 'The Only Way is Up' by Yazz. To anyone over 30 it's a shot reminiscent of an old Hovis ad of a boy pushing his bike up a cobbled northern lane. Within those opening minutes Potter produces more cantankerous outbursts than Victor Meldrew has managed in the past ten years of *One Foot in the Grave*. The string of bulbs on the club roof isn't impressive enough ('Think Las Vegas'); the builders have gone on their dinner break at half ten in the morning ('It's a bloody disgrace'); he has to settle for a *Das*

Boot fruit machine instead of the *Matrix* one he ordered ('It's the last one on the van,' says the delivery driver. 'I don't care if it's the Last of the Mohicans'); one of his staff is filling religiously sloganed balloons with helium ('Pop 'em. It's a club not a mosque'); and social secretary Jerry 'the Saint' Dignan is sat on the loo reading a pamphlet about colon care when he should be rehearsing ('Stop crappin' and get cracking. Avanti!'). The laughs come so thick you feel as if you're in fear of missing half of them. The next 20 minutes don't disappoint either, as we are introduced to the regular cast of loafers – Ray Von (an electrician who becomes the Phoenix's resident DJ), Kenny Snr (a compulsive liar who claims to have played on Centre Court at Wimbledon despite being unseeded), Potter's gormless Manchester City shirt-wearing slave Young Kenny, and the doormen Max and Paddy, whose thrill at wearing radio microphones extends to Paddy going on a bus ride while still wearing them.

Max: 'Can you hear me now?'

Paddy: 'I can see ya, you dick.'

The next day in the *Daily Express* critic Ben Walters wrote that *Phoenix Nights* 'was as perfectly pitched – and as bitterly funny – a parody of working-class lassitude as *The Royle Family*. Think of Jim Royle on wheels and armed with a random – yet weirdly resonant – list of pop culture references.' While Charlie Catchpole in the *Mirror* wrote that *Phoenix Nights* was so good he was going to tape them all so he could watch them again – quite an accolade for someone who watches TV for a living. 'Each time I spot some new, tiny detail that delights me – like Kay's wheelchair-bound club owner Brian Potter drinking whisky from a vase because he can't reach the optics behind the bar with a glass.'

Bloody Rafferty!

Picking up where 'In the Club' had left off, we discover that Brian's last club, the Neptune, had been burnt to a crisp and this was his new chance to run the best club in Bolton. Like the American sit-com *Cheers*, which had an often unseen rival bar, the Olde Towne Tavern, the Phoenix too had an adversary – the flashy Banana Grove, whose malevo-lent owner Den Perry (brilliantly portrayed by Ted Robbins) is like some dark northern gothic cut and shunt of Les Dawson and Dr No reincarnated in a double-breasted suit. Perry's Banana Grove was about profit; Potter and his crumbling Phoenix Club was about survival and not ruining the cork flooring. As Paul Sandland, the chairman of St Gregory's Social Club, where the majority of *Phoenix Nights* was filmed, explains: 'Social clubs, Catholic clubs, working men's club, everything you make on the door and at the bar goes back into running the place. You're always scraping by and improvising and worried about how much things cost.'

Indeed a lot of southern viewers, not immersed in working men's club culture (not to be confused with Culture Club) and how they operate, might have imagined Brian Potter as a tight arse, looking after his own back and giving the change in the disabled boy statue in the entrance hall a shake to see if there's enough money in it for a holiday ('Corfu for Christmas'). Potter, it seemed, was a million miles (well, at least as far away as Stranraer) from the personality of his creator we knew through his stand-up – open, warm, friendly. Kay's Potter seemed to be culled from all the unpopular bosses Peter had ever had. But there were family traits, too, like Brian's constant consumption of Teacher's whisky, which he imbibed as if it were Sprite, and his creative collection of alternatives to swearing and coyness regarding 'filth', mirroring his mother, Deirdre, and her calling of saints' names and shock at the relationship between the priest and Rachel Ward in *The Thorn Birds*.

Brian is a conservative curmudgeon, as he tells the stand-up comics getting ready to take part in the Phoenix's alternative comedy night, Funny Farm: 'There's a picture of Her Majesty the Queen out there and as far as you lot are concerned she may as well be sat on the front row.' But he is also strangely loveable.

As each episode went by, Brian Potter became less and less of a grotesque, so by the time of the singles night in episode four, where he meets Beverly Hillscopto and is hopeful of a sexual liaison with her, you are rooting for him to succeed – especially after his own admission that he hasn't seen much action in that department for years. As he tells Jerry, 'It's been twelve years. He thinks he's in for life, you know.'

'Who?' asks Jerry.

'Him!' Brian says, pointing to his crotch. 'He's up for parole soon. If he gets out I want him coming home in style.'

'TV's own' Roy Walker cut the ribbon of the Phoenix Club in the first episode and after that each week revolved around a theme night. Originally they were going to ask Bob Carolgees to do the honour, but Peter was worried about overdoing the joke. So instead they featured him as the celebrity endorser of Jerry's colon care leaflet.

In episode two, Brian takes delivery of a bucking bronco in exchange for a wonky snooker table, but improvises to create a Wild West theme night. 'Give it a couple of days and it'll be shitting money,' says Potter's provider of dodgy entertainment gear, Eric (brilliantly played by Bolton comedy and folk music legend, Bernard 'the Bolton Frog' Wrigley). 'If not it better learn how to shit snooker tables,' says Potter.

Just like classic sit-com *The Fall and Rise of Reginald Perrin*, which was awash with regular jokes ('I didn't get where I am today without …', '17 minutes late …', 'Take a letter Miss Jones …'), Peter, Dave and Neil gave the *Phoenix Nights* characters a bevy of recurring gags. Among them were Brian's malapropisms, where he'd get words just slightly wrong – acapulco instead of a cappella, 'a Catch-21 situation' instead of Catch-22. Dave Spikey's Jerry St Clair and Neil Fitzmaurice's Ray Von had their motifs too – Jerry and his string of appalling cover versions, Ray asking as if he was still at a funfair rather than calling the bingo for six old-age pensioners. There were other running gags too: the auditions at the end, such as the escapologist who couldn't escape, a clumsy fire juggler and a pair of geriatric gymnasts. These were dubbed by Peter, Dave and Neil as 'the Last Supper shots'. As Charlie Catchpole had suggested, there were things you missed out on first time around, like various signs dotted around the Phoenix Club, song lyrics dropped into conversation (such as when Brian is jilted by Beverly: 'I've bigger fish to fry. No woman, no cry'), and Jerry's obsession with bowel movements.

Jerry: 'Are you regular?'

Brian: 'As a Kennedy funeral. You could set your watch by my arse.'

'Oh, *Phoenix Nights*,' sighs Scottish comedian Janey Godley. 'I really love *Phoenix Nights*. It was just so clever and real, they captured that world so accurately. I used to run a pub just like that called the Riverside in Glasgow. I'd have bingo and bands that were as bad as Les Alanos, climbing out of the window after gigs cos they had punters chasing after them.'

'Up until that point,' says Toni Baker, who appeared in the first episode as the guitarist in the racist folk band Half a Shilling, 'I think all most people, especially down south, knew of working men's clubs was *The Wheeltappers and Shunters Club*, which was this old flat-capped variety show that was on in the seventies. *Phoenix Nights* really caught it how it really is, with all the acts and stuff. If you played at a club like that and you didn't go down well or get paid, what they'd always do was find the bingo machine, which was usually at the back of the stage, and take out this clip on top so that the next time they used it all the balls would go whizzing up in the air.' Which is exactly what happens in *Phoenix Nights*, of course, Jerry having to improvise with bucket bingo instead – pulling the numbered balls from a white pail straight out of Bolton Market.

'I love that show because I've lived with that; it's like watching my life,' says Brian Lloyd, a comedy act from the 1960s who supported the likes of Tommy Cooper and Frank Carson on the northern club circuit. 'The doormen are just right. It's absolute perfection.' Brian says he saw plenty of incidents that were straight out of *Phoenix Nights*. 'We once had a singer who had got one of the first radio mikes and he thought he was the bee's knees,' he said. 'I introduced him and he came on looking very suave. However, halfway through we heard "243 come in" on the mike. He'd managed to pick up the local taxi firm!'

Not everyone, though, was impressed by the show's absurd twist on realism. Keith Laird, the fire safety officer who claimed Kay's dog-bothering fire safety officer from the 'Eyes Down' episode of *That Peter Kay Thing* was based on him, was upset to discover, when he picked up *TV Quick* that week, that Peter had reprised the role for *Phoenix Nights*. Especially as his colleagues at Bolton Council had only recently tired of barking whenever he walked past. Fire was an essential linking factor between the Neptune Club and the Phoenix, but Peter could have changed the character, given him a different name and facial features. He couldn't resist bringing back the much-loved Lard, however: he liked the continuity and the idea of people from the mythical Bolton of *That Peter Kay Thing* continuing to exist in his new vision. The scenes with Lard – giving a fire safety speech at Den Perry's Banana Grove club – are some of the funniest moments in the first series. Attempting to get the audience of club bosses' attention he reads a letter he has received from America about a burning tower block that seems to bear an uncanny resemblance to the lyrics of 'Disco Inferno' by The Trammps. 'Burn, baby, burn, burn that mother down,' he reads. 'Another child orphaned.'

For Laird it was too much and in the week after the first episode aired it was reported across the press that Channel 4 had apologised to Mr Laird and agreed to pay him £10,000 in compensation. A spokesman from the broadcaster said, 'Channel 4 and Peter Kay would like to state that the character of Keith Lard may have led some persons to wrongly believe that the character was based on Mr Keith Laird. We wish to make it clear that this was not the case and would like to apologise to Mr Laird and his family for the distress caused.' In February, at Manchester United's Old Trafford stadium, Laird handed over cheques worth £5,000 to two charities – the National Fire Safety Charity for Children and the Fire Service Benevolent Fund – while on Channel 4's part, whenever Keith Lard appears in a *Phoenix Nights* or a *That Peter Kay Thing* repeat it is accompanied after the closing credits with a disclaimer page and information on fire safety.

For his part Peter continued to protest his innocence. On an interview on his official website, he draws a line under the matter when he is asked, 'Are any of the characters based on real people?' Answering, he says: 'No. And I can't stress that enough. No! All the characters are fictitious and any similarity whatsoever is purely coincidental. One of the most frequently asked questions is did I know Keith Laird. The answer is NO.'

Mr & Mrs
Be nice to each other
Mr & Mrs
You've got to love one another

Mr & Mrs *theme tune*

On 27 April 2001, Peter Kay realised his lifetime ambition when he spent £187,000 on a detached home in a middle-class suburb of Bolton. On the Bolton pages of the knowhere guide (<knowhere.co.uk>) some wag wrote on the message board that you can tell which house is his because 'it's always got big light on'. Possibly in preparation for this, Peter and Susan didn't get to move in till long after their wedding day because they 'had the electricians in'.

Peter and Susan Gargan were married on Friday, 7 September 2001 at St Osmund's Roman Catholic Church in the pretty Bolton town of Breightmet. If he'd had his way *Mr & Mrs* host Derek Batey would have married them, but in the event, being a sentimentalist, it was Father Flatley, Peter's priest when he was an altar boy at St Ethelbert's, who conducted the ceremony.

Despite good intentions, Peter didn't finish learning how to play 'Dancing Queen' as a wedding surprise for Susan; that duty fell to *Phoenix Nights* theme tune composer (and Half a Shilling member) Toni Baker, who performed the Abba hit on the church organ after Peter and Susan had finished signing the register and were leaving the church. Most of the cast of *Phoenix Nights* were there to see Peter and Susan on their happy day, but guitarist Eric Clapton, who was a fan of the show and was invited to the wedding, was unable to attend. At the reception, which was held at Mytton Fold Farm in Blackburn, actor Paddy McGuinness shared best man duties with an old schoolfriend of Peter's, Michael Connell.

'I think he had five best men in the end,' says Toni Baker. 'He couldn't decide between them. Peter has five or six really close mates who have stuck with him throughout his whole life. His friends mean a lot to him.'

Peter has been loyal to his pals since making it in the entertainment industry, giving many of them work as script editors, extras and in the crew on *That Peter Kay Thing*, *Phoenix Nights* and *Max and Paddy's Road to Nowhere*; a couple of his pals from Salford University – Karl Lucas (who also appeared as one of the presenters of 'Armchair Superstore' in *Phoenix Nights*) and Gordon Isaacs – were employed to help out at live shows. He has said that his friends help him keep his feet on the ground: 'To them, I'm not Peter Kay or Brian Potter, I'm just Peter.'

Peter had wanted to DJ at the wedding reception himself (his old DJ-ing partner Michael Atherton being the other side of the world in Australia), but a few weeks before the wedding he told Brian Viner of the *Independent*: 'Susan won't let me.' 'We'll have a bit of eighties, a bit of nineties, some seventies dance music, a bit of Motown,' he told Viner. 'I know I should relax, but it's important, disco. There's nothing worse than some gobshite asking for something like "Eloise", the Damned, and they mither you until you put it on, then everyone sits down and they don't even dance themselves.'

In fact Peter had been planning the sequence of songs for his wedding since he was 14-years old, originally planning to use them when he married his first girlfriend, Catherine Hurst. 'They were called things like *Beginning of the Night, Vols I & II*. When it came to the big day, I hardly changed a thing: "Xanadu" by Olivia Newton-John, "Dancing Queen" by Abba … and the first slow song was Tony Hatch's theme for *Mr & Mrs*.'

'Dancing Queen' was Peter and Susan's song and he made certain his wedding DJ had it by bringing along his own copy. For someone who had spent so long onstage discussing how people danced at weddings, what he played at his own was deadly important stuff. 'It's one song that everyone gets up and dances to,' he said. 'It were first song I danced to. You've got to. You can't be suicidal and play "Dancing Queen" without feeling a lot better. You just think, "Ohhhhh, never mind war, never mind death ..."'

As the evening wore on, Peter couldn't resist a spell on the decks and wrested control so he could play the theme tune from *Minder*. 'It were brilliant,' he told me. 'Everyone got up for that. But the thing is, it's so short by the time they got to the dancefloor it was over. So I played it again.'

After Peter and Susan returned from their honeymoon in Mexico, they had to live for a short while with Peter's mother – 'My life is like a sit-com,' he told visitors. Finally at the end of the year his *Mork and Mindy* tapes, Tony Christie albums and lifetime collection of old *Radio Times* were ready for their new home – the shed at the bottom of the garden.

'Susan said, "What do you have to keep those old *Radio Times* for? They've got little insects in them,"' Peter revealed to me. 'But you never know when you're going to have an argument over what time of night *Tenko Reunion* was on.'

On <peterkay.co.uk> Peter tells his fans that he's just 'cutting out all the effing and jeffing that tends to creep up from time to time' and then filming will be ready to begin on the next series of *Phoenix Nights*. 'I hope everybody who's reading this is well and happy,' he writes. 'If not, here's a little joke for you ... I was in the car the other day and a man asked me for a lift. I said, "Sure, the world's your oyster, go for it buddy!" I promise you that the series will be a lot funnier.'

In October 2001 Peter returned to St Gregory's Social Club in Farnworth. As before, the series had been co-written with Dave Spikey and Neil Fitzmaurice, but on top of his writing and acting duties this time he would be directing as well.

It is often remarked upon, often by people who haven't worked with him, that Peter Kay is hard to work with. He got this reputation on the sets of *That Peter Kay Thing* and the first series of *Phoenix Nights*, where his obsession with getting things exactly how he imagined them tested the patience of the film crew. 'I have heard that he became a bit difficult on *Phoenix Nights*,' says Iain Coyle. 'But I think that's the price you pay for working with a creative genius.'

'I'd like to be able to tell you about storms and diva tantrums, but I've only ever found him a pleasure to work with,' *Phoenix Nights* commissioning editor Iain Morris told the *Observer* in March 2005. 'But it's always easier to count the number of highly successful comics who are universally loved by their contemporaries than those who are resented.'

'I suppose the crew must have found me a constant annoyance,' said Peter in a 2001 website interview. 'But if the end result is something that they'll be proud of, then it's worth the hassle. Comedy is a very serious business. Everything you believe in is worth fighting for.'

Peter was annoyed by the budget constraints that hampered some of the filming in the first series. For the scene of Keith Lard giving his talk at the Banana Grove just ten extras had been booked. Unhappy that this wouldn't make the scenes realistic enough, he paid for some club regulars to turn up early and fill the seats.

Allegedly, in the making of *Phoenix Nights* series one Peter saw less than eye to eye with the experienced director Jonny Campbell. Although he has never discussed it on record, there have been hints that the pair didn't get along. In the summer of 2002, when he appeared on Toby Foster's BBC Radio Sheffield show they reminisced about Foster's time as Les the drummer in Phoenix Club house band Les Alanos.

Peter: 'It were bloody easy for you lot ... I had more grief on the first series than the second because I didn't get on with the director.'

Toby: 'What were his name, Jonny something?'

Peter: 'Don't say it, don't go stirring up trouble.'

Toby: 'You didn't like him, did you? I don't think he'd ever been this far north. He turned up on the first day of shooting and said [adopts posh accent]: "I love what you've done with this place, it's such a pastiche." We said, "No, this is how it is." '

With Phil McIntyre in his corner, Peter persuaded Channel 4 to let him direct a second series on his own. For McIntyre it was all part of the plan he had for all his clients, from Victoria Wood to Craig Cash – that they should have as much control over their work as possible. This approach was music to Peter Kay's ears; he told Brian Viner in the *Independent*: 'If you're an artist you don't just do outlines, do you, you colour it in as well.'

'Normally when that kind of thing happens there's a bit of a panic,' says former Channel 4 commissioning editor Robert Popper. 'They're a big star, they want to direct; you don't want to let them down. But you think, "Can they do it? Will they be able to act and direct; will they have enough distance from their stuff?" The stakes are incredibly high. I imagine the feeling was, "We've got to let him do it." But he pulled it off.'

Fortunately Peter's attention to detail and work ethic extended to the whole team behind *Phoenix Nights* series two.

After the first series ended with the club burning down after the evil Den Perry had dropped a lit cigar in the toilet waste basket, a disillusioned Brian Potter eventually had a flash of inspiration after visiting a friend in Blackpool who had packed in Clubland and opened a multi-purpose leisure facility on the Golden Mile – including 'lifts to all floors'. 'Lots of clubs around Bolton had turned into Italian or Chinese restaurants,' says Peter. 'The idea of the second series was to get that in. Dave brought back this article from a newspaper about a club in Blackpool that had everything under one roof – a solarium, bar, soft play centre for the kids – and so it all came from there, except with it being the Phoenix Club they'd be doing it with no money.'

After persuading the old team back to the burnt-down club – giving them a rousing 'If we build it they will come' speech to the soundtrack of the *Van Der Valk* theme tune – the stage is set for the second episode and one of the funniest scenes in British TV comedy history: 'The Phoenix Club Family Fun Day' with Jerry St Clair dressed as a giant red berry; Young Kenny with permanent tiger face – applied with a car paint spray; a portable toilet transformed into a children's play centre with a ball pond filled with a decades' worth of muddy footballs that had been kicked into Potter's back garden; and an obscene bouncy castle. As an example of the often bizarre pressures of being writer, actor and director, Peter Kay told me the full inside story of his penis. Well, not *his* penis.

'Ah, the 20-foot inflatable cock,' says Peter. 'The guy who made it, he were from Bury; all these other inflatable manufacturers had put the phone down on me. When he brought it to show it to us he was so proud of it, he says, "I'm in entertainment myself, you know", cos he makes bouncy castles. I first thought of it in about 1994. I just had this idea of this huge inflatable penis on the back of a lorry going down a back street and someone pegging their washing out and seeing it across the tops of the back walls.'

In the episode the inflatable is supplied by Eric, the man responsible for the Phoenix Club's regular deliveries of fruit machines that pay out in Deutschmarks and three-legged pool tables. Eric explains that he got it from a festival in Amsterdam, but Potter isn't impressed. 'There's kiddies around,' he says. 'They can't go jumping up and down on a … love length.' When Eric persuades him it can be disguised as Sammy the Snake, he acquiesces, but disaster strikes when a couple of mischievous kids interfere with it and it begins expanding to gigantic proportions.

'Originally at this point we wanted the cock to fly off and float into the sky but we couldn't get it to work,' says Peter.

'It's really funny because you think of these things but three or four months later you're there with it. What happens is people get numbed to what you're doing. First of all everyone sees it and they all laugh, then the novelty wears off and you suddenly find you're in the rain, in December, at ten o'clock at night, freezing cold, with a 20-foot inflatable cock that's too big to go on the back of a lorry and you've not quite measured it right and everyone's getting really angry and the producer's shouting because the guy who's working the lighting generator has got to go at ten and he's screaming and he's shouting at someone else "Can we get a move on, can we get a move on" and I just had to stop to shout, "Stop, stop, look at what we're doing. It's a 20-foot cock we're all so serious about. Can you not realise what you're doing?" '

There's more!

'I wanted it to have pubic hair, and for Brian to disguise it with weeds, but Channel 4 wouldn't allow it,' he says. 'After giving up on the floating idea, we tried to see what it would look like with the cock exploding, so we had this guy trying to use all these different methods to blow this cock up, like. And we had some of the props people, who are quite prim and proper, ringing up and going [adopts posh woman's voice], "What's the situation with the cock?" and the assistant director going, "Well, the cock's arriving at two o clock", and you'd think, "Ha, you're talking about a cock, ha, ha." Some people are really prudish and it's like "the penis" … anyway the guy who blows things up he always turns up with guns and explosives and pyrotechnics, he's a really funny guy – deaf as a post, mind. He was experimenting with all these different ways of filming it exploding for weeks and he'd come and see us with camcorder footage of him in his backyard exploding balloons. In the end we must have spent six thousand pounds just trying to blow it up.'

'Not since Austin Healey made his first clanking appearance in the Advanced Hair Studio's adverts on "Men and Motors" have I laughed so incontinently at the TV,' wrote Ally Ross in the *News of the World*. TV gold.

With the second series, *Phoenix Nights* became more and more Peter Kay's baby and less and less Dave and Neil's. Elements of his stand-up set started creeping in, too – at Le Grand Marche hypermarket in France (which was really Costco in Salford), Max and Paddy study a packet of Les Cadbury's Fingers, and Potter and co. take part in a *Crimewatch*-style reconstruction. Brian Potter even references Peter Kay's most famous catchphrase of all when he tells his doubtful troops the new reborn club will sell food.

'But not just any food, Jerry, proper food. Scampi, chicken Kievs, garlic bread.'

'Garlic bread?' asks Max.

'Garlic bread, that's right, Max, garlic bread. It's the future, I've tasted it.'

With *Phoenix Nights* painting a picture of clubland on the bones of its arse, the series had a very marked effect on reality. Encouraged by the show, takings went up in Bolton social clubs, who staged special *Phoenix Nights*-inspired cabaret evenings. There are some viewers who looked at *Phoenix Nights* and missed the comedy but loved the variety acts. Indeed, it was mooted at one point that Peter should take Talent Trek on the road to theatres across Britain. At the Farnworth club, which had been the set for the show, they suddenly found themselves opening their doors to a younger local clientele. Attempting to make the most of the club's fame, St Greg's manager Paul Barnwell dubbed his social club the Real Phoenix and started holding Sunday cabaret evenings, and with real life imitating art found himself playing host to various members of the cast who'd visit the club and meet fans.

'They are all really good people, I haven't got a bad word to say about any one of them,' he says, showing me a picture of him with his arm around Brian Potter. As a consequence of *Phoenix Nights* Barnwell has also found the club taking bookings for wedding receptions and stag dos. 'We had one bloke who had a party here and he hired a bucking bronco,' says Paul, who for a while found himself dubbed the Real Brian Potter. But visit St Gregory's on a wet Tuesday evening and it's an entirely different story. The handful of members in this formica-clad wonderland are closer in years to the Captain, who worked the door in the first couple of shows, shortly before dying in the middle of bingo, than to Young Kenny. Paul, though, is happy to show you the sights including the toilets where Den Perry dropped his cigar and the changing room to the side of the stage where Jerry popped his herbal tablets. The bar staff are lovely, the beer cheap and the pool tables empty.

'You should come on Sunday; it'll be buzzing then,' says the barwoman. 'We've got a Freddie Mercury look-alike on; he's very good.'

If people can go to Notting Hill to see a door or all the way to Scotland to see the set of *Balamory*, then why not this flat-roofed palace down a Bolton side street? Until the coach parties turn up Paul is waiting to hear if there is going to be a third series of *Phoenix Nights*. 'We'll be the last to know,' he grumbles.

'Two more lamb bhunas.'

Peter Kay, John Smith's advert

In April 2002 Peter made the switch to the big screen in *24 Hour Party People*, the tale of maverick Factory Records label boss Anthony Wilson, who split his time between discovering legendary Manchester bands such as Joy Division and presenting *The Wheel of Fortune* on Granada TV. Steve Coogan played Wilson – kind of Alan Partridge filtered through Brian Clough – while Peter played the small yet significant part of Don Tonay, the sideburned owner of the Russell Club, the venue of Factory-endorsed rock gigs in the early 1980s. Peter wasn't on screen for long, but they included his first ever sex scene, with a prostitute in the back of a van (what would his mum think?). He also managed to incorporate a few Potterisms into the dialogue.

'What sort of music is it?'

'Rock mainly, indie.'

'Indian?'

Garlic? Bread?

Peter and Steve Coogan had worked together once before, in a Comic Relief 2001 sketch. In it Coogan, as Alan Partridge, reluctantly travels to the north, or as he patronisingly puts it 't'North', to visit a boxing gym staging a 24-hour sparring session for Comic Relief, but ends up enraging the owner, Tony Maloney (played by Peter), by impersonating his accent.

Alan: ''Ey up.'

Tony: 'We're not Yorkshire, it's Manchester, flower.'

Alan: 'Just having some fun with the accent for Comic Relief.'

Tony: 'Dickhead.'

The sketch ends with Partridge in the ring with one of Maloney's boxers, none other than one Paddy McGuinness.

'With Steve Coogan,' says Peter, 'I always see it that he's in fifth year and I'm in third year, and third years don't knock about with fifth years! There's no animosity, but you do kind of look up to people like Steve in comedy, and you do sort of aspire to be them. When you do actually start to talk, you do realise they're not that different at all, you're very similar and you do get on, and you're just very very similar. I find that a lot, it's a bit disconcerting.'

24 Hour Party People wasn't Peter's first appearance in a movie. In 1999 he played a stuttering convict in *Going Off Big Time*, a Scouse gangland movie that had been written by Neil Fitzmaurice, and he'd made a cameo appearance in *Blow Dry*, a northern drama set in Keighley about a hair-dressing contest that features the worst Yorkshire accent – imagine a camp Geoffrey Boycott – in movie history, courtesy of Alan Rickman.

With movie appearances, sell-out stand-up shows and his own sit-com, Peter Kay was stretching his empire to such an extent that no one would have been surprised if he'd announced he also did a spot of modelling on the side for Versace. His multi-tasking increased in the spring of 2002, when he signed up to become the new face of John Smith's beer in a £20 million ad campaign. The £20 million wasn't Peter's fee, incidentally, that's the estimated total amount they would spend placing the ads on TV. According to Peter, all he got was a life-size replica of his predecessor (a card-board cut-out called Dave) and a tour of the brewery. With the exception of Dave, the cut-out Peter was following a great tradition of comic ads by John Smith's that had begun in the late 1970s with a flat-capped Yorkshireman who allows his terrier to sup on his pint. The dog is so overcome with glee at the taste of the beer that he jumps and does a cartwheel. Then in the 1990s, master of deadpan Jack Dee helped them launch John Smith's Extra Smooth with the help of some penguins.

Peter's adverts for the Yorkshire bitter begin airing in a well-picked slot halfway through the 2002 Champions League Final on ITV. A group of footballers at the side of the pitch are practising their impressive ball-juggling skills and catching the ball on the backs of their necks. When it comes to Peter's turn to impress, he boots the ball out of the park, where it bounces on the roof of a faraway greenhouse. "Ave it,' says Peter, shoving aside a tray of orange quarters and picking up a can of John Smith's instead. Come the start of the football season in September across the country, whenever a defender hoofed the ball into the stands for a throw-in vast sections of the crowd could be heard shouting, ''Ave it.'

A teetotaller advertising beer is a bit odd, but the 'No Nonsense' slogan and the commercials, all of which have the Peter Kay stamp, are a perfect fit. Kay's character is mean and bluff, but he doesn't know it; he's just a regular bloke who can't be dealing with pussyfooting around being nice. The other ads in the campaign are equally funny – chucking his mum out of her room because he wants to put a snooker table in it; taking two free boxes of washing powder from Danny Baker then slamming the door; telling his daughter on the phone from the curry house, 'There's no such thing as wardrobe monsters. It's burglars that break in through the window that you want to be worried about.'

Just as had happened with Leonard Rossiter's adverts for Cinzano with Joan Collins in the 1970s, and the Melanie Sykes-fronted spoofs for Boddington's in the 1990s, people talked about Peter's John Smith's ads more than the actual TV programmes between which they appeared. The campaign won awards and plaudits, but it was a genuine cultural phenomenon – sales of lamb bhuna increased, Engelbert Humperdinck made a comeback, and two divers who had won Golds at the Commonwealth Games said they'd 'like to give special thanks to Peter Kay for his top bombing'. Now in the Internet era people were emailing the ads to each other, especially when a 'banned' version of the curry scene appeared. In it Peter, while discussing how kids grow up faster these days, tells his wife that their four-year-old daughter had asked him where babies come from.

'What did you tell her?' she asks, a worried look descending over her.

'I said when a daddy loves a mummy very much he inserts his erect penis inside a woman's vagina, he ejaculates sperm, which travels through the womb, fertilising the egg, and it develops into a baby over nine months.'

Naturally not everyone found the ads hysterical; seasoned pontificator Peter York wrote in the *Independent on Sunday* that the only reason Peter Kay was chosen for the campaign was that the upper-middle-class media loveys behind it all 'love on-screen northerners because they think they're more real than themselves'. Ricky Gervais, from *The Office*, claimed he'd been offered a six-figure sum to do the ads before they asked Peter. Gervais went on to claim he'd been offered higher amounts from other advertisers, but had turned them down. 'I just don't think I should yet,' he said. 'If they ask now, they'll ask in a few years.'

Once decoded as the subtle oneupmanship of major comedy stars, the implication of Gervais's comments is: I don't need their money; you do.

Peter Kay has never been altruistic. In the early days he couldn't afford to be. As the breadwinner in the household after his dad had left, he juggled jobs as well as comedy gigs to pay his way at home with his mum (once when he was asked why he first went into comedy he joked 'crippling debt'). Then, when he started making money, it was always with the fear at the back of his mind that it would all end tomorrow, and he'd be back on the bins. Once he got the chance to earn larger sums of money he treated it with humour. In the *Live at the Top of the Tower* video there's a sketch before his stand-up set where he goes to talk to Paddy McGuinness, who is manning a makeshift merchandise stall in the foyer. The official stock looks as if it's been assembled by a three-year-old with a sticker-making set, and features Peter Kay mugs and a Peter Kay kettle that look as if they have been stolen from the Blackpool Tower staff room.

Just like his John Smith's character, when it comes to money Peter Kay doesn't mince his words: he wants it off you and more often than not he'll tell you why. He wants a car, a holiday, his own home, or he wants to pay for sister Julie's house to be rewired. Not only is it honest, it also turns the guilty situation of raking it in into a joke. It came as no surprise, then, that when the details of Peter's 2002 tour were announced it was called the 'Mum Wants a Bungalow' tour.

'Why?'

'Because she does.'

Chapter Nine

How Dare You

'Ten years ago a crack commando unit was sent to prison by a military court for a crime they did not commit. These men promptly escaped from a maximum-security stockade to the Los Angeles underground. Today, still wanted by the government, they survive as soldiers of fortune. If you have a problem and no one else can help, and if you can find them, maybe you can hire ... the A Team.'

The A Team, opening titles

'Here, as I watch the ships go by
I'm rooted to my shore'

The Kids from Fame, 'Starmaker'

On 30 August 2002, just as his 2002 'Mum Wants a Bungalow' tour was due to begin, the official website that had been started by a couple of his friends back in 1997 was taken offline. There was a message from Chris, the webmaster, telling fans that his services were no longer required; instead, a 'more official' site would shortly be taking its place. As Peter Kay's fame had grown, so had the amount of effort needed to run the website, and when Chris suggested they put ads on the site to fund their time Peter – who owned the domain name – decided to put it in the hands of his manager Phil McIntyre instead. Weeks later, in a scorched-earth policy, the personal messages from Peter had gone, the rants and jokes vanished, the episode guides were

no more. In their place were pages and pages of merchandise
– Garlic Bread T-shirts, mouse mats, calendars and mugs –
but sadly no Peter Kay kettle.

Peter Kay plc was open for business. 'Maximising your
brand potential' is what celebrities do in the twenty-first
century. The canny stars realise that, putting art to one side,
they are a commodity just like anything else. Blame
'Thatcher's Britain', as Peter's bearded doorman Max might
say. Peter Kay was one of the first comedy acts to realise he
was a brand and by 2003 Peter Kay calendars would be
outselling Manchester United, Kylie and David Beckham at
HMV stores across the country, and if they'd sold out, a visit
to the website was always possible. Peter's way of coping
with this mass burst of shameless consumerism was to treat
it with the same disdain Les Dawson reserved for *Blankety
Blank* chequebooks and pens – on some tour dates Paddy
McGuinness would come out just before the interval and
demonstrate some of the 'tat' (his word) available in the
foyer. The tour was called 'Mum Wants a Bungalow', after
all, so the more T-shirts and signed photos they sold the
closer Peter was to his target of buying his mother's new
home. Peter treated it like a one-man *Magpie* appeal for his
mother, but the merchandising was no different from how
rock bands operated (as a former tour manager, Phil
McIntyre knew all about that), he was just being more up-
front and honest about it – yet another illustration of Peter's
no-nonsense attitude to business. Although, subsequently,
Archie Kelly's request that Peter call his next tour 'The Cast
of *Phoenix Nights* Want Bungalows Too' fell on deaf ears.
They'd had enough money out of him.

While the tour blatantly seemed to be about making
money, Kay was also openly concerned about not spending
any. Appearing on Toby Foster's radio show on the eve of his
Sheffield show, he asked the listeners if there was anyone

who could lend him a Peugeot 208 because he was driving down to London and wanted to go in a nice car – recalling Brian Potter, from the first episode of *That Peter Kay Thing*, whose first thought when the Aquarius Club is sinking is to swim to the safe to collect the night's takings. One imagines him in a crisis situation saying, 'The theatre's burning down, you say? Quick, get the money from the T-shirt stall!'

The merchandising website has led many a commentator to whisper that Peter Kay is greedy, but it's not that. He's making a living; if people want to spend money on t'Internet mouse mats, let them. As stand-up comic and Kay fan Janey Godley says: 'Profit's not a dirty word! I wouldn't mind a bit more profit! What do these people think? Stand-up comedy's not a charity.'

'I'm not really surprised by his merchandising,' says Peter's old schoolfriend Michael Atherton. 'He always looks like he can't believe his luck, that somehow it isn't all real. And if his star does fade in the coming years, you can't blame a guy for grabbing what he can while it's there. It's not like he had much to start with.'

With his Internet site transformed overnight into a cyber-world-version car-boot sale, Peter began the 'Mum Wants a Bungalow' tour in earnest. Such was the snowballing success of these live shows that he could still be touring today if he had the energy and by the end he could have retitled it 'Mum Wants a Bungalow in Every Street in Bolton'. But he didn't know this when he started, playing warm-up dates at the Birmingham Glee Club, standing on a crate in front of 125 people; Leicester Arts Centre and Bury, Darlington, Maidenhead and Tynemouth followed.

He possibly didn't realise it at the time, but this was farewell to the world of fag smoke and dodgy Cher look-alikes. Instead, he was entering a new world of theatres and arenas. It was a case of goodbye Benson and Hedges, hello Maltesers and Skittles.

In Tynemouth there was almost tragedy when he ran across the stage mimicking a kid sliding across the floor on his knees at a wedding, and fell into the orchestra pit.

The warm-up dates gave him the chance to try out new material. A section he dubbed 'Surgery's open' was a chance for the audience to ask him questions, out of which popped stories (like going swimming as a kid and forgetting which locker was his in the changing room) he'd long forgotten. Jokes also came out of his attempts to ask people directions to the venues he was playing at – 'What is it about when people start giving you directions that you stop listening? They might as well be speaking Swahili.' And recalling taking his nan to see *Stuart Little* at the cinema – 'I told her it was a true story.'

In the Maidenhead show he got tongue-tied halfway through a joke about *Crimewatch* re-creations and mistakenly put one of his invented victims inside a burgled shop as the manager was opening up in the morning – 'What's Jean doing there?' he laughed. 'I'll have to change that.' In fact, because the mistake got a bigger laugh, he kept the error in, each night pretending he'd just made it.

Some may see this as a lie or a trick, but to others it is a mark of Peter Kay's genius; his ear for his own shortcomings is as finely tuned as it is to others'.

'I suppose that's the art of it,' he says, attempting not to sound too pretentious. 'Making people think you're making it up as you go along and you've just thought of these things. When in fact you've been polishing and polishing it every night.'

Thanks in no small measure to his website's promotion the first 50-plus dates of the original tour all sold out. Such was the demand that when he spied a pair of empty seats at the Hammersmith Apollo he said, 'What a waste, we could have had £600 between us on ebay for these!'

*

The 'Mum Wants a Bungalow' tour was not only his longest tour – previously his biggest was playing ten consecutive dates in 1999 just before his dad died – but also his first time on the road since *Phoenix Nights*. Not only did this give him a few new lines to throw back at hecklers – 'I'm not in a wheelchair now, son' – but also a chance to gauge the incredible popularity of the show. In Rhyl, Wales, he was delighted to see three blokes with tiger facepaint à la Young Kenny from the family fun day, and such is his godlike status in Bolton that coach parties from the town travelled as far as Edinburgh to see him.

The demand for tickets left him awestruck. On the eve of the first proper show at the Buxton Opera House on Monday, 16 September he told the *Bolton Evening News*, 'At the moment it's sold 101,000 tickets out of 111,000 and that's without any posters being printed. It's been absolutely incredible.'

It was about to get even more incredible, and as more and more dates were added to the end of the tour, which by now was stretching into the summer of 2003, he would end up playing to a staggering 380,000 people in a 180-date marathon that would eat up 11 months of his life. It was the biggest comedy tour this country had ever seen and rough estimates put the gross figure of total ticket sales at £5 million. At Bolton house prices, this was enough to buy his mother the entire suburb and turn it into a golf course, with a bit left over to buy her a Sodastream.

Despite this popularity, some critics still didn't seem to get it. Reviewing his London Palace Theatre show in the *Guardian*, journalist Brian Logan wrote, 'He is a confident and companionable stand-up, but his particular skills – a killer eye for character, and for tone of voice – seem more suited to the deadpan comedies with which, on telly, he's so swiftly made his name.' Sarah Barrell, reviewing his Edinburgh Assembly Rooms date, called him a 'cosy performer' and concluded 'Royal Variety Show, here he comes' – ignoring the fact that he'd already played the Royal Variety show four years previously.

Most of the remaining 379,998 members of the audience disagreed with these assessments and left theatres happier than when they'd entered them a few hours earlier – which is the point of going out, after all, something many critics seem to forget – stopping on the way out to buy an apron emblazoned with the legend 'Garlic Bread?' Ker-ching!

As with his rival comedians, who bemoaned the similarities between their act and his, newspaper critics have always tended to label Peter Kay as 'hackneyed' and unoriginal. The truth is that, as long as something is funny, these things don't enter an audience's head; it's about entertainment. And for Peter Kay any criticism is drowned out by ringing tills. One is reminded of Brian Potter heckling an alternative comedian and the Phoenix Club's ill-fated Funny Farm evening – 'Tell us a joke we know.' On the 'Mum Wants a Bungalow' tour he only has to mention the words 'garlic bread' and the crowd roars its approval.

The 'Mum Wants a Bungalow' tour was so popular that even famous people couldn't get in. At the Manchester Lowry Theatre the requests of several Manchester United players for free tickets were turned down. The typically forthright response from the Kay camp – 'They can buy their own.' Although this snippet has the ring of an invented newspaper story, the public voiced its approval.

In Halifax, midway through the tour, Peter's old friend from his garage days, now a writer for Manchester's *City Life* magazine, Marc Rowlands, caught up with him. Kay was frazzled – 'I haven't seen *Emmerdale* for months' – but as friendly as ever.

'Do you get bored by people coming out with "garlic bread"?' asks Rowlands.

'Well, you can't moan about catchphrases, because it's your own fault,' replies Peter. 'It's flattery really, until they won't shut up. But then we've got a couple of lads that drag 'em out by their hair.'

In his *City Life* article, Rowlands nailed Peter Kay's appeal better than any other journalist when he wrote that the genius of Peter Kay is that he 'exposes the ridiculous things we don't see in everyday life because we've become accustomed to living with them'.

'He highlights the traits in his own family that we thought were so individual as to be exclusive to our own,' added Rowlands. 'It's almost like he's grown up in your house, drinking the same drinks, shopping at the same places, reminding us of the ludicrous '70s TV programmes we'd forgotten that we used to watch together. People think they know him, because they believe that when he's talking, he's talking just to them.'

At times on the 'Mum Wants a Bungalow' tour, as you looked around at an audience equally split between young and old, it was tempting to surmise that Peter Kay is not 'Marmite' comedy – you either like it or you don't – it's 'Gravy' comedy that you either like more or less than everybody else. Prior to 'Mum Wants a Bungalow' people made the assumption that because his comedy was about working-class life, only working-class people would find it amusing – this too was debunked. Unless you're some son of a rock star or a member of the royal family, it all rings true. Maybe even Princes Harry and William got to bring Connect 4 into school on the last day of term, who knows?

The tour was supposed to end in Bolton at the Albert Halls on 3 April but such was the rolling nature of the bookings that an extra date at the vast 18,000 MEN Arena in

Manchester – where Peter once showed people to their seats and confiscated bottles of Bacardi – was added. Rather than a glorious homecoming, the Bolton gig – his first in the town since he played a benefit show at the Octagon Theatre in 1999 – ended on a sour note when his dressing room was burgled and his video camera and mobile phone stolen. If it had happened anywhere it would have been upsetting, but in Bolton?

'I am furious that someone could stoop so low,' he told the *Sun*. 'I feel like I bend over backwards to do my town proud. I love Bolton and was looking forward to playing here. Then this happens.'

He still stormed it, and with his mum, nana, Susan, *Coronation Street* stars, Bolton Wanderers footballers and loads of old schoolfriends in the audience, he recorded one of the shows for a future DVD.

The MEN Arena show, which was on his 30th birthday – 2 July – was also (rightly) captured for prosperity. Apart from Baddiel and Newman, who played a one-off show at Wembley Arena, at the height of their *Mary Whitehouse Experience* success in the 1990s (which unlike Peter's show was only half-full), it was the biggest stand-up comedy show ever in the UK. Even the enormous size of the venue seemed to have little effect on Kay's ability to connect with his audience. It was little short of astounding.

And then he went home, watched *Emmerdale Omnibus* and fell asleep for six years.

Well, not quite: the next day he was at Bolton Hospice on New Chorley Road, where he is a vice-president, telling the elderly residents that for the next few months his only plans were to grow a beard.

Not that he became a hermit. Next, he announced that Susan (who was still working in Boots in Bolton town centre) was pregnant with their first child, helped choose his mother's bungalow in Ladybridge, helped his nan emulsion her front room and even went to a football match.

Whether the newspaper story about the Manchester United players being turned down for guest-list tickets for the Lowry show is true or not, Gary Neville and co. appeared to have forgiven him. At half-time during a match between United and Fulham in October 2003, he told the 67,727 Old Trafford crowd a few jokes and looked on as a Norwegian teenager showed off his ball-juggling skills. 'Twenty-six, twenty-seven,' he counted before delighting everyone with his trademark ''Ave it!' as the kid booted the ball into the stands. 'Brian Potter can do that,' he told them as he left the pitch.

There was also validation from Michael Parkinson, for whom he once worked as a warm-up man, who called him 'Britain's best-loved young comedian'. In return Peter told him that his nan was a fan of Parkinson's. 'You know that compilation CD you've got out?' he said to Parky. 'The other day my nan says, "Ooh, he's got a copulation out." '

Nana Kay, it seems, is as prolific with the malapropism as Brian Potter. Peter told Parkinson about her criticising her grandson's handling of his car, saying, 'Your driving's a bit erotic.'

Just before Christmas 2003, Channel 4 released a DVD (or as Peter's nan put it 'a VD') of *That Peter Kay Thing*. It had been released before on video but the popular new DVD format meant that he could add out-takes, deleted scenes and an audio commentary. In the first week alone it sold a staggering 145,000 copies, dislodging the *Star Wars* trilogy and Disney's *Aladdin* off the top of the charts. A year previously, the first series of *Phoenix Nights* had sold similarly quickly, competing to top the million sales of *The Office* over Christmas. The DVD boom means that programmes can enjoy an afterlife long after they've aired, and for many people – because of the bad original scheduling and because of his rise in popularity with *Phoenix Nights* – this was the first chance they'd had to meet Leonard and Mr Softy. 'For whatever reason, and I don't know why, some people just don't watch Channel 4,' says former commissioning editor Robert Popper.

Maybe the fourth button on British remote controls is always faulty, maybe people got put off the channel when Damon Grant used the word 'pissing' in *Brookside* all those years ago (everyone's pissing these days though); who knows but this strange phenomenon was to be Peter Kay's gain. In due course the astronomical sales of his TV shows would be matched by his *Live at the Bolton Albert Halls* DVD, whose total sales of 1.3 million are double those of the previous bestselling live DVD. But it was the success of *That Peter Kay Thing* that pleased him most. Even more so when the channel gave him a breakdown of the sales figures and he saw that it was selling much more in the south of England than in the north.

'Mind you,' he said during a fan question-and-answer session on the *Live at the Top of the Tower* DVD, 'they probably get all their copies from car boot sales in the north.'

Despite his denials, it had been a fallacy concerning his career that only northerners got his humour. He even denied it during the 'Mum Wants a Bungalow' tour when he told Toby Foster on BBC Sheffield that 'people from the north live in London too, so it's OK'. But this stark evidence seemed conclusive. Although maybe there is something in Andrew Collins's argument that *Phoenix Nights* 'represents a kind of lost world to most people in the south'. Lancastrians have a chip on their shoulder about their southern neighbours – often for sound economic reasons (it's easier to close a factory in St Helens than in south London) but sometimes due to the south's perceived snobbery. As Sylvia Lovat Corbridge wrote in her book *It's an Old Lancashire Custom*: 'It is a

Lancashire custom to be on the defensive. We anticipate jokes about rain, "by gum" and Wigan; we expect people to peer at us through the thin layer of smoke they fancy they see around our heads.'

Which maybe explains why, when he reprised the role of Max the doorman a couple of years later, Kay wore a 'London is Shit' baseball cap.

At the end of 2002 Peter Kay stopped doing interviews with the press. He found them exhausting and he was fed up with their lies and the way they always made him try to slag off other shows. But most of all he was pissed off by the way they patronised him. Flicking through his clippings, it's not hard to see how he became so resentful. In the *Sunday Mirror* in January 2001 an interview with Peter begins 'It's just gone midday according to Peter Kay's watch, and his stomach agrees. "Ey oop, time for me dinner," he says. "I'm fair famished and if I don't get me dinner on t'dot I'll be good fer nothing, for t'rest of t'afternoon." '

'It's like the f***ing *Goodies* or something,' he told Toby Foster.

Worse, the *Daily Mail* once wrote, 'I know Channel 4 has to cater for minorities, but if it chooses to glorify Boltonians, subtitles might help the rest of us.'

'Once you become famous you become public property,' he told Foster. 'You can't go around moaning "I want a private life" ... go and be a plumber then, but in interviews they just want sleaze.'

As they do with many celebrities, the British tabloid press have a difficult relationship with Peter Kay. They know their readers love him, but they can't get to him. If Peter Kay can make it in showbusiness without ever leaving Bolton, he can continue to make it in showbusiness without the help of the tabloids. Like all celebrities he is sensitive about the things that are written about him – he can read a hundred great reviews but the one bad one will outweigh them all. In their frustration in recent times the tabloids have run stories like the one in the *Sun* about Peter's father. There were also pictures of Susan in the *People* still turning up for work at Boots in her 'white uniform jacket and sensible shoes' despite being married to the second richest man in British comedy (in 2005 the *Mail on Sunday* estimated his wealth to be £4.5 million).

His fame and wealth have attracted female celebrity admirers – Pamela Anderson tried to set up a dinner date with him in 2005, claiming she 'totally got his humour', and Gillian Porter confessed to a longstanding crush. He's unlikely to be impressed. As he told a woman who shouted out 'I love you' during the 'Mum Wants a Bungalow' tour, 'No you don't. Say I didn't do what I do, say I was just a bloke and I looked like this, would you love me then?'

In these celebrity-obsessed times it seems incredible to many that you can be so rich and so popular and refuse to play the fame game, but incredibly Peter and Susan appear to have achieved it. In reality it's pretty easy not to be hounded by the paparazzi – you just don't go to the Groucho Club or hang out with the 3 A.M. girls. If making it big is like winning the lottery, then the Kays haven't gone wild with their cash – they are more like the Lotto winners who say that it won't change them. This, among other reasons, is why Peter Kay demands more respect from the public than he does from people within the media. Even though he is not 'one of us', it feels like it.

In the records at Companies House, Susan is listed as a director of Peter's production company Goodnight Vienna, her profession listed as pharmacist. She worked in the store right up until the birth of their son Charlie Michael, who was born weighing 7lb 3oz at 9.01 p.m. on 12 January 2004. This project put all others on hold and, wanting to spend time with his wife and son, Peter decided to put back filming of the *Phoenix Nights* spin-off series he had written with Paddy McGuinness during the 'Mum Wants a Bungalow' tour. The decision to write a series based around the two doormen surprised some, but in series two of *Phoenix Nights* their bungled attempt at being hired killers (with a broom handle World War II Broomhandle Mauser no less) is the main story arc.

As Peter told me, 'There's something about Max that really fascinates me.' Although, here too he is annoyed by a slight continuity error. The first time we meet Max he is describing what sounds like a violent fight – ' ... quick scissor kick to the temple. Goodnight, my friend.' At this Paddy looks at his colleague and tells him, 'You see, that's why I don't go to parents' evenings, they get me angry.' Later storylines reveal that Max is a Dad.

For Paddy McGuinness the wait between *Phoenix Nights* and the new series was filled by his first rudimentary attempts at stand-up. Like a Bolton version of the Rat Pack, alongside other members of the *Phoenix Nights* team – Archie Kelly, Janice Connolly and Steve Edge – McGuinness toured venues in the north west of England on the honestly titled 'Jumping on the Bandwagon' tour. Typically, there was a suggestion in stand-up comedy land that Peter wasn't best happy with this development, but it turned out to be false and he even visited a couple of shows, joshing with his friend Paddy: 'You haven't got an act, have you? Well, I say that you have got an act, only it's mine.'

Before he disappeared into a world of Pampers and Farley's rusks, there was one piece of Peter Kay magic for us to enjoy, when on 10 January 2004 he made a welcome return to the troubled streets of Weatherfield. Peter and *Coronation Street* actress Sally Lindsay had been firm friends ever since she had been cast as Tracy Burns, the woman Ray Von was supposed to have murdered in the first series of *Phoenix Nights*. It was only a matter of time before she would manage to cajole him to appear in the ITV soap with her. Not that he needed much persuading.

'I've always been a huge fan of the *Street*. I think it's hard to live in the north west and not be,' he said. 'I've been brought up with it all my life and it still amazes me that everything stops when you hear that famous theme music at 7.30.'

He was a bit worried about continuity, having appeared in the soap seven years previously as a shopfitter – 'I'm still getting royalties from Chinese TV,' he'd tell friends: '£2.81.' The solution was a rather unflattering bowl-cut wig and some false teeth, so that he could transform himself into Eric the drayman – he couldn't have been less attractive if he were the secret love child of Albert Tatlock and Ena Sharples.

Corrie bosses first asked him to play a probation officer who would take off Les Battersby's security tag. Then he suggested the Shelly storyline because he thought she needed a date to cheer her up after her split from love rat Peter Barlow.

Despite looking like the last person in the world the Rovers Return landlady is ever likely to fancy, Eric persuades her to go out on a date with him. Their scenes together are some of the sweetest and most squirmishly embarrassing in *Coronation Street* history – from the moment he meets Shelly's mum, Bev, and says, 'You look too young to be her mother ... oh, apart from your neck' to their awkward scenes in a posh *nouvelle cuisine* restaurant – 'You don't get much, do you?'

'I'm surprised he's not asked to do more acting,' says TV producer Iain Coyle. 'He was amazing in *Coronation Street*. I know people who work on it and the speed at which they turn that round is incredible. There's no two takes, they just do it.'

Better still – and almost turning *Corrie* into a *Phoenix Nights* special – was the fact that Janice Connolly (aka Holy

Mary) played Eric's mother and surprised him by being at home when he returned with Shelly. 'Oh,' says Eric, caving in with despondency, 'I thought you were at jazzercise.'

Peter watched at home with Susan and baby Charlie – he didn't want to watch it on tape, he wanted to see it as everybody else did, running in from the kitchen with a cup of coffee (milk and two sugars) when he hears the theme tune.

He's a hands-on dad, is Peter, changing nappies – 'I went right off that Frankie Dettori when I found out he didn't do nappies' – and getting up at 5.30 a.m. when Charlie cries, like every other new father. He enjoys the whole new set of life's little mysteries that being a parent opens up, such as 'Why does everyone cheer when a child burps?' But there was some evidence that he got bored being at home so much, when he made an impromptu visit to Michelle Mullane's 'Michelle Around Midnight' radio show on BBC GMR and told them that he'd recently phoned the station to enter a competition. 'I knew the answer, "Timewarp", so I came running out of the bath to find the phone,' he told Mullane. 'Susan said, "What are you doing?" I said, "Entering a competition." She says, "What's the prize?" and I said, "Two tickets to Comedy Store", and she said, "What do you want them for?" I said, "That's not the point, I know the answer." So I got through and they answered and I said, " 'Timewarp' ", and they said, "Who's this?" I said, "Peter Kay", and they put the phone down. I'd never got through to a phone-in before ... well, except *Going Live* when Five Star were on.'

Ah, so it *was* him!

'Sponging for a living
Checking out the women
Driving on the road to nowhere.'

      Max and Paddy's Road to Nowhere theme tune

Who needs the newspapers when you've got Jonathan Ross? On bonfire night 2004 Peter Kay starred in one of the most hilarious editions of *The Jonathan Ross Show* there has ever been or is ever likely to be. During the interview, mockingly referring to the chaos he had caused, he told Ross, 'It's TV gold, this.' But the thing is, it was true. First we were treated to the surreal sight of seeing him in the dressing room next to singer Gwen Stefani and her exotically dressed female Japanese bouncers – Peter called them 'the cast of *The Man with the Golden Gun*' – especially funny, as ex-James Bond actor Pierce Brosnan was there too. Then when he emerged from the green room, he went completely off script, turned away from the sofa he was walking towards and went to join Ross's house band Four Poofs and a Piano, with whom he performed a stirring rendition of 'Starmaker' from the *Kids from Fame* soundtrack. 'Come on Jonathan, let's play about with the format,' he said, ushering his highly reluctant and dazed host over to join him. Once they eventually sat down, after a couple of verses of '(Is This the Way to) Amarillo', Peter upset Ross's star guest by saying, 'Last week I thought she were a fella.' 'I think you look spectacular,' Ross covered. 'You would, you're having a mid-life crisis.' He also gave Jonathan a Parkin Loaf, purchased for 69p from Dutson's the Family Bakers on Bury Road, Bolton. 'Not that you'd go that far north,' he told him. 'You'd need a tetanus.'

'It was a masterful act of on-air hijacking,' wrote Alex Games in the *Independent on Sunday* a day later. 'It also showed someone utterly at home in a studio, knowing which camera to face, denouncing and deconstructing the system even as he posed and mugged for it. Another, more crafty by-product of all the high jinks was that he had to answer comparatively few questions about himself.' Peter did talk briefly about his 'Mum Wants a Bungalow' tour; about Charlie, who is named after his dad; and about his new series, *Max and Paddy's Road to Nowhere*, which he described as a spin-off 'like *George and Mildred* from *Man About The House*'. 'I'm only here for the clips; roll 'em,' he said, taking even Ross aback with his sheer cheek.

When the first episode of *Max and Paddy's Road to Nowhere* aired the following Friday, it was not seen as an unqualified success by the press, and was generally deemed as a step down from the high quality of *Phoenix Nights*. Damningly, Jim Shelley in the *Mirror* wrote: 'Aptly-titled *Road to Nowhere*, it's like watching Channel Five trying to do its own imitation of *Phoenix Nights*.'

Garry Bushell at the *People* was more enthusiastic. 'The humour is cartoony – Joe breaks a leg but doesn't seem to mind. The sight gags are terrific – like the laugh-out-loud *Dirty Dancing* spoof as Paddy teaches Max to strut his stuff, to the horror of a passing family. Neat lines and new slang abound. I liked Cherry Bakewells for boobs.' But even he had his doubts and wondered: 'Are Max and Paddy strong enough to carry the show alone?'

The answer is most definitely yes – although more than one knockabout series seems unlikely. *Max and Paddy's Road to Nowhere* turned out to be a grower, with each episode funnier and better than the last – this was reflected in the ratings for the show, which began at 3.6 million, slid to 2.6 million, then climbed back up beyond 3 million again. Episode 5, where our heroes had to share their motorised home with a flatulent pig, was the funniest TV moment of the year by far – unless you counted Peter Andre 'making up' a song he'd already released in *I'm a Celebrity Get Me Out of Here*.

Meanwhile, back in Bolton, sales of Parkin Loaf at Dutson's on Bury Road went through the roof. 'We see him in here about once a week and he never plays the big star,' said Helen Dutson about their celebrity customer. 'He just orders a corned beef salad and mayonnaise bap and has a pie while he's waiting.' Yes, that's a pie while he's waiting.

Max and Paddy's Road to Nowhere picked up where *Phoenix Nights* left off, with club doormen Max and Paddy driving off into the sunset to live a new life travelling the British Isles in a motorised home. The show gave the illusion that our friends were travelling around England, but as ever most of the locations allowed Peter to be able to drive home for his tea. Much of the humour came from their discomfort at having to live with each other in such close quarters, as for example when Paddy questions Max's hygienic standards. Max: 'How dare you. How dare you. I have a good stand-up wash in that sink once a week.' Paddy: 'Once a week! Stray dogs wash more than that. And what's wrong with deodorant? It's not the work of the devil, Max, give it a whirl some time.'

The jokes were more ribald than before and the best ones came from their opposite personalities – Paddy a bit of a stud, Max a bit of a loser, Paddy an unreconstructed lad, Max struggling to be a politically correct new man. The journey was, as much as anything, a voyage of sexual discovery for Max with Paddy as his Mr Miyagi, motivating him into living *la vida loca*.

'Women love a man in a uniform,' Paddy tells his friend.

'Do they?' questions Max. 'Let's go out dressed as a couple of Nazis and see how far we get.'

There was a surprise, though: Max is actually a father. This revelation is received with incredulity by Paddy – 'You've had sex?' The mother? A girl who was 'a kind of midget'. 'Isn't that a song by Queen?' asks Paddy.

'I didn't like that storyline so much,' says sit-com writer Graham Linehan. 'I thought it was a bit too much having your cake and eating it, telling all those short jokes. But it did show another side to Peter Kay, that he wants to pull at people's heart strings.'

Peter also gave us a new catchphrase – 'How dare you'; we learned about two gents who 'operate outside the law' called Magnet and Steel (Max's idea for a TV cop show) and found out that Max's full name is Maxwell Bygraves. Best of all, there was a flashback to Bolton in the mid-1980s with Max working as a bouncer at the Aquarius Club – before the flood – and we got to see Brian Potter running, a marvellous sight.

Cross-referencing *Phoenix Nights* aside, the jokes were a bit more spelled out and obvious than Peter's previous work – in the ignoble history of spin-off shows it was closer to Ronnie Barker's *Going Straight* than Kelsey Grammer's *Frasier* – and Potter notwithstanding, there is none of the multi-character roles we'd previously enjoyed. Still, it was all good fun and Max and Paddy were a charming couple of oafs anyone would enjoy sharing a pint with.

Never one to miss out on an opportunity to sing ('Write the theme tune, sing the theme tune,' as *Little Britain*'s miniature Dennis Waterman might have it), there were also a couple of chances for Peter to belt out a 1980s standard. At the 40th birthday party of his old schoolmate, the Wolfster, he finds himself singing Elton John's 'I Guess That's Why They Call It the Blues' accompanied by Paddy on the jazz harp. It was actually pretty good. Playing keyboards in the backing band, dressed as George Michael from Wham!, was Toni Baker, who continued to write the music for all of Peter's shows. He wasn't the only one to have followed our friends from the Phoenix Club. In Episode 4, when Max and Paddy find themselves in prison, Brian Potter wheels himself to their rescue with his Free the Phoenix Two campaign. Later we see a news report of a benefit show live from Bolton, with Marc Park singing a cover of Take That's 'Back for Good' – 'Whatever they said, whatever they did, they didn't mean it ...' Holy Mary, Kenny Snr and Young Kenny also appear in the episode, but pointedly not Jerry St

Clair – even though at the end we see a banner draped over the club wall reading 'Happy Sixtieth Birthday Jerry'.

The joke didn't go unnoticed by Dave Spikey, still in his early fifties, who called it 'a bit cheeky'. In an interview on <www.chortle.co.uk>, when asked what he thought of Max and Paddy he replied: 'Not my cup of tea, I'm afraid. Hate to say it, but pretty obvious, blatant, unsophisticated comedy for me. But, hey, what do I know?'

The fall-out had been rumbling for quite some time; as far back as the 1999 British Comedy Awards Spikey had been miffed that he hadn't joined Peter onstage and he felt he hadn't got the credit his contribution deserved. In the following years he told interviewers: 'That's all blown over now. We're friends, we text each other a lot these days. It's cheaper.' Any chance of a reconciliation seemed completely blown by 2004, however, when he wrote on his website on 10 April: 'Talking of writing, I was watching the British Book Awards on TV yesterday and was shocked and stunned when *Phoenix Nights* by Peter Kay was nominated in the category of "Best TV-related books of the year". I can only presume that they took all the bits that Neil and I wrote out, but then that begs the question as to why it's still such a thick book.'

A very strange sort of rivalry seems to have developed between Dave Spikey and Peter Kay since *Phoenix Nights* and while it may well be coincidence it does seem rather odd that the man previously known as 'The Saint' is a patron of Chorley FM (the real community radio station that just happens to share a name with the not-real radio station where the listener comes first) and is the new host of *Bullseye* – a game show Peter Kay did much to bring back to public awareness during the 'Mum Wants a Bungalow' tour. Or maybe we're imagining things.

For his part, Neil Fitzmaurice has kept his own counsel, although he too has not been invited back into the Peter Kay fold and recently said that reports of a third *Phoenix Nights* series were 'just paper talk'. Furthermore, it doesn't seem to have escaped Peter's attention that Neil Fitzmaurice recently appeared in a sit-com called *Eyes Down* set in a northern bingo hall co-starring Beatrice Kelley, not to be confused with the *That Peter Kay Thing* episode also called 'Eyes Down' and also set in a northern bingo hall that also co-starred Beatrice Kelley. Peter mentions it on the DVD commentary of the second series of *Phoenix Nights* – a recording both Spikey and Fitzmaurice don't appear to have been invited to. However, Fitzmaurice is not given the treatment afforded Daniel Kitson in the commentary: every time he appears on screen, playing Spencer the mumbling barman, Peter gives him a two-word sobriquet: 'the bastard'.

The reason? Comments Daniel Kitson made to Plymouth's *Evening Herald* in February 2003, while he was on a nation-wide tour. When asked about *Phoenix Nights*, Kitson said that he wasn't happy with his work on the show. 'I didn't like *Phoenix Nights*. 'I didn't think it was absolute rubbish, but I didn't think it was the work of genius that some people lauded it as. I thought it was racist and lazy. I won't do something like that again.'

Sadly, he wasn't asked to justify his racist barb – requests to discuss it for this book were not replied to – but it can only have been intended as a comment on Ant and Dec, the Chinese asylum seekers who end up working in the Phoenix Club kitchens. 'It didn't seem to bother him at the time,' says Peter. 'The bastard.'

The rift between the pair – while comical – is such that when Channel 4 screened some *Phoenix Nights* out-takes as part of a special 'Peter Kay Night' in April 2006, Kitson's face was pixellated out in some scenes, *à la Crimewatch*. One senses that if he could erase him from *Phoenix Nights* completely, he would. He has been loyal to the same band of comics for years and helped them all, but at the same time the thought of someone profiting from him while also betraying him sends him spinning into a rage.

Like Daniel 'The Bastard' Kitson, who won the 2002 Perrier Award at Edinburgh, Dave Spikey and Neil Fitzmaurice have done well since appearing in *Phoenix Nights*. Dave Spikey finally got to make his sit-com set in a regional newspaper office (not the *Bolton Independent Leader*), *Dead Man Weds*, which was very funny but badly scheduled opposite *Desperate Housewives*, and has shone in the quiz show *8 Out of 10 Cats*. Neil Fitzmaurice managed to appear in the other great sit-com of our generation, *The Office*, as well as enjoying starring roles in T*he Bill, Holby City, Peep Show* and *Doctors*. But then everyone seems to have benefited from the afterglow of the Phoenix Club – Ted Robbins (Den Perry), Toby Foster (Les) and Justin Moorhouse (Young Kenny) all host popular regional radio shows. Archie Kelly (Kenny Snr) played Waggy, the second-hand car salesman in *Shameless* who touches up Veronica's breasts, and Steve Edge was the assistant boss in *Mike Bassett: England Manager* and ran naked across Brentford FC's pitch in an advert for the ITV Sports Channel. While some of the diminutive Bolton Wanderers fans ('How far away are they?') who caused Max and Paddy so much bother in Episode 5 could be seen in *Snow White* at the Civic Theatre in Darlington.

And Paddy McGuinness? Well, Paddy McGuinness is the new Peter Kay.

In 2006, mirroring Peter's 2002/03 'Mum Wants a Bungalow' dates, Paddy played to a seemingly endless number of full houses across Britain. Not wishing to appear as if he was riding the coat tails of his friend's success, he told audiences that he was a very different proposition. 'Peter tells you about the wedding night, I tell you about the honeymoon.' Wink, wink.

Appropriately, his tour was called 'The Dark Side', and as he told audiences a sequence of jokes about wanking, visiting an STD clinic and his lovemaking prowess (not necessarily in that order) it was not hard to see why. He did, however, reprise his act as Lord Love Rocket from the ladies' night in *Phoenix Nights* for the encore and even cajoled everyone into a sing-along of the *Minder* theme tune. It was funny, but if Peter Kay is Arthur Daley to Paddy's young Terry, then he was sorely missed. Wanna buy a mouse mat? There's loads in the warehouse.

Chapter Ten
Weeping Like a Willow

'I don't want to achieve immortality through my work. I want to achieve it through not dying.'

Woody Allen

'It's a funny thing this celebrity. If you don't wave back you're a miserable bugger, if you do wave back you're a big-headed bugger. I don't know.'

Fred Dibnah

It is often said in football that the sign of a successful team is that they keep winning even when they play badly. The celebrity equivalent of this is when you get more and more famous despite not actually doing anything. This was certainly the case with Peter Kay in 2005 and 2006: despite the fact that he wasn't writing or appearing in his own TV series or live tour for the first time since 1998, his Celebdaq stock rose far and away beyond that of any other British comedian. In the past two years he has most definitely become the 'megastar' stand-up comic Adam Bloom predicted he'd be all those Edinburgh Festivals ago. Peter's rising fame was partially due to the John Smith's adverts, which had made him an omnipresent face on mainstream TV – and not just Channel 4. But it was also thanks, in no small measure, to a song that had been following him around since he was seven years old, one his mum and dad would play over and over again on the living-room stereo.

2005 began with what could have been seen as a Prince Philip-style gaffe when he was quoted as saying, 'I don't know why they call it *Comic* Relief. They should just call it Relief because there's nothing funny about it.' With the tabloid and stand-up fraternity sharpening their swords, he stopped them in their tracks when it transpired that he was to play a major part in the fundraising marathon. Just as had happened with his awful Jill Dando joke in 1999, the remark was quickly brushed aside.

As had been shown up by Ricky Gervais's ape dance in *The Office*, while Comic Relief is an excellent charitable cause it is also imbued with telethon naffness – of wacky accountants going mad for the day and bathing in Big Bob's Baked Beans, of kids paying 10p to wear their own clothes to school and of stiff building society branch managers carrying gigantic over-sized cheques (all too aware that this rewards their employers with more publicity than the amount they are donating could pay for in advertising). But Peter Kay entered into the spirit of the event with unfettered gusto and on *The Parkinson Show* in early March 2005 showed his one-time boss a music video that was the focal point of the Red Nose Day effort. In it, Peter, dressed like a 1980s Mr Byrite model in purple suit and gaudy Hawaiian shirt (an outfit not too dissimilar to the one he wore as a dancing bear in *Max and Paddy's Road to Nowhere*), is seen marching down a corridor cheerily miming as he is joined by a riotously eclectic selection of showbiz personalities from Bernie Clifton and Keith Harris (with feathered friends) to Michael Parkinson himself. The song is '(Is This the Way to) Amarillo', as previously heard sung by Max and Paddy as they drive the Asian elders to a mosque at the start of the second series of *Phoenix Nights* and before every night of the 'Mum Wants a Bungalow' tour, where he'd sing it in the aisles with his tour manager Gordon Isaccs on backing vocals. Of course anyone who had known Peter from his schooldays would have been aware that the song had even greater significance for him. Long before showbusiness and fame called, he used it on the soundtrack to the video of his hallowed *The Wizard of Oz* appearance. '(Is This the Way to) Amarillo' was, as he had continued to do throughout his career, Peter Kay cross-referencing Peter Kay, and Tony Christie – the 1970s crooner he was miming along to – was just along for the ride. It should also come as no surprise to learn that Peter's talismanic lion suit, which he wore in *The Wizard of Oz*, features too – worn by his friend Danny Baker as he strides down the yellow-brick road to nowhere with Peter and Heather McCartney as Dorothy. On his chat show, Michael Parkinson was beside himself with enthusiasm, especially when they showed the scene where Ronnie Corbett is seen tumbling over. It was later revealed that the pairs of celebs joining Peter in his march to see 'sweet Marie' were walking on treadmills in front of a blue screen.

On Comic Relief night, Jonathan Ross was no less effusive and the video got replayed three times – with callers offering to donate more cash in return for repeat showings. Each time it was shown, the giant cheque-holding audience cheered when their favourite celebrity appeared on the screen. Somewhat hysterically, the Sooty Appreciation Society claimed that Sooty and Sweep got the biggest response, but there was no doubting who the real star was.

The '(Is This the Way to) Amarillo' Comic Relief video is a brilliant piece of fun. It reminds us that with all the sophisticated, intelligent and complex humour on our TV screens nothing beats sheer outright, uncomplicated entertainment. Well, apart from a fart gag. Two years later he pulled it off once more with a rip roaring cover of the Proclaimers' '(I'm Gonna Be) 500 Miles', again with a cast of light-entertainment superstars – including Janette Tough (aka Wee Jimmy Krankie) freshly recovered from a fall from a beanstalk at a Glasgow pantomime.

Now it seems inconceivable, but in 2005 there had been no plans to issue '(Is This the Way to) Amarillo' as a single, but public demand was such that Christie's song – which had only got to no. 18 in 1971 – was rush-released. Oddly, the cover proclaimed that it was 'Featuring Peter Kay' despite the fact that he did not appear on the version released on CD. No matter. Tony Christie's ego might have been dented a little bit but his song sold thousands, staying on top of the charts for seven weeks – a run unmatched since the days when Wet Wet Wet were in their pomp.

There was a price to pay for its success, though, as Peter revealed when he joked, 'It's ruined a good song, that.' Now, with the whole nation singing along and an army squadron doing a video spoof called '(Is This the Way to) Armadillo', the song that had soundtracked Peter's life was lost to the nation.

Thanks to the now ubiquitous nature of his fame, there was also the inevitable accompanying backlash. The bigger you get, the bigger target you become. Predictable, then, that in his *Daily Mirror* column on 21 March, offended by Kay's grandstanding on *The Parkinson Show*, Tony Parsons took a wild shot at the nation's number-one comedian, labelling him a 'slob-of-the-people'. In the article, headlined 'Please Stop Singing ... O-Kay?' the populist author bemoaned his 'charidee chortles' and wrote: 'Peter Kay is an old-school, 16-stone light entertainer of a kind that 30 years ago would have been telling crap jokes about Chinkies, Pakis and West Indians called Chalkie. For some reason (possibly because they learn their trade performing in front of pissed audiences who are stupid enough when they're sober), that type always think they can sing as well as tell jokes.' Parsons – an excellent and enjoyable columnist who loves playing devil's advocate with popular culture – did a great disservice to his wit with his scandalous comments, and the paper printed a small selection of the offended responses. However, as wildly inaccurate as his accusations were, there was a growing sense of discontent with everybody's favourite Boltonian. Jim Shelly in the *Mirror*, noting the 'Spazzy Paddy' jokes in *Road to Nowhere*, asked, 'Surely these days are long gone?' But the main difference this time was that the disquiet came not from the press or a closed circle of southern comedians crying into their shandy about some gig in 1996 but from the public. When Peter released his *Live at the Manchester Arena* DVD there were cheers as his fans rushed to buy it, but then, when they discovered that he was performing the same set as on the *Live at Bolton Albert Halls* DVD they had purchased the previous year, there were groans of consumer unrest. In the customer reviews on <amazon.co.uk> the words 'con' and 'rip-off' featured prominently. The thoughts of a 'viewer from Halifax, West Yorkshire' far from unique: 'I have watched both the Blackpool show and the *Live at Bolton Albert Halls* DVD and loved them both. When *Peter Kay: Live at the Manchester Arena* came out I was excited to watch it. I have just seen it and was not impressed, to say the least: every single part of it was repeated from the two previous DVDs.'

If anything, the mistake of the *Live at the Manchester Arena* DVD was one of bad marketing. If it had been sold as a 'Mum Wants a Bungalow' documentary, nobody would have complained; in fact they would have applauded that they'd got a bonus live set with the documentary. Instead, the behind-the-scenes film was tucked away as an extra, along with the '(Is This the Way to) Amarillo' video the whole nation had already seen more times than their own front doors, and Peter Kay ended up looking like a cheap-suit-wearing double-glazing salesman on *Watchdog*.

With all the criticism in the air surely it was time for Peter Kay's loyal fans to stand up for their man and, mimicking Brian Potter's *Spartacus* moment when Jerry is assaulted by a heckler in the *Phoenix Nights* alternative comedy club episode, pronounce as one: 'You push him, you push me.' Their chance would come, but first there was more substantial evidence that proved that, rather than falling out of love with Peter, the British public loved him more than ever. Such was his Midas touch that he was held responsible for a sudden surge in the popularity of Greggs the baker; even replicas of the Pakistan cricket shirt he wore as Max sold out across the land. He was voted Britain's Best Loved Comedian, a gay icon by the readers of *Bent Magazine*, the man most of us would like to share a bag of chips with, the person we'd most like to go on holiday with, be trapped in a lift with and have over for tea. According to a poll conducted by the Co-operative Bank his is the voice we'd most like to tell us directions on an in-car satellite navigation device. How about from Peter Kay's house to, er, the Co-operative Bank, Bolton? Laughing all the way! According to Companies House his Goodnight Vienna company is now worth £8.5 million. There was, though, one poll that Peter would have preferred not to top in 2005: he headed <chortle.co.uk>'s list of the most over- rated comics in Britain (narrowly beating Jim Davidson).

Maybe only Tony Parsons voted. It seemed very unfair.

Thankfully, incandescent with rage, Peter Kay fans bombarded the website with emails to put them right on their error: 'Your poll stinks. Peter Kay rocks,' wrote Dean Ramsey; 'You are a big load of bollocks,' scrawled someone called piroadmark, who continued: 'You load of scrotums.' While one fan simply asked the Chortle editors: 'Are you on drugs?'

Chortle probably found the inarticulate nature of these emails amusing, but there is no denying that they got it very wrong. Considering his enormous popularity and the rela- tively small number of awards he has won, there is a stronger case to make that he is the most underrated British comedian.

'The same website did a survey last year, where Peter was

named the funniest man on the planet,' voice of reason Paddy McGuinness told Teletext (a great place to find cheap holidays, by the way) after the Chortle announcement.

'Whoever is successful finds the same media that build them up like to knock them down. I don't think Peter will be bothered one bit.'

He was, but, as ever, Peter's response was hidden within his work. In April 2006, as part of the special 'Peter Kay Night', he and Paddy McGuinness filmed the links between the shows in character as Max and Paddy. Reading from a TV magazine that the *Live from Manchester* show is on next, Max says, 'He's just brought this out on DVD last Christmas, the money-grabbing bastard.'

Turning negativity into humour has been Peter's way of dealing with criticism his whole life. At school, when his teacher Paul Abbott told him, 'Life's just a joke to you, Kay', he turned it into a catchphrase, repeating it under his breath whenever he was in trouble. In 2006 he took to calling himself a 'roly poly funny man', turning a comment about him in the *Daily Star* into a gag.

Of course, the one thing that would shut everybody up would be if Peter did a stand-up tour again. Exhausted by the marathon 'Mum Wants a Bungalow' tour, he revealed in November 2004 that he was considering quitting stand-up comedy because he feared it would damage his health. 'I don't want to be dropping dead of a heart attack,' he told the *Radio Times*. 'You look at the people you love, like Les Dawson and Eric Morecambe, and you think, "Why did they do that to themselves?" They didn't have the confidence to say no.'

It is an incredible admission for a man in his early thirties to make, but a fear that Eric Morecambe's son, Gary, can sympathise with: 'Peter Kay is the same as my father,' he says. 'I don't think being funny is his job, I just think it's something he is. If he were told tomorrow he'd never be paid again to be a comedian he'd still entertain people. My father said no to nothing and it badly affected his health in the end.

'Even when he got things on a lot better level and was doing less, he couldn't resist climbing on that treadmill. I think Peter has been looking at people like my dad and like Les Dawson and he's learning from it.'

Indeed the agents at Phil McIntyre's office spend more time turning down offers for Peter Kay than anything else. True to his word, apart from the occasional charity event Peter has not performed stand-up since 2003 – not that you'd know it from the number of times his live shows are repeated on TV. When it was first shown on Channel 4 in August 2004, his 'Live at the Bolton Albert Halls' gig was watched by 6.7 million viewers – the highest ratings ever for a stand-up show.

In October 2006, talking to Radio One's Edith Bowman, he promised that he would be touring again in 2008 – 'it's going to be called "The Knives Are Out Tour"' he told her, obviously aware that his absence has been noted. When (or if) it happens it will have been a mighty six years since he last went out on the road.

One rare live performance came when he hosted a charity evening for the Teenage Cancer Trust at the London Royal Albert Hall on Thursday, 7 April 2005. Peter appeared as himself and as Brian Potter, even singing 'The Wind Beneath My Wheels' (his subtly altered version of Bette Midler's 'Wind Beneath My Wings'). But the most remarked-upon moment of the evening came when Mighty Boosh star Noel Fielding suffered a hail of unsophisticated four-lettered heckles during his set and, losing his train of thought, disintegrated into incomprehensible mumbling, leaving the stage to cries of 'Taxi' from one audience member.

Rather than sympathise with the distraught surrealist, Peter told the audience that Fielding's set wasn't his cup of tea at all and that it all went over his head. Fanning the flames, the *Mirror*'s 3 A.M. Girls painted a picture of riotous scenes backstage at the end of the show, with Peter Kay locked in his dressing room as the young Rod Stewart lookalike seethed at the after-show party. Later, Noel Fielding and his Mighty Boosh partner Julian Barrett prolonged the feud in the pages of gentlemen's journal *Zoo* (a great magazine for zookeepers). Referring to Peter, Fielding told the publication: 'There are some people who like that sort of thing. We sort of hate that shit really.' Barrett was no less forthcoming: 'My mum loves him. Whenever I go home it's just Peter Kay, Peter Kay all day long – I'm like, "Yeah, all right!"'

Organisers reminded people that the event raised a lot of money for the Teenage Cancer Trust and, wisely, Peter refused to comment.

Enjoying his semi-retirement, back in Bolton with Susan and Charlie, Peter was spotted at a Balamory live show. Despite Peter's incredible fame and wealth, the family enjoy an ordinary life. And while Peter may no longer visit the café in Bolton Market for his regular meal of baked potato with tuna mayonnaise and baked beans, he is regularly seen around town and at Asda in Astley Bridge, where he once filmed the 'Black Bin Bags' song with Dave Spikey. As a rule, the people of Bolton leave him alone as he does his weekly big shop, but if disturbed he will inform them of his love for Weight Watchers Banoffee Desserts ('just one and a half points').

In his premature dotage, Peter also made a habit of introducing live bands onstage – Keane and Elton John were both ushered from the wings by Peter Kay. At the V Festival Peter, introducing Doves, spotted a member of the audience urinating against a fence in the distance– "your mother'll be proud," he told him. As the band waited he announced: "And now it gives me great pleasure … to sit on bath taps."

Introducing bands became such a habit that it was absolutely no surprise at all to find him at the biggest rock event of 2005, Live 8. Sally Lindsay's boyfriend, session drummer Steve White, was playing with The Who, so it was decided that Peter would introduce them onstage. However, things didn't go quite as planned. As is the chaotic nature of such enormous events, Live 8 was running massively behind schedule once it was time for Peter to perform his task for the day. As the technical crew attempted to equip the stage for Townshend and Daltry's performance, Peter was prodded onstage and told to 'fill'.

He didn't know how long he was supposed to do this for; he thought he was meant just to be telling the exhausted white-rubber-braceleted mass ' ... and here's the Who'.

Instead, seconds seemed like hours as he paced the stage apologising for 'not being Robbie Williams'. Mark Sutherland, who was covering the event for BBC radio, watched from what became dubbed 'the golden circle' – the section of the audience at the front of Hyde Park filled with competition winners, the press and VIPs. 'We stood there thinking this can't be on telly, surely,' says Mark. 'He started singing "Amarillo" but then sort of wandered off, but you could still see him on the big screen talking to people and then he came back on and tried to do the song again. Then these roadies kept walking past and he kept accosting them, asking what was going on. He didn't tell any gags or anything. He said something about wanting to be on the motorway. We were all stood there saying, "What's going on here?" It looked like no one had told him what to do and he was just winging it, and he had to wing it for a lot longer than he expected to. After Mariah Carey, it was the most embarrassing moment of the day.'

Not everyone agreed and, despite witnessing Paul McCartney with U2, Coldplay, Pink Floyd and Madonna, many people found dancing around at the back of the park to Peter Kay singing '(Is This the Way to) Amarillo' the happiest moment of a strenuous day. Not one to be put off by such a setback, Peter even returned to Hyde Park a few weeks later and appeared onstage with his childhood favourites, Queen. In fact the whole of 2005 felt like this, like he'd been let out of school early. He didn't have to turn up on *The Paul O'Grady Show* dressed as a Christmas tree – he just wanted to. He didn't have to walk off the street and into the offices of Century FM and go on air completely unannounced to tell a couple of jokes, he'd just been in the area and had felt like it. And his DJ set at gay Manchester nightclub Homie Sexual helped him get out of the house for a bit.

Then in December 2005 there was news that this fallow period in Peter's career was coming to a close when newspapers – prompted by a BBC press release – started reporting that not only was a third series of *Phoenix Nights* due, but also a movie. The only downside was that 'we'll have to kill off some of the characters'.

The source of this information was an interview Peter had done for BBC 6 Music with DJ Vic McGlynn. Alongside popular indie bands the Foo Fighters, Franz Ferdinand and the Kaiser Chiefs, who had recorded similar shows, Peter Kay had been invited on to the station as controller for the day for their regular special event called 6 Music Selector. It was a huge coup for the station. In early December, Peter recorded the interview and chose his music.

Although there was some disquiet that his taste – Billy Joel, George Benson, the Flying Pickets' cover of 'Psycho Killer' – didn't exactly match the station's profile, the interview was great and was seized upon by the press office. However, what they neglected to tell us was that Peter's comments were originally very heavily laced with humour and accompanying 'maybe's, all of which would have been made clear once the show was broadcast, but it never was. Angered by the leak, Peter refused to sign a release form and the tapes were locked away in a vault never to be heard. So will there ever be a third series of *Phoenix Nights* or even a movie? Peter told Radio One's Edith Bowman just before Christmas 2005: 'I think there's more chance of them bringing back hanging.' Laughing, he did give *Phoenix Nights* fans some hope. 'Yeah, it'll be back some day. You always need something to fall back on. Hitler were a house painter. It'll be back one day ... I love Brian Potter.' Nearly a year later though, talking again to Bowman, Peter revealed that not only would there be *Phoenix Nights 3* but that it was already written, alongside a couple of Max and Paddy one-off specials. Despite being on ice as far as his own show was concerned Brian Potter made several appearances on our screens – he's even in Max and Paddy's spin-off exercise DVD (a spoof too far that would have made a funny sketch). On Monday, 16 January 2006 he even got to co-host an edition of *Top of the Pops*, singing Dead or Alive's 'You Spin Me Round' as co-host Fearne Cotton gave his wheelchair a whirl around. It was the first time people talked about the ailing pop show at work the next day for years. On it Brian gave us his verdict on some of the movers and shakers in the charts – James Blunt is 'a modern-day Gilbert O'Sullivan', Morton Harket from A-ha 'is ageing backwards', the Kooks 'need a haircut' and 50 Cent is 'a load of rubbish'. There was also a plug for the Phoenix Club: 'Junction 5 of the M61, just past Balti Towers, coach parties welcome'.

As well as Potter, we've even seen Marc Park again – reincarnated in Peter's pop video for Texas, with Sharleen Spiteri taking the place of Cheryl Avenue as the object of Marc's creative vision. Rather brilliantly, the video references *An Officer and a Gentleman* and Lionel Richie's 'Hello' video and was filmed at Farnworth Veterans Club in Bolton, the set of the first *That Peter Kay Thing* episode, 'In the Club'.

In June he made an appearance in *Doctor Who* (insert Dalek Bread gag here!) as the theatrical villain Victor

Kennedy, proving yet again that he has the acting chops on top of all his other skills. It was all good fun but one curious feature of his role was that when he transformed from human into the Abzorbaloff creature his voice also switched from Southern sophisticate to a Northern accent that wasn't so much Bolton factory floor as Newton-Le-Willows Conservative Club. It was seeing him in this part that convinced the people behind the musical stage version of *The Producers* that Peter would be ideal for a touring version of the show – that and the fact that he's been telling anyone who'll listen for the past 20 years that *The Producers* is a work of genius and he'd love to be in it. If he was willing to be a naked alien then wearing a dress would be a doddle.

Initially they wanted him to appear as the transvestite director Roger DeBris in Edinburgh, Bradford and Manchester, but, unwilling to stray too far from home and his growing family (Finley James had arrived in October 2006), he elected to appear for three months in Manchester only. So impressive was he when the show opened at the Palace Theatre in February 2007 that the man behind both the film and stage musical, Mel Brooks, offered him a deal to stay with the production. 'If he'd only leave his beloved Bolton,' said the 80-year-old icon, 'I'd take him to London – or even America. But he won't.'

Peter was in his element – and he could be home in time to watch *Bad Girls* on UK Gold. As Georgina Brown in the *Mail On Sunday* pointed out: 'Beaming like Benny Hill and basking in the bliss of being a star (both DeBris and Kay), he perches on the edge of the stage and chats to his chums. A moment of musical comedy magic.' For all his achievements and record sales there was a real feeling from Peter that *The Producers* was the proudest moment of his career.

Peter Kay is contracted to one more show for his long-time supporters at Channel 4, but the real question is what he does next. According to reports, ITV have been knocking, offering a substantial pay rise and the chance to take his pick of new dramas. Some industry insiders predict that he may be tempted to Sky. The biggest surprise of all would be if he remained at Channel 4. But if it isn't broke, why fix it?

Indeed, a return at some point to the characters in *That Peter Kay Thing* shouldn't be ruled out. At one stage he suggested that he would like to mimic Granada's *7 Up* series and return to them seven years later to see how their lives had advanced. Long-term Kay followers would much rather see this than the cameo and chat show appearances (*Catherine Tate*, *Little Britain*) he appears to prefer. Still, no rush. From the Texas video we know what's happened to Marc Park – he's a security guard dreaming of the good old days – but what of the others? Is Leonard still carrying his giant cross around Bolton, preaching the Lord's word and still failing to get a laugh from his boy-making-a-noise-like-a-frog joke? Or did he meet an unsavoury end at the hands of his mass-murderer pen pal, Walter? Was Mr Softy more successful with porn than with ice-cream (as residents of Bolton will know – the shop's still open)? And did Mathew Kelly at the Arena ever get to wear a nametag with his real name on it? Meanwhile, somewhere in a box at the BBC, Peter's uncompleted series *Seaside Stories* is hiding.

Peter's steps into the theatre and the more accessible *Max and Paddy's Road to Nowhere* indicate that his blaspheming days are behind him and that prime-time TV is his for the taking – if he wants it. As he told the owner of the Frog and Bucket, the Manchester comedy club where he cut his teeth as a new stand-up, he is destined for Saturday night at 7.30 p.m. Gary Morecambe feels this is Peter Kay's natural home. 'You do feel that what is missing on television is just wholesome family entertainment,' he says. 'It could be that he's the one that comes in and replaces the Morecambe and Wises and Mike Yarwoods.'

'His next move could be a chat show,' says author and sit-com writer Andrew Collins. 'He's so old-fashioned he could single-handedly take television back to the glory days of the 1970s, wearing a cummerbund and hosting a variety show in a big top. Game shows are his for the taking, too. There is no irony to what Peter Kay does, so at least if he did turn up on the twenty-first-century equivalent of *Bullseye* he'd do it with sincerity, and not with the knowing wink of Ant and Dec or Johnny Vaughan or Graham Norton.' Incidentally, only one of those celebrities Andrew mentions has ever been to Bury.

For those upset by the vision of Peter Kay in a cummer-bund, *Father Ted* co-writer Graham Linehan offers a more visionary career path. 'I have a feeling he will make a very successful British film at some point. He's one of the people who's capable of doing it.' Furthermore, Linehan strongly believes that our man from Bolton can succeed where Morecambe and Wise, Tony Hancock and Steve Coogan have stumbled and make an impact beyond the cosy confines of pasty and pea suppers. 'I don't think you can get the audience he gets for his live DVDs and it to just stop once it hits the coast,' he says. 'There is something about him that's touching something more than regional humour; he's touching some-thing that's human, and that's what you need when you're writing films. I don't think he should make any concessions to an international market, I just think he should make a film that feels right to him and I think an international audience will just follow along if he sticks to his guns. Morecambe and Wise were very much a pair of stand-ups messing about in front of the camera, and Steve Coogan is a very fine comedian and actor, but Peter Kay's an actor, director, writer, and the people to compare him to, the people he should be emulating, are people like Woody Allen.'

As Peter himself once said on the set of *That Peter Kay Thing* in his hometown, 'There are a million stories in Bolton, behind all those doors.' His tongue was in his cheek, but maybe he's right, and maybe he'll carry on making them and Bolton will become some mythical British Mecca for people in America and beyond. It's possible.

If anything, the past two years have proved that Peter Kay will stay famous long after *Phoenix Nights* and 'The Services' and even *Max and Paddy's Road to Nowhere* and *The Producers* become fading memories. Once people forget about garlic bread, Rola Cola and the way mums dance at weddings, he'll still be around.

He will achieve it all without compromise and quite probably without leaving Greater Manchester. The best is still to come and, as Brian Potter might say, 'The world's your lobster.'

'You know, he always imagined having a biography written about him by some journalist,' says Michael Atherton, remembering Peter Kay aged 16. 'He even had a title – When the Laughter Stops – and a mental picture of the cover, a close-up picture of his face with a wistful expression. Honestly, that's true!'

The nuns at Mount St Joseph's would have been proud of him.

To be continued ...

The Little Book of Mis-kay-lany

AS HEARD ON CHORLEY FM

Paul Owen – 'My Favourite Waste of Time' (1986)

Tiffany – 'I Think We're Alone Now' (1988)

Johnny Nash – 'I Can See Clearly Now' (1972)

Ryan Paris – 'Dolce Vita' (1983)

Aneka – 'Japanese Boy' (1981)

Mr Mister – 'Kyrie' (1986)

Rock Steady Crew – '(Hey You) the Rock Steady Crew' (1983)

Transvision Vamp – 'Baby I Don't Care' (1989)

Culture Club – 'Church of the Poison Mind' (1983)

Bananarama – 'Robert De Niro's Waiting' (1984)

Wham! – 'I'm Your Man' (1985)

Cheryl Avenue – 'I Will Survive' (1999)

Yazz and the Plastic Population – 'The Only Way is Up' (1988)

Cockney Rebel – 'Make Me Smile (Come Up and See Me)' (1975)

Waterboys – 'The Whole of the Moon' (1985)

Dennis Waterman – 'I Could be so Good for You' (1979)

Tony Christie – '(Is This the Way to) Amarillo' (1971)

Blue – 'Keep On Movin'' (1999)

Bill Withers – 'Lovely Day' (1978)

TRACKLISTING TO JERRY ST CLAIR'S SOLO ALBUM *YOUNG AT HEART*

'Sexbomb'

'She Bangs, She Bangs'

'Drugs Don't Work'

'Gangsta's Paradise'

'Martika's Kitchen'

'Lythium'
'Alphabet Street, Batdance/Get Off' (medley)
'Rock Me Amadeus' (in German)
'Belfast Child'
'Brimful of Asha'

FOR SALE ON LADIES' NITE

The Developer
Thai Beads
Female Climax Cream
Blow Job Action Couple
Mini G Spot
Man to Lamb
Oro-Stimulator
Perfect Pleasures
Sex Lube
Choc Chip Dick Lick
Love Eggs

SIGNS YOU MAY HAVE MISSED

Batteries Available at the Bar (Dildos not Included)
Banana Grove Presents … Deidra Kay
Hidden Tiger! Crouching Dragon! Peking Duck! Available here!
Big Jo's, Kings of the Road: 'Trailers for sale or rent'
Scrawled on side of van: 'If you think I'm dirty you wanna meet the wife!'
Items available from the Potter's Platter menu: Farmyard Special, Bold Yankee and Northern Beef

PHOTO OPPORTUNITIES TO USE UP HOLIDAY FILM

Mum on patio
Dad looking baffled
Dog in front of radio
Self-portrait

PADDY'S CHAT-UP LINES

Evening girls, wanna have a look into my crystal balls?

Lordy, Lordy, I wouldn't mind hanging out of that.

Here's 10p, phone your mum and tell her you won't be coming home tonight.

Pick a number between one and ten … You lose, take your tops off.

Nice legs. What time do they open?

STARS OF THE '(IS THIS THE WAY TO) AMARILLO' COMIC RELIEF VIDEO IN ORDER OF APPEARANCE

Peter Kay (Lee Lard look-alike)

William Roache (Ken Barlow)

Anne Kilbride (Deirdre Barlow)

Keith Harris with Orville (blue comedian and non-flying bird)

Bernie Clifton plus ostrich (*Crackerjack* legend, non-flying beast)

Max and Paddy (a couple of doormen)

Shelly Lindsay (Rovers Return landlady)

Jimmy Savile (Mr Fix It)

Albert Wilkinson, Trevor Jones, Craig Salisbury, Big Mick and Nick Read (Bolton Wanderers hooligan firm)

Jim Bowen (Bully's special prize)

Mr Blobby (unemployed pink rubbery lifeform from Crinkly Bottom)

Danny Baker (Daz salesman)

Heather Mills-McCartney (Macca's wife)

Geoffrey Hayes and Bungle (*Rainbow* presenters)

Michael Parkinson (chat show king)

Ronnie Corbett (One Ronnie)

Tony Christie (singer, uncertain of route to Amarillo)

Lee Lard (Peter Kay look-alike)

Shaun Ryder and Bez (Happy Mondays fellas)

Roger Taylor and Brian May (a pair of Queens)

Sweep and Sooty (argumentative glove puppets)

Ramakant Shah (Mahatma Gandhi look-alike)

Trevor Payne (thinks he's Cliff Richard)

Shakin' Stevens (singer, knows what's behind green door)

ALTERNATIVE NAMES FOR BRIAN POTTER

Ironside

Davros

Phantom of the Optics

Dr Strangelove

THAT PETER KAY THING CO-STARRING 'TV'S OWN' BOB CAROLGEES AND SPIT THE DOG

'The Services' – Due to pop in on Bolton First Services on way back from hairdresser's.

'In the Club' – Brian Potter claims to have discovered Bob Carolgees, Spit the Dog, the Krankies, T'Pau and Tom O'Connor.

'The Ice Cream Man Cometh' – Disbelieving policeman says, 'Oh yeah and my name's Bob Carolgees.'

'The Arena' – Steward Mathew Kelly is co-starring in *Oliver!* with Lulu, Lennie Bennett and Bob Carolgees

'Leonard' – Special guest presenting Leonard with his reward.

'Lonely at the Top' – As Marc's career spirals downwards he learns that he has been replaced on 'Night Fever' by Carolgees. 'What's he got that I haven't got,' he asks, 'apart from a spitting dog?'

Phoenix Nights Series One – Endorsing colon care on a leaflet Jerry is reading while on the toilet.

Phoenix Nights Series Two – Hosting daytime chat show on teenage pregnancy being watched by Brian Potter.

Max and Paddy's Road to Nowhere – Paddy is tuning in the radio when he briefly pauses on a radio announcer saying 'and Bob Carolgees'.

YOU LOOK FAMILIAR

Deirdre Kay – Peter's mum enjoys Alfred Hitchcock parts in all Peter's shows. Featured on poster on wall of Den Perry's Banana Grove club.

Susan Kay – Peter's wife appears in many crowd shots and played Clinton Baptiste victim Sonia in *Phoenix Nights*. Last seen grooving to a couple of dancing bears.

Dougie – If there's any phoning to be done in Peter Kay-land, you'll need to phone Dougie.

Cowardly Lion suit – Peter's *The Wizard of Oz* suit appears in 'The Services', *Live at the Top of the Tower* and '(Is This the Way to) Amarillo'.

WEATHERFIELD GAZETTE: LATEST NEWS

'It's people like Jim McDonald that keep me going' – Brian Potter finds hope in *Corrie* survivor.

'I've got narrow veins like Jack Duckworth, but it doesn't stop me' – just one of Leonard's ailments.

'In memory of Alan – Died 8th Dec '89' – flowers tied to Blackpool lamp-post in honour of Alan Bradley.

'It worked for Deirdre Rashid' – Brian Potter launches his Free the Phoenix Two campaign.

I'M NOT FEELING MYSELF

Waitress in 'Leonard' has been off with the runs, which were 'very loose'.

Harry Haroon can't make it to Leonard's award night because his wife's not feeling so good; 'her foot's come back'.

Tom Dale in 'Eyes Down' hasn't taken a day off in 14 years. Even when the doctor suspected he had meningitis – 'put that on your film'.

'Adeena's phoned in with a water infection' so she can't work at 'The Services'.

Jerry St Clair thinks he's 'ruptured an artery'.

The words 'Stranraer' cause sudden angina symptoms in Brian Potter.

I ♥ '80S MOVIES – TEN FILMS PETER KAY HAS PARODIED

Mannequin

Karate Kid

Cannonball Run

Taxi Driver

Dirty Dancing

Midnight Cowboy

Ghostbusters

ET

An Officer and a Gentleman

Ghost

Dirty Harry

Shawshank Redemption

FIVE PEOPLE WHO LOOK LIKE PETER KAY

Joe Royle (football manager)
Alf Roberts (*Coronation Street* grocer, deceased)
John O'Shea (Manchester United defender)
Mungo (canine in *Mary, Mungo and Midge*)
Billy the Fish (goalkeeper)

CITY LIFE COMEDIAN OF THE YEAR WINNERS

1990 – Sister Mary Immaculate (Caroline Aherne)
1991 – Dave Spikey
1992 – Shared by Steve Vernon and Paul Glasswell
1993 – Tony Mills
1994 – Dave Rothnie
1995 – Chris Addison
1996 – Peter Kay
1997 – Shared by Neil Anthony (aka Neil Fitzmaurice) and Dom Carroll
1998 – Steve Harris
1999 – Jason Manford
2000 – Justin Moorhouse
2001 – John Bishop
2002 – Phil Walker
2003 – Seymour Mace
2004 – John Warburton
2005 – Andy Watson

THINGS THAT ANNOY PETER KAY

People who point at their wrist while asking for the time.
People who say, 'Oh you just want to have your cake and eat it too.'
When people say, 'It's always the last place you look.'
When people say, while watching a film, 'Did you see that?'
People who ask, 'Can I ask you a question?'
Rich Tea biscuits.
When something is 'new and improved!'
When people say, 'Life is short.'

When you are waiting for the bus and someone asks, 'Has the bus come yet?'

GREAT DOUBLE ACTS

Maxwell Bygraves and Paddy O'Shea (the Maxster and Padster)

Mary and Joseph (Holy Mary's kids)

Les and Dennis (Mick Bustin's two lads)

Ben Dover and Phil McCracken (what now?)

Rose and Theresa (bingo groupies)

Trigger and Minnie Ha Ha (Cowboy and Native American bride)

Tippit Twins (lesbians before it was popular)

TOP FIVE *THAT PETER KAY THING* MOMENTS

Paul LeRoy's girlfriend saying 'Stop looking at her tits' in the Talent Trek 99 Final.

Alan McLarty drunk on the hard shoulder of the M61.

Keith Lard's fire safety speech.

'I don't care whose it is. I don't care what it is. It's floating.' Pearl, 'The Services'

'She's took it out off me this morning, she's thirsty, she'd 80 gallon for breakfast.' Utah, 'The Services'

Marc Park's speech about being a ladies' man: 'I used to have them hanging off my cock. I was like a human cup tree, I'm not deformed or anything like that ...'

LEONARD'S FRIENDS

The Duke

Turkey George

Carl Who Waves at Cars

3-2-1 Tommy

Jackie Busher

POTTERISMS

'Are my eyes dreaming, Jerry, or have you got two of my builders singing acapulco?'

'The world's your lobster.'

'You're a bloody hypodermic Jerry.'
'We're in a catch-21 situation.'
'Like a bull to a red rag.'
'We've got to grab the cow by the horns and pull together.'
'I want everything shit-shaped and Bristol fashion.'
'Rubber burns? Isn't he a Scottish poet?'
'Jerry St Clair. Licensee and my left foot.'
'Like St Paul, the road to Domestos.'

TEN COMEDIANS WHO HAVE INFLUENCED PETER KAY

Eric Morecambe
Steve Martin
Steve Coogan
Victoria Wood
Caroline Aherne
Les Dawson
James H. Reeves
Ronnie Barker
Leonard Rossiter
Robin Williams

'OL' TOILET MOUTH!' SOME ALTERNATIVE SWEARING

Sweet baby Jesus and the orphans!
Shine a light!
Shut up you girl
Jesus H
You're twisting my melons man
Sweet Jesus and the Mary Chain
Get bent

ITEMS FOUND IN KEITH LARD'S BAG

A ball with a bell on
A muzzle

Dog chews

Chloroform

THE TAO OF LEONARD

1. Don't die with any fun in the bank. You're a long time dead, live your life, cockers.

2. Do all the good you can by all the means you can in all the ways you can in all the places you can at all the times you can so long as you ever can.

3. Tell a lie, lose an eye.

4. Live life to the max.

5. Life's an adventure.

6. A home without a Bible is like leaving the door ajar for the devil to call.

7. Many a good tune can be played on an old fiddle providing the strings don't break.

8. How can you get bored of life when you don't know what's coming next?

9. Life is like a motorway. Sometimes it might seem like you've chosen the wrong lane, it might not be a smooth ride, but keep driving. Sometimes it might feel like you're going too fast. Slow down, pull into services and have a toasted tea cake.

10. If you fancy a jar, forget the car.

BULLSEYE PRIZES

In 1 – Sodastream

In 2 – library video cases

In 3 – Ferguson Videostar

In 4 – George Formby grill

Special prize – a speedboat

'DANCING QUEEN' (ALTERNATIVE VERSION)

'Dancing Queen young string bean only seventeen / Dancing queen feel the meat on a tangerine/ Dancing queen eating Chinese with Mr Bean oh yeah / You can dance in your underpants.'

WISDOM OF POTTER

Dancers are not drinkers.

The higher a monkey climbs the more you can see its arse.

Clubland will never die.

It's amazing what you can do with a computer and access to t'Internet.

The secret to running a successful club is to cater for the family. Nothing offensive, nothing blue …

Would you suck a 10-year-old banana? No. Exactly.

Battery acid is a good remover.

TOP FIVE *PHOENIX NIGHTS* SERIES 1 MOMENTS

The horse mating the Bucking Bronco.

Brian asking Jerry for romantic advice while in the toilets, then the whole of his answer inaudible due to hand-dryer noise, except the end of his tale '… covered in piss'.

Clinton Baptiste turning the Phoenix Club audience into an angry mob … 'Now I'm getting the word nonce.'

Max and Paddy being attacked by a gang of seven three-foot-tall Bolton Wanderers fans.

The Robot Wars when they dispense with technical wizardry and start axing the other robots by hand.

JUST OUT ON LIMITED EDITION VIDEO

Beverly Hills Cock

Shaving Private Ryan

Forest Dump

Willy Wanker and the Chocolate Factory

Party Pissing

Look Who's Porking

Charlie's Anals

Phantom Penis

TOP FIVE DUNKERS

Hob Nobs

Ginger Nuts

Malted Milk

Digestives

Bourbons

SONG LYRICS IN DIALOGUE

'Well my heart definitely belongs here, in First Services Bolton. She's my first, my last, my everything.' Pearl, in 'The Services'

'She's a grafter, she's my bridge over troubled water, that's what I always tell her. She's my night in white satin and she drives the van.' Marc Park, in *That Peter Kay Thing*

'I always thought that love was true in fairytales. Meant for someone else but not for me.' Brian Potter, in *Phoenix Nights* Series 1

'One god and one love, let's get together and feel all right. Bob Marley.' Leonard De Thompkinson, in *That Peter Kay Thing*

'Burn baby burn, disco inferno. Burn baby down, burn that mother down, another child orphaned.' Keith Lard, in *That Peter Kay Thing*

'This old heart of mine, been broke a thousand times.' Brian Potter in *Phoenix Night*s Series 1

'You'll find a girl, if you want you'll get married: look at me, I'm old but I'm happy.' Max, in *Max and Paddy's Road to Nowhere*

'Come on Billy, don't be a hero.' Max, in *Max and Paddy's Road to Nowhere*

'Ooh, it's bootylicious.' Brian Potter, in *Phoenix Nights* Series 2

CAN BRIAN POTTER WALK?

The case against:

Seen standing as the Neptune Club burns.

Sells shopmobile for Cadillac.

Car is clamped outside a gym.

Clinton Baptiste says, 'You can walk.'

The case for:

Cannot feel Beverly playing footsie with him under the table.

Uses vase instead of glass.

Says: 'I'd like to moonwalk but life's a shithouse.'

Soils himself while trapped on stair lift.

Clinton Baptiste says, 'You can walk.'

TOP FIVE *PHOENIX NIGHTS* SERIES 2 MOMENTS

When Brian Potter first sees the inflatable cock and balls.

Brian running into Jerry singing about black bin bags in Asda.

The fortune cookie incident at the grand opening of the Golden Phoenix.

Brian stuck on his stair lift and asking, 'What would Thora Hird do?'

When confused members of the audience do actually 'stand up' when Jerry sings, 'I'm the Real Slim Shady please stand up' as Eminem during the 'Stars in Your Eyes' show.

THINGS WORTH REMEMBERING

You only get a bucket and a half.

Laugh or burn, it's up to you.

Where there's tragedy there's trade.

Life is for the living.

Slippers make you run faster.

Take the C off chips and what have you got?

Never trust a man in Farah.

There's no maternity leave in showbusiness.

PETER KAY'S FAVOURITE TV SHOWS AGED 12

'Allo 'Allo

Porridge

Gentle Touch

Only Fools and Horses

Coronation Street

No Limits

Bullseye

3-2-1

Minder

Mork and Mindy

BOLTON INDEPENDENT LEADER COMMUNITY AWARDS 1999 BEST LOLLIPOP LADY NOMINEES

Doreen Gash

Heather

Diane Purdy
Rita Chalk

THINGS PETER'S NAN SAYS

'Your driving's a bit erotic.'
'Have you got Harry Potter on VD?'
'When you going t'Egypt?'
'Donnie Osmond is a Moomin.'
'I've got a smashing copulation CD.'
'Don't put those bloody cameras on me!'
'See them George Formby grills?'

PETER KAY'S FAVOURITE FOOD

Pear drops
Weight Watchers banoffee pie desserts
Chicken in black bean sauce
Baked potato with tuna and baked beans
Fish and chips
Holland's meat and potato pie
Cauliflower grills
Hob nobs
Parkin loaf
Tuna bap
Häagen-Dazs Bailey's ice cream

TRUE FACTS ABOUT THE PHOENIX CLUB'S KENNY SNR

Used to bag dead bodies in Vietnam
Has slept with Bonnie Langford
Is very friendly with the SAS
Absolutely hammered Robert De Niro at swingball
His surname is Dalglish
Homebrew has won awards
Has seen the Lord's face in a pepperoni pizza
Knows what horse shit tastes like
Main supplier of wood chip to Chuck Norris
Can blow up a bouncy castle with his mouth

FILMS IN WHICH SEAN CONNERY WEARS A WIG (ACCORDING TO MAX AND PADDY)

The Rock
Never Say Never Again
Highlander
Highlander II: The Quickening
Zardoz
The Hunt for Red October
The Avengers

NOT AVAILABLE IN THE SHOPS: SOME ITEMS FROM KAY'S CATALOGUE

Piagra (helping gentlemen last all night long. Available in aniseed, spearmint and linament flavour)

Tantasy (the tanning aid that's not a fantasy)

Invader 2000 (get back you bastard)

Spray Maine (full Sean Connery-style hair thickness)

Umbrella hats (they're umbrellas and they're hats)

Les Cadbury's Fingers (taste exactly the same as Cadbury's Fingers. It's incredible)

Rola Cola (4p for 30 litres)

Kamikaze lager (lifetime supply available now)

Gaspeén (mineral water bottled in the mountains of Afghanistan)

One Dips (our new name for Rich Tea biscuits)

Big Bob's Baked Beans (also known as Big Bob's Bastard Beans)

Snake Eye Pie (actually just chicken and mushroom)

Camerilla Biscuit-Flavoured Condoms (sadly past sell-by date)

Millennium Cone (now with seven flakes)

Hoverboards (available from 2015)

CONTENTS OF MAX'S POCKETS

A pound-coin holder (empty)
An afro comb
I've Stroked a Beaver at Drayton Manor keyring

CONTENTS OF PADDY'S POCKETS

Pornographic magazine (*The Finger Club*)
One pack of condoms (ribbed for the ladies' pleasure)

SPOT-ON PETER KAY OBSERVATIONS

The first item on an airport carousel is always a pram.

Answer machines and old people are not a good combination.

When you're drunk at a wedding you think those white bits of card from the bottom of Party Poppers are pound coins.

When someone tells you directions you go deaf.

When somebody's giving you a phone number you always use a pen that doesn't work.

Mums call you by everyone else's name in the family before they get to yours.

TEN MOVIES PETER KAY BOUGHT ON VIDEO

It's a Wonderful Life
Airplane!
The Man with the Golden Gun
Finding Forrester
Blazing Saddles
The Producers
The Odd Couple
Dr No
Escape to Victory
The Wizard of Oz

THE WAY TO AMARILLO ... FROM BOLTON

Train: Bolton Station to Manchester Airport
Plane No. 1: Manchester to Las Vegas McCarran International Airport
Plane No. 2: Las Vegas to Dallas Fort Worth Airport
Plane No. 3: Dallas to Amarillo International Airport
Taxi: Airport to Amarillo

RAY VON'S FINEST MOMENT

'Fun is the key, but keep seated at all times or you may die.'

TOP FIVE *MAX AND PADDY'S ROAD TO NOWHERE* MOMENTS

Max showing Paddy his notebook filled with childish pictures of two detectives he's created called Magnet and Steel.

The TV theme tune face-off.

The cow flying through the air when they run into it.

Brian Potter being sprayed down outside the Phoenix Club shouting 'I am Brian Chelsea Potter and I am not the Taliban.'

When the pig they are transporting to market starts farting and Max resorts to wearing swimming goggles to stop his eyes burning.

NOT REAL SHOPS

Kebabylon

Tantastic

Porn Again

Plaice Your Orders

Sweet Truck Haul Ltd

Balti Towers

Only Foals and Horses

You Can Call Me Halal

UTAH THE COACH DRIVER'S RULES

1. If you're going to be sick you mop it up yourselves.
2. No solids in the toilets.
3. Only a leg stretch at services, no food.
4. No bottles.
5. No buggering about with the emergency exits.

MAX AND PADDY'S ROAD TO NOWHERE LOCATIONS: ALL ROADS LEAD TO BOLTON

Episode One: White Cliffs Shopping Centre is Crompton Place Shopping Centre in Bolton

Episode Two: Safeways supermarket (now a Morrisons) in Breightmet, Bolton; Mick Bustin's Garage is Radcliffe Tyre Centre in Radcliffe, Bolton

Epiiode Three: The Wolfster's 40th birthday party in London is Dobbies Sports and Social Club on Bradley Fold Road, Bradley Fold, Bolton

Episode Four: Magistrates Court is Swinton Civic Centre on Chorley Road, Swinton

Episode Five: The Beadle's Arms pub is the Farmer's Arms on Manchester Road, Swinton

Episode Six: Newcastle is Lower Market Street, Farnworth, Bolton; service station is Bolton West

GAMES SANS FRONTIÈRES (SUPPLIERS OF QUALITY TAT TO THE LICENSED TRADE)

Pool tables with one short leg

Das Boot fruit machine

Flavoured condom machines (six months out of date)

Foxy boxing

Indoor golf

Mechanical bulls

Six-feet-high-Kerplunk

Inflatable Sammy the Snake, fun for all the family

LITTLE THINGS YOU MAY HAVE MISSED

When Holy Mary's mobile goes off while she's in church the ringtone is 'Hot Stuff', as heard on *The Full Monty* soundtrack.

In Brian Potter's address book (seen while he's calling round his staff) there are some curious entries – 'Big Julie, afternoons only, ramp fitted', 'Sluts R Us' and 'Rubber Pants', No. 1 Leakers Road.

In *Peter Kay Live at the Bolton Albert Halls* we see him driven to the venue in a car marked BS Taxis – the cab company owned by Marc Park's manager in *That Peter Kay Thing*.

When Max and Paddy emerge from the Phoenix Club 'Sarolium' they are wearing white gowns embroidered with Le Ponderosa – the name of the hotel complex in Blackpool that Brian visits.

Brian's doorbell chime is 'Tears of a Clown'.

When Jerry is having his sigmoidoscopy the song playing on the radio is 'The Whole of the Moon' by the Waterboys.

One of the salesmen on the fictional Armchair shopping channel is called John Lennon.

When Marc Park goes back to being a greengrocer he keeps his 'personalised' number plate – MEMPC2.

The road recovery van attending to Alan's broken-down truck is marked ARC (Alan McLarty from *That Peter Kay Thing*'s alternative to RAC).

Holy Mary's son, Joseph, is 'doing a BTEC in joinery down the college'.

The green Ford Cortina in the Phoenix Club car park gets vandalised further with every episode.

In *Max and Paddy's Road to Nowhere* the registration plate of their motor home is BOL 10X.

CHEAP POP THAT'S WORSE THAN ROLA COLA

Suncharm

Panda Pop

Quattro

Hey Brothers

Quenchie Cups

PETER KAY'S FAVOURITE THEME TUNES

1. *Minder*

'*Minder*'s a brilliant theme, I've always loved *Minder*. It's a great one for singing along in the car. *Minder* always reminds me of Wednesday nights at nine o'clock, Benny Hill would be on at eight. I'd go to bed at 8.30 and I'd always hear *Minder* through the floor, then I'd hear the front door close and my dad going out and I knew where he'd be going. He'd send us to bed and then go and get fish and chips and he'd come back and I'd always come down and go, "I can't sleep … ooooh fish and chips" and he'd go, "All right, you can have a butty", and I'd stay and watch a bit of *Minder*.'

2. *Mork and Mindy*

'Lovely theme. Boulder, Colorado. I saw it recently and the theme came on and I had this rush of being a child and I remember my dad just laughing and laughing at it so much. I loved *Mork and Mindy*.'

3. *Fall Guy*

'*Fall Guy*'s a cracking theme. [Sings]: "I never spent much time in school, but I taught ladies plenty" … bit saucy there, cos it's Lee Majors singing you know. [Sings]: "When I wind up in the hay it's only hay, hey, hey". I thought yeah, you were up all night writing that one, Lee. He was a stuntman, a bounty hunter who kind of operated outside the law and he went off and did his own thing. That was a sing-along one that. That were Friday nights, half seven to half eight, then *Gaffer* were on or *That's My Boy*, then at nine o'clock it were either *Shine On Harvey Moon* or *Gentle Touch* or *Flambards*, with *Winner Takes All* at seven.'

4. *This is Your Life*

'Oh yeah, *This is Your Life* is a really great theme. Someone once told me *This is Your Life* is the best format for a programme in the world – there's suspense, surprise, tears, it will never die, it will always be on, always. Everyone flicks it on and says, "Just see whose life it is."

5. *Sportsnight*

'That was another one you heard through the floorboards. I was always hearing *Robin's Nest*. *Sportsnight* was like a vivid waking-up dream. They had *Closedown* after *Sportsnight*.'

6. *Hill Street Blues*

'Ah, all Mike Post's themes are good, but this one's best.'

7. *The A Team*

'Everyone loves *The A Team*. They were Vietnam vets and you hired them for free; if you were in trouble you'd call the A Team and they'd come and help you. Why? *The Equaliser* was very similar. Where he got his money from I'll never know. He had a New York apartment, massive apartment with a panic room; the rent on that alone must have crippled him, plus he did it all for free … you'd come and find the Equaliser and he'd come and balance the odds. I remember thinking, "How can he run this?" '

8. *The South Bank Show*

'My favourite show of all time, *Porridge*, didn't even have a theme, just loads of gates and doors slamming and "Norman Stanley Fletcher, you have been found guilty …" – very serious. *Two Ronnies* was always a good theme. *South Bank Show*'s a classic, it's great: you get all excited and then Melvyn Bragg comes on: "Blah blah, Czechoslovakian poet". Flick that shit off ... but the theme comes on, here we go!'

9. *Superstars*

'Thursday eight o'clock that were on; 7.30 *Top of the Pops*, eight o'clock *Superstars*. It's bizarre cos I must have been about four, but I remember *Superstars* like it was yesterday.

10. *The Pink Panther*

'This is a great theme tune. It reminds me of Saturday nights; we used to have breakfast at night-time. That was my dad's day to cook and that was all he could make, so we'd have full English for tea. We'd have tea watching *Pink Panther* and *Dr Who* then my mum and dad would go and my grandad would baby-sit and we'd watch *3-2-1* or a film. I remember watching *American Werewolf in London* with my grandad. I knew that scene with Jenny Agutter were coming up and I had to leave the room. I couldn't watch muck with my grandad. Besides, I'd already seen it about eight times. I'd come back and my sister would be reading back of tissue box: "Are they two-ply, these tissues?" '

'Peter Kay's Favourite Theme Tunes' were originally published in *The Guardian* in an interview with Johnny Dee.

Acknowledgements

That Peter Kay Book includes a substantial amount of exclusive material, including an unpublished transcript of my own two-hour interview with Peter Kay. Many people spoke to me off the record – you know who you are, cheers – and many kind people agreed to talk openly about Peter, over the course of numerous meetings, emails and phone calls. I would like to give very special thanks to Peter's old school pals Michael Atherton and Karen Peel, who gave up a great deal of time to help with the book.

This book would not have been possible without the help of three very special people: Chris, Jacqui and Dorrie. I thank you for appearing like angels at my hour of need. I am very fortunate to know people as thoughtful as you. Also to Kathy, Holly and Annie – sorry for becoming a Peter Kay-obsessed lunatic! Dad and Jo – much love to you. You can phone me now, it's OK, I've finished.

The generosity of Jon Wilde was most crucial. Jon, go and take your dog for a walk. Much gratitude also to the lady at Bolton Library who I had running up and down stairs fetching books like a madwoman – you are doing a great job looking after those crazy family tree folk. A multitude of high fives to Ian Gittins and Miranda West.

Thanks, in no particular order, to: Gary Morecambe, Andrew Collins, Graham Linehan, Sonia Hurst, Adam Bloom, Doreen Gash, Billy Bedlam, Lisa White, Dawn Panton, Iain Coyle, Cheryl Avenue, John Marshall, Lloyd Peters, Mathew Kelly, Paul Barnwell, Steve Alcock, Toni Baker, Robert Popper, Janey Godley and Marc Rowlands.

Finally, thank you for the music, the songs I'm singing. Thanks for all the joy they're bringing. Who can live without it? I ask in all honesty. What would life be? Without a song or a dance what are we?

Oh, and thank you to Peter Kay.

Bibliography

BOOKS

Allen, Woody *Without Feathers,* Ballantine
Cook, William *The Comedy Store – the Club That Changed British Comedy*, Little, Brown
Corbridge, Sylvia Lovat *It's an Old Lancashire Custom,* Dennis Dobson
Double, Oliver *Stand-Up,* Methuen
Margolis, Jonathan *Bernard Manning: A Biography,* Orion
Nevin, Charles *Lancashire, Where Women Die of Love,* Mainstream
Peter Kay's Phoenix Nights: The Scripts Series 1 and 2 (4 books)
Thompson, Ben *Sunshine on Putty*, Harper

VIDEO/DVD

Peter Kay, Live at the Top of the Tower
That Peter Kay Thing
Blow Dry
Going Off Big Time
24 Hour Party People
Ted Robbins, Live and Large in Blackpool
Phoenix Nights Series One and Two
Peter Kay, Live at Bolton Albert Halls
Peter Kay, Driven to Distraction
Max and Paddy's Road to Nowhere
Peter Kay Live in Manchester
Max and Paddy's The Power of Two
Wallace and Gromit: The Curse of the Were-Rabbit

INTERNET SOURCES

<peterkayonline.com>
<peterkay.co.uk>
<davespikey.co.uk>
<chortle.co.uk>
<offthetelly.co.uk>
<bbc.co.uk>

<channel4.com>
<theguardian.co.uk>
<billybedlam.co.uk>
<peterkayforum.com>
<thecustard.tv>
<ruscoe.net/maxandpaddy>
<peterkayfan.co.uk>
<www.northstarproductions.co.uk>
<thisislancashire.co.uk>
<thisisbolton.co.uk>
<manchesteronline.co.uk>
<hoscar.demon.co.uk>

CREDITED ARTICLES

Banks, Martin: 'Peter Kay, Glee Club' (2000), *Birmingham Evening Mail*; Jackson, Nick: 'Funny Man Peter In The Big Time' (1997), Ackerley, Chris: 'Peter's Show Is a Record Breaker' (2002), Savage, Ian: 'Peter's Tour de Force' (2002), all *Bolton Evening News*; Bennett, Steve: 'Review' (2002), *chortle.co.uk*; Burgess, Marissa: 'Contrast and Compere' (2003), Rowlands, Marc: 'Those Peter Kay Things' (2003), 'Once Upon a Time In The North' (2003), all *City Life*; Paterson, Peter: 'Animals Before Humans' (2001), *Daily Mail*; Fulton, Rick: 'Peter Kay's Phoenix Nights' (2001), 'Paddy Power' (2006), Morgan, Kathleen: 'Quickfire Peter' (1998), Robertson, Cameron: 'I Don't Want To Die Laughing' (2004), all *Daily Record*; Jefferies, Mark: 'Ricky Turned Down TV Beer Deal' (2003), Jefferies, Mark: 'Peter Chaos' (2004), Morgan, Gareth: 'Humour? I'm Working On It' (2001), all *Daily Star*; Spikey, Dave: 'That Peter Kay Connection' (1999), 'News' (1999-2006), 'Dave On Chain letters' (1999), all *davespikey.co.uk*; Roberts, Wendy: 'Telly Stardom Won't Drag Peter Away From Home' (1999), *Derby Evening Telegraph*; Atherton, Ben: 'Comedian Kay Comes Clean on Sick Jill Joke' (1999), Somerville, Colin: 'Cereal Filler' (1998), all *Edinburgh Evening News*; Lee, Veronica: 'It's Another Kay Thing' (2001), *Evening Standard*; Beacom, Brian: 'Peter's a Sound Bloke' (2001), *Glasgow Evening Times*; Donohue, Simon: 'Cool Venue' (1996), *Lancashire Evening Telegraph*; Gould, Phil: The Rise and Rise of...' (2002), *Liverpool Daily Post*; Viner, Brian: 'Motorway Services With an Ironic Smile' (1998), *Mail On Sunday*; Barnes, Anthony: 'Laidback Liam Sits it Out' (2001), Donohue, Simon: 'The Rise and Rise Of Peter Kay' (2003), all *Manchester Evening News*; Neild, Andy: 'Comic Peter's Shock at Award' (2000), *Newsquest*; Walliams, David: 'Noel Gallagher Interview' (2005), *Observer Music Monthly*; Lyons, James: 'Anger Over Dando Joke' (1999), *PA News*; Freeman, Martin: 'Comedian is Funny

Peculiar' (2003), *Plymouth Evening Herald*; Jinks, Peter: 'Fringe Comics Go Channel Hopping' (1997), *Scotland On Sunday*; Jagasia, Mark 'Bolton - The New Showbiz Capital of the World' (2000), *Sunday Express*: Laws, Roz: 'Living On The Edge' (2005), *Sunday Mercury*; Donnelly, Claire: 'How Peter Kay Became the King of Comedy' (2004), Ellam, Dennis: 'I Owe It All To Bolton...' (2001), Hewett, Rick: 'Man U Can 'Ave It' (2002), Hyland, Ian: 'Royle Ructions' (1999), all *Sunday Mirror*; Davies, Mike: 'Northern Magic Is a Kay Thing' (2000), *The Birmingham Post*; Born, Matt: '£10,000 Damages For Fire Officer' (2001), Lee, Veronica: 'The Comedian With 16 Faces' (2000), all *The Daily Telegraph*; Gibson, Janine: 'Four Seasons Its Schedules' (1999), Logan, Brian: 'Peter Kay' (2002), Margolis, Jonathan: 'Shut Up, Dad' (1999), McLean, Gareth: 'Peter Kay Profile' (2004), Moore, Emily: 'My Inspiration' (2000), van der Zee, Bibi: 'He Could Have Been a Bingo Caller' (2000), Walsh, Collette: 'Funny Ha Ha' (1997), all *The Guardian*; Barrell, Sarah: 'Assembly Rooms' (2002), Byrne, Claire: 'Chorley FM Under Fire' (2005), Lee, Veronica: 'Meet The New Les Dawson' (1998), 'Something Funny's Going On' (1998), 'Have You Heard The One About the Warm-up Act' (2002), 'Laugh - By Order Of The Committee' (2000), Rampton, James: 'Edinburgh Festival '98' (1998), Rudebeck, Clare: 'Graduate Careers: How I Got Here' (2002), Viner, Brian: 'Podgy Peter Pulls It Off' (2000), 'The Gag With The £10,000 Punchline' (2001), 'Viva Johnny Vegas' (2003), all *The Independent*; Games, Alex: 'Funny Bones' (2004), York, Peter: 'John Smith's Bitter' (2004), all *The Independent On Sunday*; Carroll, Sue: 'The Funny Thing About Bolton' (2000), Catchpole, Charlie: 'Britcoms Have The Last Laugh' (2000), 'Potter's Stairlift To Heaven' (2001), Parsons, Tony: 'Please Stop Singing... O-Kay?' (2005), Purnell, Tony: 'Peter's Too Much of a Good Thing' (2000), Ridley, Jane: 'Family Night Out' (2002), Robertson, Cameron: 'Coronation Pete', Shelley, Jim: 'Shelleyvision' (2004), all *The Mirror*; Flett, Kathryn: 'Don't Turn Your Noses Up' (2000), Woodcraft, Molloy: 'Wednesday TV Review' (2000), Merritt, Stephanie: 'Special Kay' (2005), all *The Observer*; Bletchley, Rachael: 'Don't Give Up The Kay Job' (2005), Bushell, Garry: 'Peter Hits Bullseye' (2004), 'Phoenix Nights Is Working Class Act' (2002), all *The People*; Smith, Aidan: 'This'll Make You Laugh' (1998), Synnot, Siobhan: 'Flight Of The Phoenix' (2004), all *The Scotsman*; Dowell, Ben: 'That Thing He Does' (2000), *The Stage*; Brockway, Sally: 'Chat's Showbiz' (2002), Compton, Louise, 'Bizarre Workout DVD' (2006), Hockney, Karen: 'I'd Sooner Give It Up Than Move To London' (2002), Patrick, Guy: 'TV Peter's Theft Fury' (2003), Yates, Charles: 'Peter Kay Buys His Mum That Bungalow' (2005), 'Peter Kay's Secret Heartache' (2005), all *The Sun*; Phelan, Stephen: 'Perrier? Who Needs It?' (2003), *The Sunday Herald*; Fanshawe, Simon: 'Pride Of The North' (1998), Nicol, Patricia: 'The

Surreally Useful' (1998), all *The Sunday Times*; Oliver Wilson, Chris: 'Smash Wit' (1999), *The Times*.

UNCREDITED ARTICLES

The majority of the quotes in this book are from my own transcripts and sources. When this is not the case, where possible I have credited the writer and/or publication. However, some of the articles researched on the Internet did not have complete credits, plus many news stories do not name the journalist. My heartfelt apologies to anyone I miss out in the following list of research material.

'Comic Kay boosts Baker's profits' (2005), 'Comedian's dressing room burgled' (2003): <bbc.co.uk>; 'Bolton comic scoops top award' (1996), 'Comic Peter slammed over Dando joke' (1999), 'Comic to make his directing debut' (2001), 'Comic's a real wag' (1996), 'Corrie Cameo' (2004), 'Film fans honour movie buff Leslie' (1996), 'Fire adviser hands over TV cash' (2001), 'For Pete's sake have a laugh' (1998), 'Funnyman bids for fringe benefit' (1998), 'Funnyman Peter is big news back home' (1999), 'Funnyman Peter misses the fun to help Omagh fund' (1998), 'It all adds up to comic Peter' (2005), 'Laugh? I nearly choked to death' (1999), 'Life's a bundle of laughs ...' (1998), 'Peter announces Bolton shows' (2002), 'Peter becomes master of mirth' (1996), 'Peter friends up for Comic Relief' (2001), 'Peter Kay' (2002), 'Peter Kay to be a dad' (2003), 'Peter Kay's joy ...' (1998), 'Peter's big mistake' (1999), 'Peter's friends' (1999), 'Peter the Great' (1997), 'Peter's top billing on Parkinson' (1998), 'Peter's voice is key to success' (1999), 'Spikey's a real wag' (1996), 'Spitting image' (2000), 'Star turns down new offers ...' (2002), 'The big breakthrough' (1998), 'Welcome to the Wild West – Houghton that is' (1998), 'Young folk set the scene' (1996): all *Bolton Evening News*; 'That Peter Kay Thing' (1999), <channel4.com>; 'A Bitter Man' (2005), 'Dave Spikey' (2002), 'Dave Spikey' (2003): all <chortle.co.uk>; 'Comedian horrifies guests with Jill joke' (1999), *Coventry Evening Telegraph*; 'Wicked whispers' (2005), *Daily Mail*; 'Say sausages' (2005), *Glasgow Evening Times*; 'Rock-Kay mountain high' (2000), 'Laughing all the way to London' (1999): *Lancashire Evening Telegraph*; 'Pride of Manchester' (2002), *Manchester Evening News*; 'Peter cheers up sad Reds' (2003), *Stockport Express*; 'Phoenix jail nights' (2004), 'Krackers from Kay' (2002): *Sunday Mirror*; 'Fancy a pint?' (2003), 'Producer's Choice' (2003): *Televisual*; 'Home entertainment' (2000), *Guardian*; 'Phoenix will not rise again' (2005), *Independent*; 'Gagged by model mum' (1997), *Mirror*; 'The new faces of TV comedy' (1999), *Observer*; 'Bolton wanderer' (2005), *Sunday Herald*; 'Peter Kay special' (2004), *Zoo*.